Philosophy of Mind: An Introduction

Introducing Philosophy

Introducing Philosophy is a series of textbooks designed to introduce the basic topics of philosophy for any student approaching the subject for the first time. Each volume presents a central subject of philosophy by considering the key issues and outlooks associated with the area. With the emphasis firmly on the arguments for and against a philosophical position, the reader is encouraged to think philosophically about the subject.

Philosophy of Mind:
An Introduction

Second Edition

George Graham

BLACKWELL *Publishers*

First published 1993

Second edition published 1998

2 4 6 8 10 9 7 5 3 1

Blackwell Publishers Inc.
350 Main Street
Malden, Massachusetts 02148
USA

Blackwell Publishers Ltd
108 Cowley Road
Oxford OX4 1JF
UK

Library of Congress Cataloging-in-Publication Data

Graham, George, 1945-
    Philosophy of mind: an introduction/George Graham. — 2nd ed.
    p. cm.—(Introducing Philosophy)
    Includes bibliographical references and index.
    ISBN 978-0-631-21205-8 (pbk.: alk. paper)
    ISBN 0-631-21205-1 (hbk)
    1. Philosophy of mind. I. Title. II. Series.
BD418.3.G73   1998
128'.2—dc21   98-13851
                                                                          CIP

British Library Cataloguing in Publication Data

A CIP catalogue record for this book is available from the British Library

Contents

Preface to the Second Edition

*For you will do me much greater good by putting an end to ignorance of
my psyche than if you put an end to an affliction of my body.*
Plato, *Hippias Minor*

This is a book to begin with: to begin the philosophy of mind. It tries to
make the main ideas of the subject available to readers with little or no
previous exposure to philosophy. It is primarily intended for under-
graduate students and the inquisitive general reader.

The first edition appeared in 1993. This is the second edition. What
changes have been made?

The most visible change is that the book is longer. A chapter on
epiphenomenalism about consciousness has been added. The discussions
of personal identity, materialism, freedom of will, and conscious experience have been substantially revised. The chapter on computer belief and
the mind of God has been split into two chapters. Both discussions have
been expanded, the first with consideration of functionalism. Paragraphs
prompted by philosophic interest in psychopathology, neuroscience, and
cognitive science have found their way into different chapters. Sections
of various chapters have been rewritten, either because they contained
mistakes or because the quality or clarity of argumentation wanted
improvement. In all, about a third of the book is new or different.

The structure is the same. Each chapter addresses topics which are
distinguishable from topics addressed in other chapters. So someone
who is interested in whether persons can survive bodily death could read
the second chapter without reading the first, whereas someone who is

curious about freedom of will could turn immediately to the ninth chapter for a self-enclosed guide to the rudiments of that concept. While the chapters stand alone, however, the book can be read from front to back. When read in order a narrative unfolds (with some redundancies as seem unavoidable). A cautious and, no doubt, incautious train of my own thoughts, indeed, there is.

The first chapter provides, to begin with, a working definition of philosophy of mind as well as representative discussion of a topic within the subject. This is the question of whether knowledge of conscious experience is essentially subjective or first-personal. The book is then divided into ten main chapters, each of which deals with a specific family of topics central to the subject. Both the choice of topics and their treatment is influenced by current philosophic research and activity. The current influence is perhaps most clearly shown in the organization of the second through sixth chapters, which directly mirrors contemporary concern with the attribution of mind to others: the disembodied, other human beings, nonhuman animals, computers, and God. This is followed by discussions of rational action, materialism about Intentionality and supervenience, freedom and personhood, and the issues and debates which these topics have inspired. The tenth chapter applies philosophy of mind to ethical debate over animal liberation. It employs theses about animal consciousness to support critical moves in the debate. It also addresses the question of whether conscious experience is a brain process. The eleventh and final chapter locates debate about the causal power of consciousness within the broad confines of contemporary psychopathology and neuroscience.

Several important figures in past and present philosophy of mind are discussed, although this is not an intellectual history text. My own convictions and preferences are present, sometimes visibly in certain remarks, always invisibly in underlying editorial decisions, but this is not a personal philosophy of mind. I try to let positions and arguments speak for themselves. I also try to maintain contact with puzzlement and perplexity about the mind. The mind/body problem, for example, may be made genuinely interesting to novices when bound up with questions of survival of bodily death (as attempted in the second chapter) and of mental illness and suicidal depression (as attempted in the eighth). It is less interesting, perhaps even uninteresting, if people simply walk through the Philosopher's Museum of Mind/Body 'Isms' (materialism, dualism, etc.) without the partner of perplexity.

A long paragraph about footnotes, endnotes, citations, and reading lists: To offer a visually uncluttered text, there are no footnotes. When a particular reference is part of the narrative progression or development of an idea, I offer citation in the main text. Otherwise references are in endnotes. Endnotes, as the name suggests, are relegated to the backs of chapters, where they help the author to acknowledge sources and the curious reader to track down references and suggested readings. In this book they also function as notes. They add information to the text, which seems useful to a student, who otherwise may wonder why various authors or works are mentioned. Readers eager to read more philosophy of mind may consult 'A philosophy of mind bookshelf' at the back of the book. By examining citations, endnotes, and the philosophy of mind bookshelf, students should find ample bibliographic orientation for term papers and other academic projects.

Although the book is written in a non-technical style, I include a glossary.

George Graham
University of Alabama at Birmingham

Acknowledgments

Support for the revised edition came, in part, from the Rockefeller Foundation as well as from a sabbatical leave from my home university. The Foundation deserves special thanks for two consecutive invitations to write at the Foundation's Study and Conference Center, Bellagio, Italy, both of which I had to decline, but each of which provided symbolic reinforcement for my work. Special thanks are owed to Ms Susan Garfield, Secretary to the Bellagio Committee.

The second edition has benefited from the counsel and suggestions of many people. My editors, Steve Smith and Mary Riso, and staff at Blackwell Publishers deserve special thanks for their interest in the book and encouragement to pursue a second edition. Several people helped me to improve the book substantially. Reinaldo Elugardo published a detailed review that led me to revise my reading of John Searle on Intentionality and to assume a more explicit burden of proof in my discussion of inverted qualia. I also profited greatly from reactions of Gareth Matthews, Rita Nolan, David Sanford, and Lourdes Valdivia.

I feel most fortunate to have such excellent philosophers as William Bechtel, Owen Flanagan, Max Hocutt, Terence Horgan, Robert Kane, Ullin Place, James Rachels, and G. Lynn Stephens as friends. I am grateful to them all for helping me to think about mind. Special thanks go to Richard Garrett for insight and inspiration.

My wife, Patricia, has endured my time and preoccupations with both the first and second editions. By reading the first edition she reinforced my efforts to write readable prose. I re-dedicate this book to Patricia, in renewed appreciation for her efforts on its and my behalf. My good thoughts would be lost without her.

1

What is Philosophy of Mind?

In reading this book you are using your mind. When you ponder this page your mind is at work. As you sit in your chair you are having experiences. When you see the color of the book cover you are having a visual experience. When you notice the sounds in the next room you are having an auditory experience. Your mind enables you to read, ponder, see, and hear.

Now think for a minute of what it would be like if the world, our Earth, was mindless. What if the world was devoid of experience and thought? At the very least, a mindless world would be, to borrow a phrase of the poet John Keats, a wide quietness, 'with buds, and bells, and stars without a name'. It would be a world in which nothing was named, in which nothing was either thought of or experienced, for there would be no one. There certainly would be no you and me.

Fortunately, the world is not mindless. Indeed, it is thickly populated with minds. In the world, moreover, minds not only name but are named. They are named by type, such as The Human Mind or The Animal Mind, and by individual, such as My Mind, Your Mind, and the Minds of Charles Dickens and Emily Dickinson. Indeed, minds are not just named, they are studied and examined in science, novel, and verse as well as philosophy.

The purpose of this book is to introduce the area of philosophy which studies mind: the philosophy of mind. I write for those coming to philosophy of mind for the first time.

1.1 Beginning Definitions, Elementary Ideas

What is philosophy of mind? Philosophy of mind is the area of philosophy which strives for comprehensive and systematic understanding of that which thinks and experiences, namely the mind. It tries to understand what mind is, what it does, and how to uncover it.

Although philosophy of mind is a single subject, it has many parts or aspects. The aspects serve as bases for the chapters to follow. Meanwhile, one can learn something about the subject before reading the book by looking at various concepts used in the preceding definition. Let us look first at 'philosophy', then at 'mind'; then, we shall return to the complete expression 'philosophy of mind'.

Philosophy is the subject or academic discipline which attempts to comprehensively and systematically understand the most fundamental areas of human experience. These include mind as well as religion, science, art, language, and morality, among others. The key words are 'comprehensive' and 'systematic'. Comprehensiveness and systematicity help to distinguish philosophy from other subjects of intellectual and theoretical endeavor such as, for examples, physics and history.

Comprehensiveness has two dimensions. One is breadth; the other is depth. Breadth? Physics studies matter in motion but not belief in God. History studies the recorded memory of humankind but not the difference between right and wrong. Philosophy studies (among many other things) belief in God and the difference between right and wrong as well as, for examples, the central features of physics and history. So philosophy covers a lot of ground. It covers more ground – in a systematic manner – than any other discipline. In covering a lot of ground philosophy possesses breadth.

What of depth? Philosophy penetrates beneath the ground which it covers. It tries to get to the core. Sometimes, in fact, a philosopher will argue that something close to the heart of another mode of inquiry, such as science, should be rejected or replaced. This typifies the drive for depth. Philosophy may recommend or urge changes in other disciplines, because it probes deeply into the foundations of those disciplines. To take a brief illustration, most psychologists probably agree with Susan Blakemore, a psychologist at the University of Bristol in the United Kingdom, that after the death of our physical body 'there will be no more experience; no more self'.[1] Philosophers, however, may challenge psychologists to re-examine the belief in non-survival. A philosopher may argue, rightly or wrongly, that a probing analysis of experimental and clinical data together with what is known of other areas of human experience shows that the self or mind can survive. The self is not necessarily snuffed out when the body dies.

I do not mean to convey the impression that philosophy contradicts established convictions of scientists and psychologists. Many philosophers share Blakemore's skepticism about survival. What I am concerned with here is philosophy's comprehensiveness and, in particular, its drive for depth. Philosophy attempts to penetrate even if this means challenging doctrines of other disciplines.

Thus far we have considered the comprehensiveness of philosophy. What of systematicity? The simplest way to describe systematicity, which states the basic idea but does not attempt to clarify it very much, is this: in aiming to be systematic philosophy strives to be both consistent and coherent. It aims for ideas or theses which are free of contradiction (that's consistency) and which stand in relationships of mutual reinforcement and support (that's coherence).

The elements of systematicity, mainly consistency and coherence, sound very abstract, and in truth they are difficult to describe with precision. At the same time, philosophy requires consistency and coherence. Anything less is unsystematic and unacceptable. To illustrate, consider the following three philosophic claims about mind, brain, and death.

C1   The mind is one and the same as the brain; mind and brain are identical.
C2   The mind survives bodily death.
C3   The brain fails to survive bodily death.

C1, C2, and C3 cannot each be true; thus, they are inconsistent. It is not possible for the mind to survive while the brain, if mind is one and the same as brain, fails to survive. Compare with the following: I am one and the same as George Graham. Then, I cannot travel to Scotland while George Graham journeys to China. If we are one and the same, then whatever I do George must do, for he is me.

What can be done to rescue or achieve systematicity? In the case at hand, one option is to subtract C1 and then add C4:

C4   The mind is *not* one and the same as the brain. Mind and brain are distinct.

C2, C3, and C4 are consistent. Each member of the set can be true. This is not to say that each really is true. However, it is to claim that the set is free of contradiction. C2, C3, and C4 even support or cohere with one another. If, for example, mind is not one and the same as brain, then something is true of the mind which is not true of the brain. What is that something? C2 and C3 offer a possible answer. 'The mind survives bodily death whereas the brain does not survive.' C2 and C3 thus reinforce or support C4. They help to explain why C4 might be true. So, C2, C3, and C4 stand not only in consistent but coherent or mutually supportive relationships.

Unfortunately perhaps, as Gilbert Harman, a philosophy professor at Princeton University, is fond of pointing out in another context, there are no fixed rules which reveal how to achieve consistency and coherence.[2] The search for systematicity suggests that something in C1, C2, and C3 must go. But what? Should we substitute C4 for C1? Should we abandon the C2 conviction that the mind survives? How about the C3 claim that the brain fails to survive? Either alternative produces a consistent and coherent set of theses or claims. However, even without strict guidelines for systematicity, it is clear that a philosophy which is neither consistent nor coherent fails to be systematic. Philosophies can be unacceptable on a number of different grounds. Failure to be systematic is one of them.

I hasten to add that if two distinguishing features of philosophy are comprehensiveness and systematicity, these are not the sole distinguishing features. Philosophy is different from other subjects such as physics and history not merely because it systematically covers more ground, but because of its method and motive. Physics, for example, relies on mathematics and laboratory experiments; philosophy doesn't rely on mathematics or experiments. History rests on the record of the past; philosophy doesn't rest on the past. There isn't even reliance on the great thinkers of the past, philosophers like Plato (427–347 bc) and Descartes (1596–1650), despite appreciation for their ideas. The heart of philosophic method is reason and argumentation. The motivation or source – the reason people do philosophy – consists of features of the world and human experience which people naturally find worrisome, perplexing, and puzzling, such as the mind. 'What is the relation between mind and brain?' 'Does mind survive bodily death?' 'Is mind nothing over and above brain?' True, perplexity and puzzlement also motivate disciplines like physics or history, but in other subjects human puzzlement is more limited than in philosophy. In physics, it is confined to the physical world, whereas in history it is focused on the recorded past. Philosophy, like human intelligence itself, is first and last driven by *expansive* puzzlement and perplexity. The topics of philosophy cover the total spectrum of basic human concerns. Hence, when I contend that philosophy aims for comprehensive and systematic understanding, I don't mean that only comprehensiveness and systematicity distinguish it from other subjects. My statement represents the bare bud of philosophy. It does not reveal how philosophers try to achieve that understanding (the method) or what stimulates or motivates it (the motive).

We have just learned something about the nature of philosophy. We have learned that it is both systematic and comprehensive, and we have learned something about the nature of these features. What of mind?

Before offering a definition, let's consider an instance of what may be called mind at work. Suppose you are cracking walnuts with a nutcracker, and the cracker misses the shell of a walnut and you squeeze its pivoted jaws on your thumb. What happens? First there will be pain. Then probably anger. Then eventually the belief that you made an imprudent mistake. All three – the pain, anger, and belief – are activities of mind or events which take place in or because of mind. A mindless creature could not feel pain, be angry, or believe that it had made a mistake. This is not to say that only creatures who feel pain, get angry, and believe they make mistakes have minds. Nevertheless, such events or capacities are possible only for minded creatures.

Ponder the pain. You squeeze your thumb in a nutcracker. You feel pain. Pain is among the clearest examples of mental events philosophers and others classify as 'sensations'. In particular, pain is a bodily sensation, since, as in pain produced by squeezing your thumb, the pain seems to the person in pain to occur in a part or region of the body, in this case the thumb.

Consider the example of anger. You get angry at yourself for squeezing your thumb. Anger is among the clearest examples of mental events philosophers and others classify as 'emotions' or 'emotional feelings'. In particular, anger is a directed emotion, because, as in anger over squeezing your thumb, it is aimed or directed at something which is its source or cause, for instance, squeezing your thumb.

Consider the example of belief. You believe that you made an imprudent mistake. Belief is among the clearest examples of mental events philosophers and others classify as 'thoughts' or (more technically) 'propositional attitudes' (which expression will be explained shortly). In particular, belief is a thought or attitude with a specific content or character to it, since, as in belief in your own imprudence, it is *about* something. In the example at hand, the belief is about yourself as imprudent thumb squeezer, not about yourself as curious reader of this book, although you are reading this book and probably have beliefs about yourself with that content as well.

A fact to notice about thoughts or attitudes with content is that the same content can occur in different types or sorts of thought. So, to illustrate, I can believe that I made a mistake, I can remember that I made a mistake, or I can fear that I made a mistake. In each example, there is the same content, viz. that I made a mistake; but the content occurs in different types of thought or attitude: believing, remembering, and fearing respectively. Furthermore, since content can be expressed in the form of a proposition or statement, such as 'I made a mistake', philosophers often refer to thoughts with content as 'propositional attitudes'. The attitude may be interpreted as an attitude towards a proposition or towards the state of affairs expressed by a proposition: believing that *I made a mistake*, fearing that *I made a mistake*, and so on.

It should also be noted that sensations and emotional feelings are among the clearest examples of mental events which normally, typically, perhaps even necessarily occur in consciousness and which are consciously experienced. By contrast, propositional attitudes are among the clearest examples of mental goings on which may not occur in consciousness. Think of the difference, for example, between your belief (when not planning a tour) that Radio City Music Hall is in New York City, and the sensation of pain or the feeling of anger on squeezing your thumb in a nutcracker. The belief may be non-conscious. You may have it when asleep, unconscious and unaware. It is part of your memory store of background information. By contrast, the pain lashed into consciousness with anger resounding immediately thereafter. It would be hard or even impossible to imagine having *this* pain and being *that* angry while asleep or unconscious.

Let us label conscious mental events or activities 'experiences' (for emphasis 'conscious experiences'). Let us reserve 'propositional attitudes' (or 'thoughts') for mental goings on such as beliefs which possess propositionally expressible content and of which we can be unaware. Propositional attitudes can be conscious or non-conscious. They can be experiences or non-experiences. Experiences, by contrast, are conscious.

Defining mind is not easy. But it is not impossible. By using the concepts of thought and experience, I propose the following definition. Mind is that which thinks and experiences. Mindless creatures neither think nor experience. Since you and I are minded, or have minds of our own, we think and experience.

Now back to the definition of philosophy of mind introduced several paragraphs ago. What is philosophy of mind? The following answer may now be offered: *Philosophy of mind is the area of philosophy which strives for comprehensive and systematic understanding of that which thinks and experiences, namely the mind.*

Our definition of the subject gives us, among other things, a picture of the terrain to be covered in this book. The book will portray how philosophy aims to comprehensively and systematically understand mind. We will explore from a philosophic vantage point what mind is, does, and how to uncover it.[3]

Before we start, with a brief example below of a problem in philosophy of mind, I should mention one thing that philosophy of mind is not. Philosophy of mind is not psychology. Psychology is science; philosophy is not science. Compared to scientists philosophers, for example, do not conduct laboratory experiments or observations of empirically or clinically controlled sorts.[4] Furthermore, rarely if ever does psychology support theses in philosophy of mind in a direct or immediate manner. A psychologist may be either friend or foe, for example, of the thesis that mind is brain. However, philosophy of mind has traditionally given and received assistance in the development of psychology. Philosophic arguments advance and enrich psychology, while facts and lessons from psychology make philosophy of mind more coherent and trustworthy.

One means whereby philosophers and psychologists give and receive assistance is formal interdisciplinary activity. Formal interdisciplinary activity consists of two or more disciplines working cooperatively on problems of mutual interest. Members of cooperating disciplines may teach the same courses, attend the same professional meetings, and publish in the same academic journals.

One currently popular form of interdisciplinary activity of relevance to the philosophy of mind is known as cognitive science. Cognitive science engages philosophers, psychologists, neuroscientists, computer scientists and others, all devoted to how best to understand intelligent thought and behavior and the cognitive aspects of mind.[5] These include features such as reasoning, perception, and memory, among others.

Various cognitive science hypotheses about intelligent thought and behavior have been proposed. To put one at its simplest, when people think intelligently they operate like a computer executing the rules of a program: intelligence is a matter of computational processing and so is best exhibited by a computer. Philosophers have contributed to both the defense and criticism of this hypothesis (a topic which we will examine in the fifth chapter). Since cognitive science is grounded not just in empirical science, but in speculation about intelligence, thought and computation, and much else besides, philosophers of mind are welcome alongside psychologists and others as contributors to cognitive science. So although philosophy is not science, there is no radical discontinuity between philosophy of mind and psychology.

1.2 Color in Black and White

Have you ever tried to describe to another person what some conscious experience of yours is like? One day a friend of mine tried to describe for me what his migraine headaches are like. 'They feel *awful*, positively *dreadful!*' he reported, evincing the sad and sorry character of his headaches. I tried to understand them in terms of my own luckily undramatic history of aches and pains. I complained that some of my headaches have to be quieted by double doses of aspirin. However, he was insulted by my complaint. 'You obviously don't know what mine *feel* like', he protested. 'If yours are relieved by aspirin, yours are very different from my own. Mine are dreadful; *nothing* relieves them.'

Apparently some of his headaches are nothing like my headaches. The raw feel of his headaches seemed to elude me. But why? Why did his describing his headaches do so little to communicate their character to me? A natural, intuitive explanation for this sort of phenomenon goes as follows:

> Experience is the necessary educator; a description of experience is no substitute for experience. The very feel of a conscious experience eludes us unless we have had the experience ourselves. In the headache case, I can grasp the character of migraine only by having a migraine myself. Since I have never had a migraine, I do not know what the headaches are like.

Whatever merits this explanation – which I shall call the *experience explanation* – has in accounting for my friend's frustration, as an interpretation of the character of conscious experience it is incompatible with an objection advanced by several philosophers fond of physical science. The objection goes as follows:

> The experience explanation neglects an important additional way in which to discover what conscious experience is like: through natural science. Physical, chemical, and biological science can describe consciousness and thus what the experience of migraine is like. You don't have to *have* a migraine. Science can describe it for you.

Imagine, then, that I, having located the most advanced neuroscientific texts on migraine, open one of these texts. Will I find there a description of the character of migraines through which I can grasp, as the migraine sufferer did not help me to grasp, what migraine is like?

That is the hope of some scientifically minded philosophers. I shall call it the *optimistic science position*. According to the optimistic position, to know each and every physical scientific fact about conscious experience is to know, among other things, what experience is like. Still, is the optimistic science position reasonable? Will it survive critical reflection? One trouble with the position is that we can outline an opposing (what I shall call) *pessimistic science position* in a plausible fashion, according to which even if we know the physics, chemistry, and biology of consciousness, we still will not know what consciousness is like. This is because consciousness is subjective or first-personal: we need to *be* conscious before we can know what consciousness is like. No amount of impersonal physical scientific information about migraine is sufficient to communicate what the headache is like.

To see how the pessimistic science position may be developed, let us consider one of the most famous defenses of the position in recent philosophy of mind. This is the so-called Knowledge Argument of the Australian philosopher Frank Jackson.[6] Jackson's argument is provocative, and much has been written about it. I shall spend only a few moments with it. The topic it raises – conscious experience – is discussed again in the tenth and eleventh chapters.

Jackson defends the pessimistic position with a direct, vivid story, which focuses on the visual experience of color rather than the experience of migraine. It goes roughly like this:

Imagine that we live in the Golden Age of Completed Physical Science. Imagine Mary, a super-duper neuroscientist of the golden age, who has spent her entire life cloistered within a strictly controlled room which displays only various shades of black, white, and gray. Mary nevertheless (through black and white television and colorless books) has become the world's greatest expert on the physics, chemistry, and biology of the visual experience of color. She knows everything knowable physically, chemically, and biologically about color perception. For example, she knows (assuming for the sake of illustration that the following thesis holds true) that all color experiences are the product of the interplay of three retinal cones. Each experience of a particular type of color or shade is produced by unique ratios of activity in the cones. She also knows everything else that physical science can grasp about color experience. If physical science can uncover a color fact, Mary knows it.

Jackson believes that the two sets of phenomena – color experience and everything there is to know of the physics/chemistry/biology of color experience – are stuck together in a gappy or incomplete manner. The physical sciences cannot capture everything there is to know about conscious experience. There are some facts about color experience which escape Mary's scientific understanding. To continue:

In knowing every physical scientific fact about color experience does Mary know everything there is to know about it? Consider what would happen if Mary were suddenly released from her black and white chamber and shown a ripe red tomato for the first time. Mary would discover something she did not know before. She would learn facts of the form 'this is what red color experience is like' or 'red color perception is this', where 'this' picks out the experience of color. The knowledge or fact she gains on release she did not possess in the chamber. However, since she already knew the physical science of color experience, the 'what it is like' of the experience is something which cannot be known by physical science.

Spelled out schematically, Jackson's argument looks like this:

1   Prior to release Mary knows everything about the physics, chemistry, and biology of color experience. She knows every physical scientific fact about the visual experience of color.

2   Prior to her release there is at least one fact about color experience which Mary does not know, for she learns this fact only upon release. This is what it is like to see color (red).

3   So, there are some facts about color experience which cannot be known by physical science.

If Jackson is right, then the 'what it is like' of *any* conscious experience – not just of color – cannot be revealed by physical science. This is because analogous Mary stories can be told for sensations of migraine, perceptual experiences of heat, sound, and taste, emotions of fear and hope, and so on. Virtually any sort of conscious experience cannot be completely comprehended by physical science.

Consider the following variation:

> Imagine Harry, a brilliant neuroscientist, who has spent his entire life in an environment in which he has never suffered a migraine. Harry nevertheless, through books, has become the world's foremost expert on migraine headaches.

The variation can be abbreviated since details are obvious. What the variation boils down to is as follows:

1*   Prior to experiencing migraine Harry knows whatever can be known from physical science about migraine.

2*   Prior to migraine experience there is at least one fact about migraines which Harry does not know. This is what migraines are like.

3*   So, there are some facts about migraines which cannot be known by physical science.

Jackson's knowledge argument has not gone uncontested by philosophers who are optimists about physical science and believe that physical science leaves *nothing* out.[7] For them everything there is to know about the world, including conscious experience, is contained or containable in completed physical science.

Scientific optimists object to the Jacksonian argument on a number of grounds. I shall briefly discuss two.

(1) One objection is that Mary is presumed capable of visual experience but incapable of visual color experience because of the absence of color in her room. But why can't Mary visually experience red when she

rubs her eyes or when she dreams? Merely being in a colorless environment does not ensure the absence of color experience. Color experience
can be had by other means.

In response it may be conceded that Jackson has not described a
situation which necessarily precludes color experience. Nevertheless,
Jackson can readily amend his description of Mary's situation so that
color experience is ultimately left out. To do this Jackson needs to
describe Mary's position more carefully. He could stipulate, for example,
that Mary's ability to experience color somehow atrophies by virtue of
being in the room and is restored only on release. The point of Jackson's
story is that being a color-blind or profoundly color-deficient perceiver,
for *whatever* reason, precludes knowing what color experience is like even
if one knows everything that physical science can reveal about color
experience. The story is intended as a vivid way in which to make a
scientifically pessimistic point. It can be amended accordingly.

(2) A second objection cuts more deeply. Consider, to set up the
objection, what may be said if Mary emerges from the room as follows:

> She takes one look at the tomato and announces: 'The books I had in
> that room were wonderful. I knew exactly what looking at red would
> be like. I have discovered nothing new by perceiving the tomato. I
> appreciate that it is difficult for you outsiders and scientific pre-golden
> agers to imagine how I could know of color visual experience in a
> colorless environment, with atrophied color vision, but of course
> unlike you I know absolutely everything physical science can reveal
> about color experience. Your knowledge of the physical science of
> color is pitiably puny compared to mine. So although it's tough for
> you to imagine how I could grasp what looking at red is like, I am not
> in the least surprised.'

Of course Jackson would be surprised; indeed, he would be both
dumbfounded and skeptical. He would suppose that it just can't be done.
But why not? Why can't Mary know what color experience is like
beforehand? If, for example, we imagine a fictional future in which Mary
knows *everything* physical science *can* reveal about color experience, as
Jackson imagines, one temptation – contrary to Jackson – is to say that
what color experience is like is knowable independent of color experience. 'Information through the senses', says the philosopher Anthony
Kenny, 'and the discriminations performed with their aid, may be

acquired . . . by means other than the senses.'[8] Just as it is not necessary to perceive planets and numbers in order to know that there are nine planets which orbit around our sun, it is not necessary to have a red color experience to grasp what red color experience is like. One can acquire this information by relying on scientific books.

I shall refer to the second objection to the knowledge argument as the means of acquisition objection. It has many variations.[9] According to the objection 'what color experience is like' expresses information which can be acquired by means other than by undergoing color experience. The information can be known by physical science.

Is what Mary lacks merely a means of knowing what red color experience is like? Are there other ways of getting the *same* information? Here, in a nutshell, is a Jacksonian response to the means of acquisition objection.

Consider again such facts as what red color experience is like. 'What red color experience is like' is a fact whose understanding depends upon having certain experiences – visual sensations or perceptions of red – for the information is information about the like-thisness of red visual experience. It cannot be separated from its (visual experiential) means of acquisition. By contrast, information that there are nine planets can be separated from its means of acquisition. Planetary information is not information about what an experience is like. It is information about facts (the number of planets) which are independent of how or even if they are experienced. One can get planetary information from a book. Planets exist independent of human experience; human color experience does not.

If all this is right, and barring other objections to the knowledge argument, then the proper conclusion is that 'red visual experience is like this' and 'what color experience is like' express information which cannot be known by physical science. The information can only be acquired in first-person experience. The pessimistic science position is preferable to the optimistic position.

Note, I said 'barring other objections'. Jackson's knowledge argument is controversial and the literature which it has inspired is complicated. Jeff McConnell in a paper entitled simply 'In defense of the knowledge argument' modestly sums up his own defense of the argument as follows:

My aim here has not been to argue for the Knowledge Argument but to show that a ... version of it can be constructed that withstands the best attacks made so far by critics ... If it is to be defeated, this will happen only with arguments more subtle ... than any previously made.[10]

I will not introduce 'arguments more subtle' here, although (as said) I will return to the topic of consciousness (more than once) later in the book. Our discussion of Jackson is meant to offer a small but tantalizing slice of debate surrounding the knowledge argument. If after reading this first chapter, you decide to advance through successive chapters, you will notice how much more there is to say about topics in the philosophy of mind than I say about Jackson's argument. That information, new reader, will more than suffice for a bright red migraine!

NOTES

1 Susan Blakemore, 'Minds, brains, and death', in *Frontiers of Science*, ed. A. Scott (Blackwell Publishers, Oxford, 1990), pp. 48–9.

2 See Gilbert Harman, *Change in View* (MIT Press, Cambridge, Mass., 1986).

3 This does not mean that we will develop a *fully* systematic and comprehensive philosophy of mind. A fully systematic and comprehensive philosophy of mind requires examination of topics ill-suited for an introduction, and it would be committal about matters towards which this book is not committal. However, the book will contain some measure – a healthy dose – of both systematicity and comprehensiveness.

4 On the relation between the empirical methods of science and the critical practice of philosophy, see Bertrand Russell, 'The value of philosophy', in *The Problems of Philosophy* (Hackett, Indianapolis, 1912/1991), pp. 153–61.

5 For additional information about cognitive science, including the role of philosophy within cognitive science, see W. Bechtel, A. Abrahamsen, and G. Graham, 'The life of cognitive science', in *A Companion to Cognitive Science*, eds. William Bechtel and George Graham (Blackwell Publishers, Oxford, 1998), pp. 1–104.

6 For the original presentation of the argument, see Frank Jackson, 'Epiphenomenal qualia', *The Philosophical Quarterly*, 32 (1982), pp. 127–36; 'What Mary didn't know', *The Journal of Philosophy*, LXXXIII, 5 (1986), pp. 291–5. See also Thomas Nagel, *The View from Nowhere* (Oxford University Press, Oxford, 1986); 'What is it like to be a bat?', *Philosophical Review*, 83 (1974), pp. 435–50.

7   See Paul Churchland, 'Reduction, qualia and the direct introspection of brain states', in *A Neurocomputational Perspective: The Nature of Mind and the Structure of Science* (MIT Press, Cambridge, Mass., 1989), pp. 61–6; David Lewis, 'What experience teaches', in *Mind and Cognition*, ed. W. Lycan (Blackwell Publishers, Oxford, 1990), pp. 499–519; Michael Tye, 'The subjective qualities of experience', *Mind*, 95 (1986), pp. 1–17; Robert Van Gulick, 'Understanding the phenomenal mind: are we all just armadillos?', in *Consciousness: A Mind and Language Reader*, ed. M. Davies and G. Humphreys (Blackwell Publishers, Oxford, 1992). These optimisms are not all of the same order or type. However, they all share aversion to the Jackson argument.

8   Anthony Kenny, *The God of the Philosophers* (Oxford University Press, Oxford, 1979), p. 32.

9   See, for example, C. S. Hill, 'Imaginability, conceivability, and the mind-body problem', *Philosophical Studies*, 87 (1997), pp. 61–85.

10 J. McConnell, 'In defense of the knowledge argument', *Philosophical Topics*, 22 (1994), pp. 182–3.

2

Death and Identity

At some point, everyone who reads this book will be dead. Must that mean that we also will have ceased to exist? Is life after death possible? Or is it absolutely out of the question?

Some people abhor the fact that they will cease to exist: that they will 'die' in the sense of being snuffed out or extinguished. Miguel De Unamuno (1864–1936) in *The Tragic Sense of Life* (1921) says, 'I do not want to die – no; I neither want to die nor do I want to want to die; I want to live for ever and ever.' Unamuno's sentiments are shared by the great Russian novelist, Leo Tolstoy (1828–1910), in *A Confession* (written in 1878–9). Tolstoy says that life would be utterly empty and meaningless if we cease to exist at death: 'Today or tomorrow sickness and death will come (they had come already) to those I love or to me; nothing will remain but stench and worms. Sooner or later my affairs whatever they may be, will be forgotten, and shall not exist. Then why go on making any effort?'

In this chapter we shall discuss the major philosophical questions concerning whether life after death is possible. These include questions about personal identity as well as about the possibility of disembodied personal existence. Such questions surround a great many people's religious beliefs, and they are by no means 'academic' questions of concern only to philosophers. One important religious tradition which has attended to them is Christianity.

2.1 Christianity and the Problem of Survival

In November 1976, Jimmy Carter, then candidate for President of the United States, spoke in a much-publicized interview in *Playboy* magazine. The interview revealed Carter's attitudes toward adultery, as one expects in *Playboy*, but it also contained a revealing remark about Carter's freedom from fear of death.

Playboy: You don't fear death. Why not?

Carter: It's part of my religious belief. I just look at death as not a threat. It's inevitable, and I have an assurance of eternal life. There is no feeling on my part that I *have* to be President, or that I *have* to live, or that I'm immune to danger. It's just that the termination of my physical life is relatively insignificant in my concept of over-all existence. I don't say that in a mysterious way: I recognize the possibility of assassination. But I guess everybody recognizes the possibility of other forms of death – automobile accidents, airplane accidents, cancer. I just don't worry.

Carter's relaxed and candid expression of religious faith certainly appears normal and even healthy. Indeed, it is usual among Christian believers, and Carter is a Christian, to believe in everlasting life after death. According to Christianity, individual persons continue to exist subsequent to bodily death; and they persist permanently. Once people come into existence, they never go out of existence. Death fails to annihilate.

Why do Christians believe that people never go out of existence? Surely the reason is not that our bodies do not die and decay. Obviously the human body (including brain) dies and rots. There is a deeper reason why persons are regarded as having a capacity for everlasting existence. In Christian thinking, person and body can be separated and once separated the person can survive without the body. Indeed, a person can survive without material embodiment of any kind. Hence, just because the body dies does not mean that the person extinguishes. Then an extremely powerful or omnipotent God exists who ensures that the person does not extinguish after bodily death. Apart from God's intervention death would destroy the person. As Iranaeus, a Bishop of Lyons in Gaul in the second century, writes: 'Our survival forever comes from his greatness, not from our nature.'[1] With God's intercession, personal survival is guaranteed independent of bodily death.

What is or would be involved in surviving bodily death? First, since the person survives, whatever makes the person the person he or she is – namely, his or her personal identity – must be present after death. If the survival of something, anything, means the survival of me, then 'the survivor' counts as George Graham. According to this first condition, which I shall call the *identity condition*, the survival of something non-identical with me (such as the survival of my children or ashes) cannot count as the survival of me. Second, there must be psychological awareness or recognition of personal survival after death. Carter expects in post-mortem life to recognize that he has survived. This awareness can be ensured, at least in part, by consciousness of who one is and the presence of true memories about pre-mortem life. For instance, Carter may remember having been President of the United States and his former life in Georgia. According to this second condition, which I shall call the *recognition condition*, if something unaware of survival survives, 'the survivor' fails to count as a surviving person. Personal survival requires recognition of personal survival.

Within Christianity the identity and recognition conditions are interconnected. The recognition condition means that pre-mortem and post-mortem life are linked by the memory and self-awareness of the person. Hence the person's mind or that which recognizes and remembers must survive. Christianity then identifies personal identity with the mind. On the Christian conception, what makes me me is my mind, including my capacities for memory and self-awareness. Post-mortem survival essentially is psychological survival.

There is considerable room for variation here. We do not find a single understanding of personal survival within Christianity. But traditionally there have been two main approaches to the topic. Although both assume that the person survives if the mind survives, both also presuppose that the mind or person reunites with the body. The term used to refer to reunion is 're-embodiment'.[2] The term used to refer to a person or mind capable of disembodiment is 'soul'.

(1)   The first approach to understanding survival relies on introducing a distinction between the complete or full person and the incomplete or truncated person. It holds that a complete person is a union of both mind or soul and body, whereas an incomplete person is just the mind. Hence people who survive bodily death bodilessly are incomplete persons and require re-embodiment to be full persons. I can survive partially without

my body; but absent embodiment I am not altogether myself.

The philosopher Daniel Dennett has noted that what one is *asked* to imagine, what one *can* imagine, and what one *really does* imagine may be three distinct things. It is not clear whether we *can* imagine existing in disembodied form, but let us try imaginatively to enter the alleged possibility for a moment. You now have, I presume, a body. However, because a disembodied person would be immaterial, if you were disembodied, existing only as soul or mind, you would not have a leg to stand on, nor lips to kiss, nor smile to shine. Arguably, you would also lack the five senses: sight, hearing, smell, taste, and touch. This is because you would lack the organs (eyes, ears, etc.) which, arguably, make perceptual sensation (sight, hearing, and so on) possible.

Mentioning candidate deprivations of the disembodied is not meant to imply that the capacities which require embodiment are absolutely essential to you or for your survival. Blind people live without sight; amputees persist without legs. But it is to point out that according to the first option you are incomplete if disembodied. You persist through disembodiment; but disembodiment, according to the first option, is truncated.

Let me add one extended personal note. To me it is not surprising that many Christians look forward to the Resurrection. The term 'resurrection' refers to the divine reconstitution of the embodied person. 'Resurrection', with a capital 'R', refers to the Second Coming of Christ and to the general resurrection which is supposed to accompany it.

Disembodied existence is unappealing to many Christians. They expect to exist for a time apart from the body, merely as souls; but soul existence may seem unattractively lean and barren. Taking a walk, kissing one's lover, singing sacred music: these sorts of enjoyable activities would be impossible. Indeed, the Apostle Paul holds that the body with which a person is reunited on Resurrection will actually be a spectacularly improved version of the pre-mortem body. 'It is sown in dishonor, it is raised in glory; it is sown in weakness, it is raised in power' (1 Corinthians 15:43).

Surely reconstitution of the body in exactly the same condition as before death would be pointless, for it would quickly rot and disintegrate. On Paul's account, then, resurrection is no mere reunion; rather, it is bodily reunion plus enrichment of the body's health and power. Christians expect to experience the body as 'raised in glory'. Just how glorified?

The Reverend Billy Graham, popular evangelist and television personality, describes glorification as follows:

> The body that lies in the grave has been neglected. It may be worn out with age, abused by disease, or broken by accident, but in the resurrection that body is raised in glory! It will be free of all infirmities ... Those who are burned or maimed in wars will be whole. Old people will be young and virtuous.[3]

Reverend Graham speaks for a large number of Christians who feel that there is not only little or nothing desirable in disembodiment, but little or nothing desirable in regaining the body if it remains subject to the same infirmities as before death.

(2) The second approach to survival interprets persons in exclusively spiritual or immaterial terms. According to the second approach, the human body is not essential to the (whole) person; the body is utterly and absolutely dispensable. The full person in complete powers can survive purely mentally – as a mind.

The second approach is more problematic, from a philosophic point of view, than the first. It is difficult to explain how a person – a sighted, hearing, talking person – can survive permanent loss of embodiment. (Temporary disembodiment is also problematic. The topic of disembodiment will be examined in detail later in the chapter.) Within Christianity, belief in the more dramatic form of personal survival represented by the second approach is less popular than belief in the first, viz. reunion in order to recover full personhood. The first is the more traditional Christian option. Nothing in the second approach, however, is meant to deny reunion. Even if reunion is not necessary for full survival, it might be essential for other post-mortem purposes, including divine reward or punishment. A disembodied person may be unable to reap the joys of heaven or suffer the torments of hell.

In any case, let's welcome back Carter. It is easy to appreciate what Carter as a Christian expects if we remember the identity and recognition conditions. When viewed from the perspective of someone who pictures death as the end of personal existence, life can seem dangerous and fragile, fraught with the threat of annihilation. In the words of novelist John Cowper Powys, 'There is the appalling possibility that the "I" upon whom this whole world of immediate impressions depends ... will be nowhere at all.'[4] From Carter's Christian perspective, however, things look very different. He expects to survive bodily death and to realize that he has survived. He expects to remember his Presidency and former residence in Georgia. Before death, he will not feel frustrated and upset (at least for himself) whenever he thinks that he may be assassinated. He will not deem his death a personal annihilation.

Thus far we have seen that there is widespread agreement among many people (Christians are the example employed here) that personal life does not terminate at death. Persons survive (although perhaps only with God's help) the rot and disintegration of their bodies. But if the anticipation of disembodied afterlife is reasonable or justifiable there must be argument for it. Only if strong, coherent reasons can be given for the prospect of post-mortem disembodied survival is it reasonable to believe with Carter and others in personal persistence beyond the grave.

What of disembodied survival? Can a person exist without material embodiment? René Descartes (1596–1650) is famous as an advocate of *substance dualism* (also known in his honor as *Cartesian dualism*). The main idea behind substance dualism is that bodies are material and disintegrate, but they can be separated from minds which do not. Souls or minds are independent of the physical world and have the potential to last forever. In the words of philosopher Richard Watson, 'The theological demand that human souls be immortal drives Descartes to his dualism of kinds of substances.'[5]

Maybe Descartes is right. Perhaps minds (souls) survive intact; no doubt bodies do not. However, leaving Descartes' main idea aside, the arguments he provides for the independence of mind from body are vulnerable to serious criticism. We will examine one of those arguments (the so-called 'first argument for dualism') in the eighth chapter. Like other critics, we will find the argument weak and insufficient.

Is there argument for disembodied survival which does not involve a conceptual journey through Cartesian dualism? Can we look elsewhere for warrant that disembodied survival is possible? The hypothesis that minds or disembodied persons can survive would actually be best confirmed if it could be shown that people actually do survive.

Consider the following analogy: Suppose someone asks 'Can Great Blue Herons survive winters in Alaska?' Friends of the Audubon Society know perfectly well that they can. While most Great Blue Herons migrate south in the autumn, a few remain in Alaska during the winter.

The actual presence of Herons in Alaska in the winter confirms that wintry Alaska survival is possible.

In general, if we know that something really does happen, then we know that it can happen. In thinking about disembodied survival, is there anything which shows that it occurs?

2.2 The After-Death Experience

St John of the Cross, a Christian poet and mystic of the late sixteenth century, once remarked that 'God is wont to enlighten and spiritualize [persons] . . . by means of certain supernatural visions.'[6]

What reason can be given for counting post-mortem survival possible? Why should anyone suppose that he or she can survive bodilessly or immaterially, if only for a time, beyond the grave? Perhaps the answer lies, as John mentions in the above quote, in experiences or visions, whether supplied by God or not. Experiences or visions may reveal the actual occurrence of disembodied survival.

Let us begin by looking at a sort of case which appears to show that people do survive without a body. The type of case is a so-called 'after-death out-of-body experience' (or 'near-death experience' depending upon one's favored interpretation of the time of death) in which a person purports to have left their body at or near death and returned. The example I am about to discuss is a fictional composite adapted from reports of individuals who actually claim to have had after-death out-of-body experiences. These reports have been widely publicized in the media and popular press. They have also been studied by physicians such as Elisabeth Kubler-Ross and Michael Sabom.[7]

Gloria G., at the age of only 39, had been diagnosed as having brain cancer and struck with the bombshell that she had only a few weeks to live. Her sole and slim chance for survival was if she submitted to a dangerous neurosurgical operation to remove the tumor. She did. This is how she reported the operation after recovery.

As I was lying on the table I heard the doctors pronounce the operation a failure and pronounce me dead. I then remember them frantically trying to resuscitate me. But what I recall, which seems funny in retrospect, is that while they were trying to bring me back to life, I was just floating up near the ceiling. It was a weird feeling because I was up there and this body was below. I could see them trying to get my heart started. From where I was looking I seemed to float higher, above an enormous fluorescent operating room light . . . and it was quite dirty above the light. Then I seemed to wander up through the floors of the hospital. I saw plainly, for instance, a young man who had been injured in an automobile accident crying with a woman, perhaps his wife or mother, at the news that he would lose a leg. Then everything began to get dark: I passed through what seemed to be a spiralling tunnel – long, very narrow, and dark – until I seemed to come to a place illuminated by an immensely bright light. Not an artificial light; more inviting and warm like the sun. Then suddenly, and this was the weirdest sensation of all, the light revealed wonderfully beautiful and spacious surroundings – flowers, trees. A tremendous peace overcame me. My grandmother, who had died nine years before, was there. I couldn't see her – for she seemed behind me – but I could feel her presence and hear her voice. She spoke in a combination of English and Hungarian, as she had while alive. I don't recall literally speaking to her, but I seemed to communicate without making noise. She told me that I was not going to remain with her at that time. That I would visit later. I pleaded with her to let me stay because I was beginning to feel an indescribable joy. But then I was thrust back into my body. I don't know how or why. My next recollection is of the nurse standing near me in the recovery room.

Gloria's after-death experience as reported by her has four important features:

1 She experienced herself leaving and living out of her body.
2 She experienced herself witnessing from 'out of her body' her body.
3 She experienced herself capable of moving around her body's immediate physical surroundings.
4 She experienced herself encountering completely different 'otherworldly' surroundings and returning to her body from those surroundings.

When all these four features are present, we have the clearest and most typical description of after-death out-of-body experience. And while it is common after the experience (itself apparently uncommon) for the person to report feelings of happiness and joy and to report meeting departed relatives and friends, sometimes people report no such feelings or meetings. Some individuals undergo much discomfort.

British philosopher A. J. Ayer (1910–89) expressed how astonished he was to have an after/near-death experience, but how equally anxious he was not to savor it. At age 77 Ayer's heart stopped for four minutes in a hospital in London. During the experience he seemed to emerge into a bright red light which was distressingly painful. At the time, he thought, 'the painful red light was a warning that the laws of nature were not working properly'. Having 'returned' to his body he was dismayed at the prospect of having to die and perhaps experience the harsh light again. In an article which appeared in the *National Review* in 1988, he wrote: 'My recent experiences have slightly weakened my conviction that my genuine death, which is due fairly soon, will be the end of me, though I continue to hope that it will be.' Ayer was an atheist. In a lead-in to the article written by editors of the *Review*, they ask, 'What happens when the world's most prominent atheist dies? A first-hand account.'

Doubtlessly, people (philosophers and non-philosophers alike) have after-death out-of-body experiences. The problem is how to understand and explain them. Just because a person has an experience does not mean that the experience is trustworthy or reliable. Under the influence of alcohol, for instance, I may complain of the pink elephant visually experienced astride my computer. Although the huge creature appears terribly real to me, no beast straddles the machine.

Are there good reasons to doubt the reliability of after-death experience? It is tempting to dismiss the experience as non-veridical or untrustworthy – as hallucination. Experiencing images of one's body as if outside the body occurs more than occasionally in cases of drug abuse, brain tumors, alcoholism, and other pathological conditions.

In the history of the psychology of religion, unsympathetic readings of religious experiences and visions enjoy considerable currency. Sigmund Freud (1856–1939) in *The Future of an Illusion* (1927) depicts religious beliefs as 'illusions, fulfillments of the oldest, strongest and most urgent wishes of mankind.' God, for example, for Freud, 'is nothing other than an exalted father' whom we invent so as to bury ourselves in perpetual infancy, trying to protect ourselves – in our own mind – against the cruel and bitter forces of nature. Under the influence of doubts, hopes, and fears we believe in God, but no Supreme Being answers to the belief. God does not exist.

Perhaps after-death experiences can be explained as Freudian projections, fueled by false hope for survival and sparked by traumatic experience (e.g. surgery). However, while the projection hypothesis may cover certain cases, at least some experiences are tough to explain in the projectionist manner. Some subjects of after-death experience report no religious feelings or strong religious or anti-religious hopes or fears prior to the experience. One investigator of after-death experience claims that nearly a third of his subjects were agnostic and gave no indication of anxiety about death.

Perhaps after-death experience can be explained in terms of physical conditions of the traumatized subject: as a form of delirium caused by over-medication or oxygen deprivation. Again, while this sort of explanation may bear on some cases, it seems irrelevant to others. As claimed by Ian Wilson in his book *The After Death Experience*, 'There are many instances of [such] experiences in which the patient received no form of drugs or other medication'.[8] What about oxygen deprivation or, more exactly, the condition of 'hypoxia', which is a delirium caused by diminishing oxygen supply to the brain at the beginning of the death process? According to a Columbia University physician reported by Wilson, the typical experience of hypoxia is sluggishness, irritability, and poor memory recall, 'a far cry from the euphoria and clarity so consistently reported in near-death experiences'.[9] One subject of an after-death experience was recorded as having normal blood-oxygen and carbon-dioxide levels at the reported time of his experience.[10]

Other facts seem to support a sympathetic reading of the experience. Some survivors of after-death experience report alleged information about physical surroundings near their body which they could not have discovered if restricted to the body's location. Recall Gloria's purported recollections of dirt on the operating theater lights and of the accident victim in the hospital room. Others sometimes claim to encounter people after death whom they did not previously learn had died, but who actually had died. Isn't this information which could only have been available to them out-of-body? In the world of the disembodied? It seems so.

Still suspicion persists. Another source of skepticism is that there are distinctively 'Christian' visions in the after-death experience and these clash with the visions of people in other religions. Christians, for example, often report the bright light as Jesus, Hindus as Hindu deities. Presumably one and the same light cannot be both Jesus and Vishnu. An unsympathetic interpretation of this divergence would be that Christians experience dying in terms of Christian images, which seem to them to require leaving their body but which in fact leave them absolutely embodied. A Hindu expecting reincarnation makes the same rash inference in their own terms. They never really leave their body; they merely feel as if they do. There are, however, striking similarities in the experiences of people from different religions (viz. the four typical features mentioned above) and data from the reports of young children who have had after- (or near-) death experiences seem to confirm a pre- or non-cultural bedrock of commonality within such occurrences. Perhaps descriptions of Jesus or a Hindu deity are misguided attempts within the experience, or memory of it, to describe leaving the body in culturally familiar terms, rather than a genuine clash in what really is experienced. A sympathetic view is that people from different cultures actually do leave their bodies, but descriptively go out on an imaginary limb. Under cultural influence they conceptualize and report things they really do not observe. A bright light is seen; radiant Jesus or luxuriant Vishnu is not.

Where does this leave the possibility of disembodied existence? I confess that my own dispositions about the significance of after-death experience are elusive. At times I am prepared to argue that the experience cannot be dismissed out of hand. Skepticism enjoys no prior plausibility. Reports of the experience should be treated like reports of any other alleged observation and subjected to unbiased scrutiny. After-death experience is not the obvious result of projection, drugs, oxygen deprivation or anything else of a contrary nature. So disembodied survival may well be possible. One should keep an open mind and let the evidence speak for itself.

At other times I am disposed to allow skepticism prior control and then I find myself saying that disembodied survival is impossible. It is too dissonant with the rest of our experience. It is the proverbial pink elephant sadly astride a dying machine.

Part of the puzzle of understanding out-of-body cases is the difficulty of finding independent confirmation. In the experience I described above of Gloria G., a fictional composite drawn from real life, she claims to have seen dirt above the surgical light. Perhaps while Gloria herself did not see *that* dirt, her general knowledge of hospitals and lights led her to expect dirt in certain spots, such as above the light. Reports of surroundings may stem from background knowledge rather than disembodied acquisition of information. The same suspicion may attach to Gloria's 'recollection' of the accident victim; just the sort of scene one expects to confront in a hospital.

It would help in assessing the significance of after-death experience if investigators followed up survivor reports by trying to fit them together with evidence obtained or checked by other means. The credibility of Gloria's claim to acquire out-of-body information depends on her lack of relevant background knowledge. Did she possess such background knowledge? If the answer is no, then provided there really was dirt above the light, her claim gains in warrant. Similarly, subjects who provide indication of bodily surroundings should have their observations confirmed. Is there a young male accident victim in the hospital whose leg will be amputated? These claims to information should be treated like parts of a jigsaw puzzle that, taken in isolation, offer no evidence of anything except the active imagination of the reporter, but when glued together with warranted hypotheses about background knowledge and other relevant evidence could produce the confirmation needed to justify a sympathetic interpretation of after-death reports.

Alas, with few anecdotal exceptions whose significance is ambiguous, the jigsaw approach has not been taken by investigators. Investigators tend to be impressed by the vividness, sincerity, and occasional detail of reports, but do not track the facts claimed to be witnessed outside the body but present in physical surroundings. Perhaps no one can travel with Gloria through her luminous forest, but someone should walk upstairs to the second floor to learn if a mother's son must lose his leg.

I turn now to my thinking in moments of more dismissive skepticism and here I find myself pessimistic about whether the jigsaw approach will warrant anything except saying that sympathizers of the experience are cursed with an unhealthy superabundance of sentimentality and credulity.

2.3 Dissent from After Death

Imagination may tempt us into believing that disembodied personal existence is possible. We have all, I suspect, imagined ourselves losing or being stripped of various physical features or characteristics: hair, feet, arms. If we can think of someone whose every physical characteristic is stripped, the possibility of disembodied survival seems ensured.

Philosophers worry, however, whether a person can be stripped of physical attributes without therein squeezing to a vanishing point and altogether ceasing to exist. Many philosophers deny that disembodied existence is possible. Three arguments for skepticism concerning the possibility of disembodied existence have been proposed. The third turns on the notion of personal identity.

(1) The first points out that stories of after-death experience implicitly violate the assumption that the person is disembodied. Suppose, as in the case described by Gloria, someone claims to pass through a tunnel and into a luminous forest. What does it mean for a person to move *through* space? To be *in* a tunnel? A forest? Isn't this physical activity? The stories are at odds with the idea that people truly are out-of-body, for they are framed in the language of embodiment: of passage, movement, and so on. The moral to emerge from such descriptions, so the first skeptical argument goes, is that descriptions of disembodied existence really do not depict disembodied existence. They make it sound like the person is embodied, albeit perhaps not in the former body.

(2) The second line of argument is to point out that advocates of disembodied personal existence need to explain how people can interact – see, hear, communicate with – each other in a disembodied condition or world. Supposedly, people are expected to commune with others after death, just as, for example, Gloria claims she interacted with her grandmother. However, once stripped of the body, there may be no coherent or truly intelligible way to interact with other people. One benefit or function of the body is that it enables us to see and observe other people. But how is communion accomplished while disembodied? .

Jimmy Carter's nemesis during the 1980 US–Iranian crisis, Ayatollah Khomeini, was bearded; Carter was (and is) clean-shaven. Any confusion between Carter and Khomeini could have been resolved by reference to their physical features. We would have refused to recognize Khomeini as Carter in part because the Ayatollah sported a beard. After death, how would we be able to recognize these two former political leaders?

Interaction is unalloyedly mysterious in a disembodied world. It may be enticing to believe in disembodied interaction, but isn't the truth harsher? Physical communion is the only communion there is; without embodiment interaction is impossible.

(3) The third, related, and most subtle line of argument against disembodied existence rests on the idea of *personal identity*. The argument rests on a conception of what is necessary if disembodied (post-mortem) existence is possible. It is possible only if disembodied persons retain their (pre-mortem) identities. For this reason I shall call the argument the *identity argument*. It goes like this:

1 Different persons have different personal identities.
2 Suppose your body (including brain) dies. Then either (a) you are snuffed out or (b) you personally survive.
3 If option (a) is true, then we must concede that disembodied personal existence is impossible.
4 If option (b) is true, then the survivor is you. The survivor is *identical*, personally, to you.
5 However since your body is dead, you have lost embodiment.
6 So, you must either be re-embodied (reincarnated) or exist in a disembodied condition.
7 Reincarnation does not occur.
8 The concept of personal identity does not apply to the disembodied.
9 Therefore the assumption that you exist in a disembodied condition cannot be true. You are snuffed out. Disembodied personal existence is impossible.

This argument, and others like it, purport to show that disembodied personal existence is unintelligible. If the argument is sound, we do not survive the death and decay of our body.

Obviously, the identity argument is a long and complex argument. Also there is not a single independent step or premise in the argument which is uncontroversial. Some philosophers, like Derek Parfit in his *Reasons and Persons* (1984), reject the first and fourth premises. Concerning the fourth, Parfit claims that personal survival does not require that the pre-mortem and post-mortem person are the same person. Independent of the issue of disembodied existence, it makes sense, Parfit says, to think of someone surviving (or persisting) without presupposing application of the concept of personal identity. If Parfit is right, young Georgie Graham, who grew up on the streets of Brooklyn, New York in the 1950s, may survive now as George Graham, the professional philosopher, without Georgie being the same person as me. Other philosophers reject the seventh premise. If, for example, someone is burned to death in a cremation oven, they claim, subsequently the person can be incarnated in another body perhaps even of a different sort. No period of disembodied existence occurs.[11]

Full-scale defense of the above argument would have to defend the first and fourth premises against Parfit and the seventh against the reincarnationists. Those chores are beyond the scope of the present discussion. I shall assume that contrary to Parfit premises 1 and 4 are true. I shall assume that contrary to reincarnationists premise 7 is true.[12] I will focus instead on premise 8.

The point of the eighth premise is this. If we accept that disembodied existence is possible, we are caught in a trap. We cannot explain how the post-mortem survivor can be *us*. Therefore, as the conclusion maintains, disembodied personal existence is impossible. Let's examine the premise.

2.4 The Idea of 'Personal Identity'

The eighth premise says that the idea of personal identity does not apply to the disembodied. Why not? This is a complicated matter. We need to describe the concept of personal identity, offer a theory about how best to understand the concept, and then show why this understanding – such a theory – precludes disembodied existence.

The main purpose (Parfit aside) of the idea of personal identity is to describe what happens when a particular person, you or me, exists at different periods of time and survives throughout an entire personal lifetime. Consider the following two sets of statements:

'Roger' (said while calling someone's attention to Roger) 'was my best friend in graduate school. That was thirty years ago.'

'I' (spoken by yours truly) 'plan to shed 5 pounds by March of next year.'

The first presupposes that Roger and my school friend are the same person. The second presupposes that me today and minus 5 pounds in March are the same person.

The concept of personal identity should not be confused with the related notion of personhood. The question 'What is personal identity?'

should be distinguished from the question 'What is a person?' That I am who I am (George and not Roger) is one fact; that I am a person *period* is another. The first fact is an identity fact; the second is a personhood fact.

The concept of personal identity should not be taken as necessitating that there is some unchanging characteristic or quality which remains absolutely the same throughout our lives. Roger is the person whom I befriended in graduate school, even though he has undergone crises, transformations, and upheavals since receiving his degree. Indeed, little or nothing about Roger may strictly be the same, except of course that he is Roger.

Befuddled? How can someone be the same without possessing qualities which are the same? To remove befuddlement, we should distinguish two notions that, in English, are expressed by the word 'same'. We need to distinguish being *similar* from being *numerically one and the same*. The first is a notion of shared qualities. To be the same as Roger is to be similar to him. I am the same as Roger in that just as he has a Ph.D., I have a Ph.D. We are the same in being similar. The second sense of 'same' is, by contrast, the personal identity notion. To be the same as Roger is to *be* the person Roger. If Roger is my friend from graduate school, he is one and the same as that person, no matter how he has changed.

People who exist at different times, like you, me, and Roger, possess identities. We can be described using the concept of personal identity. We remain (if we remain at all) numerically one and the same (self-same) over time. The philosophical challenge is to specify in what personal identity consists. Philosophers have long debated how best to understand personal identity. They have felt that there must be *something* to personal identity. But if so, what?

One answer, which identifies the main idea but does not try to refine it, goes as follows: Our personal identity consists in our being living human bodies, living human organisms. My living human organism is me; your living organism is you. Just insofar as my organism exists at different times, I exist at different times. We may call this the *flesh and blood theory* of personal identity.[13]

A corollary of conceiving of ourselves as living human bodies or organisms – a corollary of flesh and blood theory – is that reference to our body is reference not just to *where* we are but to *who* we are. Our bodies are ourselves.

Flesh and blood theory is, without a doubt, one of the most intuitively appealing theories of personal identity ever conceived. It is remarkably simple. Only one thing is taken to be the person and that is the living body of the person. Moreover, from a philosophical point of view, flesh and blood theory has several pleasing virtues. Let me mention four.

First, it seems to mesh with *common speech*. We usually talk and act as if we are living human bodies. We don't say, 'He says he is Napoleon, so he must be Napoleon'. We say, 'He cannot be Napoleon; Napoleon is dead and buried'. We don't say (except in special circumstances), 'I don't like the way he touched my arm, but I am pleased that he didn't touch me'. We say, 'I don't like the way he touched me'.

Second, it seems to solve what may be called *the divine duplication problem*. Imagine that after the death and burial of my body, God creates, with another body, a person psychologically indistinguishable from me. The person shares all my mental characteristics. He even calls himself 'George Graham'. Could this New George be *me* – Old George? Aren't we inclined to say that although the duplicate has a psychology indistinguishable from mine, New George is not Old George. New George is not the philosopher who wrote this book; he divinely mimics me without being me. Indeed, if God was miraculously to bring my old body back to life, and it was to behave indistinguishably from me as well as from New George, isn't *that* much more likely to be me, New George notwithstanding?

This is just the sort of reflective response to the divine duplication problem which we should expect if flesh and blood theory is correct. If I am my living human body, and my body is dead and buried, duplication of my psychology fails to reproduce me. I am snuffed out.

Third, since personal identity does not require persons to possess unchanging characteristics, we need a concept of personal identity which permits *change*. Permission is more than granted by flesh and blood theory. The cellular matter which composes the body is constantly undergoing transformation and replacement. This is quite analogous to a watch or table remaining the self-same watch or table even though the atoms which constitute it change from one moment to the next. Neither watch, table, nor body is composed of an unchanging thing; each has an identity compatible with qualitative change.

A fourth and final positive feature of flesh and blood theory is based on our need (discussed in the Carter–Khomeini case above) to *identify* people in social interaction with them. Persons can be identified in a variety of ways: by fingerprints, personality profiles, behavior, parents, birthmarks, and so on. Some modes or manners of identification are coarse-grained; others are fine-grained. A mode is coarse-grained when, even if adequate for practical purposes, it leaves room for other persons to be misidentified as the person in question. A mode is fine-grained when it leaves no room for confusion or misidentification. Suppose you identify me by reference to a birthmark on my shoulder. 'That's Graham in his swim suit. Just look at his birthmark.' Reference to the mark helps to distinguish me from you since you lack the mark. However, it fails to distinguish me from my sister since she and I share the mark. So picking people out by birthmarks is coarse-grained. It fails to capture me as the Graham I am. I am not my sister.

What, then, identifies people in a fine-grained manner? What serves to specify me uniquely? A fine-grained identifier is unshareable. A coarse-grained identifier (such as a birthmark) is shareable. Are there unshareable identifiers?

The psychological characteristics of persons may seem unshareable. But they are not. If I am sad, you, too, could be sad. If you are afraid of flying, I, too, could harbor the fear. Choose your favorite psychological characteristic and someone else may be discovered with the very same sort of characteristic. Indeed, in theory, *all* your psychological characteristics can be shared by another person, as the divine duplication problem makes clear. So psychological characteristics do not offer fine-grained modes of identification.

What does? One natural answer is our living human bodies. The body affords fine-grained distinctions among people. You and I may share fears and birthmarks, but no one else shares my flesh and blood (at least not at the same moment as me).[14] My body distinguishes me from other people; your body distinguishes you.

Once again this is just the sort of response we should expect if flesh and blood theory is correct. If the theory is correct, I am my living human body. My body identifies me finely because it *is* me essentially.

Flesh and blood theory is attractive. But it is not unblemished. Nothing in philosophy ever is. Cleansing (modification) is necessary.

Consider when life begins. A living human body comes into existence at conception, but does the person? I came from a fertilized egg, but was that egg *me*? No less a Christian than St Thomas Aquinas (1225–74) claimed that the human fetus is not a person until several weeks after conception. For Thomas people begin to exist *after* bodies have come into existence. We may disagree with the venerable saint about other matters to which he was committed, but his worry about the beginning of personal existence appears legitimate. Personal history seems to commence after bodily history. How so? Crudely put, the life of a body involves biochemical processes – those making up self-maintenance and self-organization. These begin at conception. But the life of a person seems also to involve psychological processes – those making up thinking, perception and conscious experience. Those begin after conception.

If Aquinas is right and personal existence begins after conception, we should distinguish two notions that are expressed by the same English words 'is alive'. We should distinguish being merely *biologically* alive from being also *psychologically* alive.[15] A psychologically–biologically alive human body has a life of conscious experience, whereas a (merely) biologically alive body is just a functioning, self-preserving organism. Alas, I do not know criteria for making the psychological/biological distinction with precision, but perhaps an example suffices here. My biologically self-regulated bodily temperature is part of my biology; my perception of the world around me is part of my psychology. Some biological organisms, like simple sea slugs, are not psychologically alive, but others of course, like you and me, simultaneously participate in both forms of life. We are both biologically and psychologically alive.

We need not identify being a person with being a psychologically alive (human) organism in order to use the psychological/biological distinction. But let us call a flesh and blood identity theory amended so that being a person *is* being a psychologically alive human organism *psychologically modified flesh and blood theory* (or simply *modified flesh and blood theory*). Versions of the modified flesh and blood theory of personal identity have been defended by a number of philosophers, arguably dating back to Aristotle (384–322 bc) in the *De Anima*. According to the modified theory, biology, psychology, and personal identity go together. We are our psychologically alive human body (or that part responsible for psychological processes).[16] My identity consists in being such a body (or that part responsible for psychological processes). Your identity consists in being such a body (or that part responsible for psychological processes). According to the modified theory, Aquinas is fundamentally correct. I came from a fertilized egg but that egg itself was not me. I began to exist just when the fetus became psychologically alive.[17]

Various virtues of flesh and blood theory apply to modified flesh and blood theory. In addition, there is no mystery, or at least no general conceptual puzzle, about when personal existence ends. Just as we begin to exist when fetal psychological life commences, our existence ends when our body (and brain) stops (permanently stops) being psychologically alive. Modified theory treats our body as the place in which, as it were, we enter and exit existence. In personal identity as in real estate, location is everything.

Now what about the eighth premise in the identity argument? Remember our goal in discussing personal identity was to buttress that argument. Modified theory is not the only theory of personal identity incompatible with saying that persons can exist in a disembodied condition. But it is one such theory. It helps to explain both why the concept of personal identity fails to apply to the disembodied and why this failure implies that disembodied personal existence is impossible. Simply put, without embodiment we are nothing at all. Since persons cannot exist without being psychological organisms, disembodied personal existence is impossible.

2.5 Glorifying the Afterlife

Suppose we discover on another operating table an exact psychological and physical likeness of Gloria G. Suppose this likeness perfectly like Gloria thought for thought, feeling for feeling, attitude for attitude, and birthmark for birthmark. For illustration, just as Gloria fears flying and loves oranges, so her likeness fears flying and loves oranges. Just as Gloria calls herself 'Gloria', so the likeness calls herself 'Gloria'. For convenience, however, we shall refer to the likeness as 'Floria'. Floria may not be a divinely created duplicate. (Let's be agnostic about her origin.) However, Floria does resemble Gloria from her mind right down to her molecules.

If we return for a moment to Gloria's after-death experience, suppose, remarkably, that at the exact same moment and in the exact same words, Floria also reports an after-death experience. Just as Gloria reports passing through a tunnel and perceiving flowers and trees, Floria reports passing through a tunnel and perceiving flowers and trees. Nothing in the reports, not even their respective grandmother descriptions, is different.

Who *really* had an after-death experience? Who *really* passed through a tunnel? Who interacted with a grandmother? Neither? Both? One but not the other? Which one?

How should we answer these questions? What is at stake here are the identities of Gloria and Floria. Those with sympathies for disembodied survival must suppose that no matter how much alike Gloria and Floria are psychologically – and despite the fact that after death they are disembodied – *something* finely individuates them. But what can that something be? If we grant that Gloria and Floria are absolutely alike psychologically, and that they are disembodied, we end up with no way to individuate them. By contrast, so long as persons are embodied, personal identity is secured and preserved. No matter the match between Gloria and Floria, while they rest on separate tables, they are distinct and distinguishable (if temporarily non-conscious) persons – distinct and distinguishable living human bodies.

The problem raised by the case of Floria is not that disembodied people are hard to spot. The problem is that there is *nothing* to spot. The concept of personal identity does not apply to the disembodied. Disembodiment snuffs out persons.

2.6 Solace and Annihilation

I am not absolutely sure where the above reflections leave the topic of whether life after death is possible – supposing that this requires at least temporary disembodied survival. As I mentioned at the outset, my own attitudes are elusive. One should attend to the empirical evidence, and it is quite possible that skepticism about survival will be displaced by the jigsaw puzzle approach to after-death experience. If (a big 'if') the best explanation of the experience (or of anything else for that matter) requires reference to disembodied survival, then we should endorse the conclusion that life after death is possible and that persons can persist without embodiment, even if the problems associated with formulating a conception of disembodied survival are formidable. From an evidentially open-minded perspective, a theory of personal identity like the modified theory might end up being false; some sort of theory – perhaps a Cartesian theory – which somehow permits disembodied existence might be acceptable. 'Coherent, I suggest, is the supposition that a person might become disembodied.'[18] So says one optimistic advocate of disembodied existence.

Of course one should also attend to the power of argument. The great unanswered question which advocates of survival must face is whether and how disembodied people can maintain identities. Under disembodied conditions, personal identity and thus personal existence seem impossible. Advocates must make disembodied survival seem possible.

Or must they? The insistence that believers in disembodied survival must explain how disembodied existence is possible would be resisted by some Christians. Some Christians countenance the omission of *any* obligation to explain.

'But', says perhaps a wishful gentleman, an earnest man, who would gladly do something for his eternal happiness, 'could you not inform me what an eternal happiness is, briefly, clearly and definitely. Could you not describe it "while I shave" ... '[19]

Hardly. The quote just mentioned is an ironic quip from the trenchant nineteenth-century Christian philosopher, Søren Kierkegaard (1813–55), who adds that you cannot seek information about life after death 'in a textbook of geography'. Kierkegaard warns in another context, 'Thou can well conceive how abhorrent it is to God that people want to wipe his mouth with formulas.'[20]

Was Kierkegaard thinking of formulas like 'no me without my body'? Or 'if deprived of embodiment we are snuffed out'?

For the devout Christian St Paul's example is often cited as something to emulate. Paul urges that life after death from the viewpoint of pre-mortem life must always remain a huge mystery. So, we should not try to plumb its depths or describe its possibility. He says, 'No eye has seen, no ear has heard, no mind has conceived what God has prepared for those who love him' (1 Corinthians 2:9). For Paul, God not man decides whether there is life after death; and God successfully divines whether survival is possible. Such, Paul suggests, is the theological virtue of faith, that it permits trust in God to supersede the bounds of human conceivability.

Although Paul's example may be admired by the religious sympathizer, his admonition to trust in God rightly offends the non-religious person. Tough-minded atheists resist temptation to believe let alone trust in God. For them, if you want to discover the truth about survival, there is only one way this can be done, namely, by weighing up the evidence and arguments – not by believing in God and letting it end in that.

What can we say from the point of view of the person who believes that life altogether ends in death; there is no disembodied post-mortem survival? Philosophers have proposed an immense range of attitudes appropriate in the face of death understood as annihilation. The major division is between those, like Unamuno, who center upon abhorrence and fear, and those who deny that death should be feared. For them, fear of death is an unworthy and undignified attitude for a reasonable and courageous person. One philosopher writes: 'A free man, that is to say, a man who lives according to ... reason alone, is not led by the fear of death. ... His wisdom is a meditation upon life.'[21]

People vary considerably in their ability to meditate upon a life which permanently ends in death and it is hard to do this without sounding like someone who fondles the morose. So I ask poets how to do it and am reminded of Swinburne's haunting, gentle, and courageous meditation *In the Garden of Proserpine*:

> From too much love of living,
> From hope and fear set free,
> We thank our brief thanksgiving
> Whatever gods may be
> That no life lives for ever;
> That dead men rise up never;
> That even the weariest river
> Winds somewhere safe to sea.

Should a person want to cling to life *forever*? Swinburne's message is resonant: If we have done all we can to live, death marks the point when we should feel we have lived *enough*.

NOTES

1   Quoted in Stephen T. Davis's fine article 'Christian belief in resurrection of the body', *New Scholasticism*, LXII (1988), p. 74. An instructive comparison of Christian attitudes towards death may be found by contrasting Billy Graham, *Facing Death* (Word, Texas, 1987) with Milton McC. Gatch, *Death: Meaning and Mortality in Christian Thought and Contemporary Culture* (Seabury, New York, 1969).

2   I will not address questions about how the post-mortem body can be one and the same as the pre-mortem, original body. Within Christianity the fundamental idea – or, should I say, *one* of the fundamental ideas – has been

that God collects the ultimate material components of the body, which may have been scattered since death, and omnipotently remakes it a human body, rejoining it with the mind. Since the very same matter composes the body, the body (it is believed) is the very same body as the pre-mortem body. This is a fascinating and controversial idea, but one which I cannot explore here. As will be evident, I wish to examine how the person – on the traditional Christian view – is supposed to survive while disembodied.

3   Billy Graham, *Facing Death*, p. 251.

4   Quoted in Ronald Blythe, 'Introduction', *The Death of Ivan Ilyich by Leo Tolstoy* (Bantam Books, New York, 1981), p. 10.

5   Richard Watson, 'What moves the mind: an excursion in Cartesian dualism', *American Philosophical Quarterly*, 19 (1982), p. 73.

6   As quoted in Anthony Kenny, 'Mystical experience: St. John of the Cross', in *Reason and Religion* (Blackwell Publishers, Oxford, 1987), p. 88.

7   For information on relevant medical work, see Michael Sabom, *Recollections of Death: A Medical Investigation* (Harper and Row, New York, 1981); Ian Wilson, *The After Death Experience* (Morrow, New York, 1987) as well as the books cited in note 10.

8   Wilson, *After Death*, p. 130.

9   Ibid., p. 128.

10 Ibid. Wilson is less a direct investigator of after-death experience than a reporter or surveyor of the research of others. Among investigators whom Wilson most frequently cites are Raymond Moody, *Life after Life* (Mockingbird Books, Covington, Georgia, 1975); Kenneth Ring, *Heading Toward Omega: In Search of the Meaning of the Near-Death Experience* (Morrow, New York, 1984); and Sabom, *Recollections*. See also Susan Blakemore, *Beyond the Body: An Investigation of Out-of-Body Experiences* (Heinemann, London, 1982).

11 For defense of the possibility of reincarnation, see Robert Almeder, *Death and Personal Survival: The Evidence for Life After Death* (Rowman and Littlefield Publishers, Maryland, 1992). Almeder's sympathetic reflections on reincarnation are associated with equally sympathetic reflections on out-of-body experiences, possession states, communications from the dead and a variety of other so-called psychical phenomena.

12 These assumptions are made without defense but not arbitrarily. In my judgment Parfit should be faulted for imposing overly stringent conditions on identity as a possible (and in his mind, failed) general basis of personal existence and survival. Reincarnation's mistake is to celebrate the conscious mind at the expense of the living body (and brain).

13 For more on flesh and blood theory, often called biological theory, see E. Olson, 'Is psychology relevant to personal identity', *Australasian Journal of Philosophy*, 72 (1994), pp. 173–86; 'Human people or human animals?',

Philosophical Studies, 80 (1995), pp. 159–81; 'Was I ever a fetus?', *Philosophy of Phenomenological Research*, LVII (1997), pp. 95–110; P. Van Inwagen, *Material Beings* (Cornell University Press, Ithaca, New York, 1990).

14 Really? No one? We sometimes speak of two or more people inhabiting the same body. What about Multiple Personality (or Dissociative Identity) Disorder? In MPD (with some exceptions) clinicians tend to speak of the body as going back and forth between two or more persons. It is important that two or more people are not in the same body at the same moment. A case for skepticism about the reality or legitimacy of MPD may be found in Nicholas Spanos, 'Multiple identity enactments and multiple personality disorder: a sociocognitive perspective', *Psychological Bulletin*, 116 (1994), pp. 143–65.

15 Something close to the biological/psychological distinction may be found in various papers of Gareth B. Matthews. These include his 'Aristotle on life', in *The Philosophy of Artificial Life*, ed. M. Boden (Oxford University Press, Oxford, 1996), pp. 303–13; 'The idea of a psychological organism', *Behavior and Philosophy* (formerly *Behaviorism*), 13 (1985), pp. 37–51'; 'Life and death as the arrival and departure of the psyche', *American Philosophical Quarterly*, 16 (1979), pp. 151–7. The distinction is similar to a distinction drawn by the moral philosopher James Rachels between being biologically and biographically alive; see his *The End of Life* (Oxford University Press, Oxford, 1986), pp. 5–6, 24–7. Biographical life is a complex form of psychological life involving (among other things) a capacity for autobiographical memory. If one were to insist upon biographical life for personal existence (Rachels does not), this would err, in my judgment, on the side of being too restrictive psychologically in the analysis of personhood. A human organism would not count as a person until childhood. It could not be said of someone that he or she was born.

16 The parenthetical reference to 'part responsible' is meant to permit modified theory to consider the psychologically functioning brain as 'the flesh' we are. But one must be careful here. Our brains are not brains-in-vats but brains of socially and environmentally situated creatures; the boundary between brain and body may look fuzzy if we emphasize the overall setting of neural flesh. See Andy Clark, 'Epilogue: a brain speaks' in his *Being There: Putting Brain, Body, and World Together Again* (MIT Press, Cambridge, Mass., 1997), pp. 223–7.

17 I cannot here discuss when psychological life begins, but a good guess, based on information about the development of the fetal nervous system, is about 7 months. See H. Morowitz and J. Trefil, *The Facts of Life: Science and the Abortion Controversy* (Oxford University Press, New York, 1992).

18 The quotation is from Richard Swinburne, 'Personal identity: the dualist

theory', in S. Shoemaker and R. Swinburne, *Personal Identity* (Blackwell Publishers, Oxford, 1984), p. 23.

19 See Søren Kierkegaard, *Concluding Unscientific Postscript*, tr. W. Lowrie (Princeton University Press, Princeton, 1968), p. 351.

20 The quotation is from Kierkegaard's *Attack upon 'Christendom'*, tr. W. Lowrie (Princeton University Press, Princeton, 1968), p. 153.

21 The quotation is from Baruch Spinoza, *Ethics*, tr. W. H. White and A. H. Sterling (Oxford University Press, Oxford, 1930), p. 235. Spinoza (1632–77) is generally regarded as one of the most important figures of seventeenth-century philosophy. Although Spinoza endows the 'free man' with freedom from fear of death, this is not because he believes that persons themselves are immortal; he denies that there is personal post-mortem survival.

3

The Problem of Other Minds

This chapter courts scandal. As students of philosophy quickly discover, more than occasionally the claims and denials of philosophers run foul of common sense. Some philosophers say that the external world does not exist or that every event which has occurred will occur again or that involuntary euthanasia is morally defensible; I could add to the list. Therein lies flirtation with scandal.

Fortunately, there is no scandal unless you make a certain background assumption. You must assume that the way people ordinarily think is the way that they should think. You must assume that common sense and truth are in harmony. If you do not, then there is nothing scandalous in someone defending involuntary euthanasia or the unreality of the external world, no matter how strange such claims may be. There is even nothing scandalous in denying that other minds – thinkers and conscious subjects other than yourself – exist. It may sound odd to deny other minds and it would certainly amuse if vigorously debated in public. However, from a philosophic point of view, what matters is how well the claim stands up to examination and analysis, not whether it squares with common sense.

Of course, the vast majority of philosophers do not deny the existence of other minds. In fact, denial is more often encountered in imaginary example than actual advocacy. My purpose in this chapter is to make the rudiments of the denial available to the reader, and to explore its implications for philosophy of mind. Before turning to this task, let me set the stage by briefly describing our own imaginary example.

3.1 The Loneliness of Skepticism

Imagine the following. Thomas Doubting is a student. More accurately, he is a philosophy student with, as one of his teachers graciously puts it, a mind all of his own.

Thomas is reading this book in the university library. The library is filled with dozens of other people. However, Thomas is convinced that he is alone, for he believes that others are mentally vacuous automatons, or robots, completely mindlike in behavior, but whose behavior arises from something other than states of mind. Indeed, Thomas is convinced that he possesses the only genuine mind in the whole wide world. When he travels outside the library, he denies the presence of other minds wherever he goes.

Thomas's convictions are as simple as they are startling. One mind exists: his. No other mind exists.

It is tempting to dismiss Thomas on grounds that his denial contradicts common sense. According to common sense, the library is filled with other minds, other persons. Imagine, for example, that your husband or wife is sitting next to Thomas. However, lest we dismiss Thomas as scandalous, crazy, or absurd, let us remind ourselves that each of us has felt at least some of the skepticism or doubt about the minds of others which infects Thomas. Some skepticism about other minds is familiar to everyone.

How much do you really know about another's mind? You watch what others do and the sounds they make. You notice how they respond to their environment – what things attract them and what things repel them. None of this, however, reveals their conscious thought and experience with the immediacy or directness with which your own mind is revealed to you or Thomas's mind is revealed to him. If you believe anything about the minds of others, it is on the basis of observing them and by drawing inferences from what you observe. From bodily damage and moaning, you infer that they are in pain. From smiles and laughter, you infer happiness. From gazing at books in the library, you infer reading. From the complex and appropriate manipulation of book pages, library cards, entrance and exit doors, you infer beliefs. But you can't crawl inside others' heads to confirm that what you suppose they experience they actually do experience. You can't peer into their minds. So a problem emerges: What justifies or warrants the sorts of inferences cited and beliefs held, when all that is obviously and directly revealed is another's public behavior? Is your spouse reading a book or planning a divorce? Is your husband or wife studying calculus or pondering the dissolution of marital bonds?

The difference – indeed, the seeming gulf – which separates the access you have to your own mind from the inferences you make about others can produce heartache in personal life. Does your spouse really wish to remain married? Apparently yes. But suppose your spouse hungers to be liberated from what he or she secretly thinks of as 'the shackles of wedlock'. You can only surmise or infer on the basis of evidence: on the basis of what your mate says and does. The fact that you cannot get inside another's mind seems to preclude access to feelings or thoughts which would decisively settle the presence of a desire to divorce. Accordingly, the inaccessibility of other minds may pose personal problems. You may, for example, remain married, sadly later to learn that your spouse really wished to divorce and now is having a tempestuous affair. Skepticism has a foothold in this sort of interpersonal misfortune. Observation suggested to you that your spouse wanted marriage. The affair, alas, shows that you were wrong. You feel like a fool.

Of course, Thomas's skepticism explodes far beyond the interpersonal skepticism of doubting whether your spouse wishes to remain married. Thomas is skeptical about your spouse's mind *period*, as well as about the minds of everyone else. Thomas is no minor skeptic; Doubting is Big Time. Therein lies the potential for scandal. Although Thomas shares in familiar skepticism, he does so only because he raises skepticism to an uncommonsensical degree.

To Thomas you are not merely unwarranted in believing in your spouse's desire to remain married. You are unwarranted in believing in other minds. In describing Thomas's skepticism, therefore, it is important to distinguish between the denial of *particular* ascriptions of beliefs, desires, and other states of mind ('Your wife really wants divorce, not marriage') and the *general* denial of other minds ('Your wife is a mentally vacuous automaton and so is everyone else'). Thomas embraces the second denial.

The *problem of other minds* is the problem of how to defend our common-sense belief in other minds against the general denial of other minds. How can we show that this belief is warranted and that wholesale skepticism about other minds is wrong? How should one decide whether something other than oneself – a denizen of the library – is really a thinking, conscious being and not an automaton devoid of genuine mentality?

Philosophers have been struggling with the problem of other minds at least since Descartes in the seventeenth century. Descartes believed that there is a realm of mind distinct, and for him separable, from that of the behaving body upon which the mind acts. Cartesian dualism of mind/body is not just a means of dividing the universe into two domains (the mental and the physical), it also gives primary warrant to the mind. We *know* that we have minds or at least I know that I have a mind. I experience it within myself. According to Descartes, my own mind is what I primarily am and know best. But what about others? Couldn't they just be mindless physical bodies going through the motions?

Partly because of the influence of Descartes in the history of philosophy of mind and partly because of the desire to avoid scandalizing common sense, there is no shortage of attempts to defend belief in other minds and to show that the belief is warranted. So, luckily, if one is uncomfortable with skepticism about other minds, philosophers offer several reasons for asserting that belief in other minds is warranted.

3.2 How Not to Solve the Problem of Other Minds

There are four sorts of reasons or arguments by philosophers designed to show that belief in other minds is warranted. Let us start with three reasons which fail, although from which important lessons may be extracted. I shall begin with the simplest which is also the least intuitive and appealing.

(1) *What you directly observe is all there is.* We find out about the minds of others only through observing what they say and do: through observing their public behavior. Being restricted to public behavior, however, is not a liability. It is an asset, since minds just are what people say and do. Pain is moaning. Happiness is smiling. If we could subtract behavior from mind we would have nothing left over. So, there is no problem of whether belief in the existence of other minds is warranted. If you observe what another says and does, since saying and doing is mind, you are amply warranted in believing that the person is minded.

To illustrate. Suppose I see a young man at the beach with a deep cut on his knee. The cut is bleeding profusely; he is bent over clutching his knee with his hands. He looks pale and tense, and has beads of sweat on his brow. He also moans and groans.

I believe that the young man is in pain. Am I warranted in believing this? If 'what I directly observe is all there is', I am richly warranted, for such pain behavior is pain. Indeed, there is no superior reason. To observe the behavior is to witness the pain. To ask whether he is in pain is about as ridiculous as asking, for instance, whether a father is a male parent. Fatherhood is male parenthood; pain behavior is pain.

The claim that only outward appearances matter, the 'what you directly observe is all there is' argument, has been dubbed by philosophers 'logical behaviorism' or 'peripheralism'.[1] This is because its basic idea is that outward or peripheral bodily behavior (including speech and sounds) constitutes mind. Logically or conceptually speaking, the two are equivalent.

Today there are not many logical behaviorists. There are two objections to the position; the first is that logical behaviorism misunderstands the nature of mind. Mind is not overt; it is internal, 'in the head'. A person can be entirely stripped of the capacity to behave – to speak, to do – by being given a paralytic drug or perhaps by having his brain removed from his body and placed in a vat. However, he still may think and experience. Indeed, he may suffer psychological torment in paralysis, perhaps because of total restriction in bodily behavior.

The second objection is that there are insurmountable difficulties specifying the behavior which allegedly constitutes thought and experience. Falling off a cliff is behavior but not mind; it just is physics. Whereas, according to logical behaviorism, moaning is both behavior and mind; it is pain. So some behavior is mind, whereas other behavior is not. But which is which? Why is moaning mind but falling physics? How can one tell when behavior witnessed is mind observed?

Which act or behavior is believing that it will rain? Staying indoors? Grasping an umbrella? Walking Aunt Tilda home? What behavior constitutes anger over foolishly smashing your thumb with a hammer? Screaming at the manufacturer? Throwing the hammer against the wall? Crying and going to bed? Even experiences, such as pain, which seem to have typical or natural expressions in behavior, such as moaning and grasping the injured part of the body, can have atypical, unnatural manifestations. A stoic in pain tells jokes and plays the violin. A suffering saint sends money to the poor. Appearances also deceive. The moaning actor on stage is merely pretending, not truly in pain.

Of course, the second difficulty is connected with the first. Since mind is inner and behavior outer, the outside may not reveal or express the inside. Appearances both confuse and deceive. Stoics suppress; professional actors merely simulate pain.

The 'what you directly observe is all there is' argument does not solve the problem of other minds. It magnifies the problem by reminding us, unintentionally, that mind is not directly or straightforwardly revealed in behavior. For behavior to reveal mind, the right sorts of things must happen *inside* a person. Moaning reveals pain only if the person genuinely is in pain. Doubting should be unmoved by peripheralism.

(2) The second argument is both more challenging and more difficult to describe with precision. It says that knowledge of one's own mind presupposes warranted belief in other minds. It goes as follows.

A humbling disclosure about self-revelation. The problem of other minds arises because it seems that I can be aware of the existence of my own mind without being warranted in believing in other minds. But this appearance is an illusion, since knowledge of one's own mind presupposes warranted beliefs in other minds. To grasp myself is already to apprehend others. Hence there is no problem of other minds. Since I know my own mind, I am warranted in believing in other minds.

Although this argument has been offered by a number of philosophers (for example, there are claims for it in Ludwig Wittgenstein's *Philosophical Investigations* [1953] and in writings of various philosophers influenced by him such as P. F. Strawson),[2] it is 'more often encountered in the oral tradition than in published writings', as American philosopher Alvin Plantinga has noted.[3] Like much that is oral it metamorphoses in successive retelling. This is unfortunate, for the plain truth is that the disclosure is hard to assess without its clarification and explanation. We should try to assess it, however, for the disclosure would solve the problem of other minds if correct.

First, it is important to note what is *not* disclosed by the second argument. The main idea is not that knowing one's own mind sometimes depends on knowing others. Surely, self-knowledge is sometimes dependent on knowing others. Consider a humorous sort of case. A man under hypnosis is given a posthypnotic suggestion to the effect that he must stand on a chair after coming out of the trance. Later, when fully conscious, he gives some completely bizarre motivation for his behavior. He says, for example, 'There are tiny gremlins crawling around on the floor', during which he climbs onto a chair. He doesn't know his own mind, for the real motivation for climbing onto the chair is to satisfy the demands of the hypnotist. We say, 'You intend to do what the hypnotist wants.' He says, 'I want to avoid stepping on small creatures.' He is wrong. His unconscious thoughts are not directly revealed to him. If he wishes knowledge of his own mind, he does best to ask outside observers. He does best to assume that we have minds of our own and can tell him what is happening inside his own head.

The problem of other minds can hardly be resolved by appreciating that some thoughts are not conscious and that other minds (friends, therapists) may need to help us uncover unconscious motives, for the problem of other minds is generated by thoughts and feelings which are conscious and directly observed. Access to our own conscious experience and thought seems to require absolutely no support from others. All mental phenomena that are in consciousness, in experience, to adopt the phrase of the influential German philosopher Franz Brentano (1838–1917), are 'immediately evident'.[4] The immediacy or directness of conscious thought and experience creates the gulf between knowledge of ourselves and inference to others. Our convictions about our own experience seem to wear their warrant on the sleeves of our own awareness. Recall, for example, some typical experience of being in pain and then ask yourself, 'Could I have an experience *like this* and not realize it?' There is neither need nor temptation to survey the opinions of friends or therapists here; there is the immediacy of pain.

The humbling disclosure is not about need for outside help in revealing the unconscious. The disclosure is much more bold. It is that knowledge of one's own *conscious* thought and experience depends on apprehending other minds. Only if I recognize other minds can I consciously apprehend my own. Is this true? As I mentioned above, no philosopher has offered a definitive formulation and defense of the disclosure. Wittgenstein's signs of the disclosure, for example, are difficult to interpret. He claims that everything we know of our own experience has its source in a social context. But his defense of this claim consists in one of the most famous, controversial and yet obscure arguments in twentieth-century philosophy, the so-called 'Private language' Argument. So I shall try to develop a defense which is representative of typical defenses without, I trust, lapsing into obscurity. The defense will be Wittgensteinean in spirit if not letter. It runs as follows:

1   If skepticism about other minds is correct, then I know my own mind

but am not warranted in believing in other minds.

2 I cannot know my own mind without applying 'mind' concepts to myself. If, for example, I think of myself as angry, then I self-ascribe 'anger'. When I feel pain, then I conceptualize my experience as 'pain'.

3 I cannot apply 'mind' concepts to myself without apprehending or realizing that they apply equally to others. I cannot self-ascribe without other-ascribing. If, for example, I possess the concept 'anger' and apply it to myself, I must realize that others, too, experience the very same emotion.

4 Therefore, to know my own mind is to realize that others are minded, too. It is to have warranted belief in other minds.

5 I know my own mind.

6 So, skepticism about other minds is incorrect. I am warranted in believing in other minds.

The preceding argument may seem discouragingly long and complicated. Yet the heart of the argument is easy to penetrate. The argument combines the knowledge which I have of my own mind together with a thesis about mental concepts into an attempted solution to the problem of other minds. To illustrate, suppose I see a person with a nail stuck in his foot groaning and writhing on the floor. If, so the argument goes, I apply the concept of pain to myself, when, for example, I am in pain, then I must appreciate that it applies to the person with the nail in his foot as well. If 'pain' applies to me, it applies to him. He has pain of his own.

Two features of the argument are worthy of pause. The first concerns the difference between having a concept of something and lacking it. If I have a concept of something, then and only then can I classify it; without concepts, I cannot classify. For instance, if I believe that Descartes is a great philosopher, I classify Descartes as a great philosopher. The classification 'great philosopher' depends upon my having the concepts of great and philosopher. Without these concepts, I could not believe 'Descartes is a great philosopher'.

The idea behind premise 2 is that in knowing my own mind I apply concepts of mind, pain, anger, and so on, to myself. I classify this experience as anger, that experience as pain, and classify myself as minded. Meanwhile, the gist of premise 3 is that self-application presupposes other-application. Classification bridges over the potential warrant gulf which separates self from other. Concepts used in my own case must be used in the case of others. Mental concepts are, as it were, public or social concepts rather than private concepts.

The second feature of the argument concerns the fact that it cuts against common sense. Ordinarily, we suppose that self-awareness affords me an inside or superior look at myself, whereas I possess only an outside or inferior look at others. I immediately grasp my own pain, but I infer pain in another. However, if the humbling disclosure is sound, observing other minds is most unlike what we ordinarily suppose. According to the argument, the outer demotes the superior and independent warrant position of the inner. I know my own pain only if I have prior or simultaneous grasp of pain in others. I must grasp the pain of the other, so to speak, before or as I conceptualize myself in pain.

The humbling disclosure sounds like an argument which is too good to be true. Simply to self-ascribe mental concepts is to be apprised of other minds. Frankly, it is too good to be true. The argument has two serious flaws.

In the first place, the requirement of applying concepts to others as or before I self-ascribe has an expensive price tag. Applying concepts to others goes hand in hand with observing behavior (presumably the only access we have to other minds); and, thus, advocates of the disclosure have difficulty avoiding *some* form of logical behaviorism. They have difficulty avoiding some form of the thesis that 'pain' means *pain behavior*, 'anger' means *angry behavior*, and so on. Perhaps this is what Wittgenstein means when he says, metaphorically, 'The human body is the best picture of the human soul'. To witness the body is to perceive the mind. But if that is what Wittgenstein means, he is mistaken. Mind is something inner and not behavioral. Behavior may be the best or only intersubjective evidence of another's mind, but it is not mind itself.

There is a second problem. Premise 3 commits a type of reasoning error which philosophers call 'begging the question'. We may characterize the mistake in different ways. But the heart of the error is that premise 3 assumes what needs to be proven. In particular, it assumes that mental concepts cannot self-apply without other-applying. It presupposes that when I classify my experience as anger or pain I must appreciate that others, too, such as the writhing person with the nail in his foot, have experiences which should be classified in the same way.

Philosophers are displeased when questions are begged. Questions should be answered, not begged. Critical solutions should be defended, not assumed. Anything less isn't comprehensive; anything less lacks depth. Isn't it conceivable that my concept of pain just does not apply to others? Isn't it possible that I have private mental concepts which enable me to know my mind without applying those concepts to others? Isn't it possible that the writhing of the nailed person arises from something other than pain? Skeptics argue that this is exactly why we are unwarranted in believing in other minds. We don't know whether others employ terms such as 'pain' and 'anger' in the way that we employ them, that is, for certain sorts of conscious feelings, since we cannot check by having another's feelings. The writhing person may be a mentally empty robot. 'Pain' may mean one thing to me, nothing whatsoever to the denizens of Thomas's library.

Examples help. Imagine a person who has for some reason been held captive all his life, alone in a small, bare, windowless room containing a dictionary which rests on a table. The prisoner spends most of his waking hours turning pages in the dictionary, not understanding that it is a dictionary, of course, but turning pages. Sadly, the volume falls off the table and smashes his toe. He knows that he is in pain: he feels dreadful, awful. However, since the prisoner has not gotten outside of the room, he does not appreciate such things as that there exist *other* minds. So, his concept of pain does not require him to apply it to others. The dictionary contains concepts which apply to others, but the 'dictionary' in his head operates in a language – a private language – utterly his own.

The painful prisoner is of course a farfetched case, which may be impossible in practice. Still, it seems that such a case is perfectly imaginable. If skepticism is correct, our *normal* situation with respect to pain ultimately is like that of the prisoner. Just as the prisoner is painfully aware without being apprised of other minds, so we are painfully aware without good and sufficient reason to believe in other minds. 'Pain' self-applies to me without my being justified in believing in other minds.

The disclosure begs the question. It hides an unproven assumption as well as a commitment to logical behaviorism. Doubting should be unrelieved by Wittgenstein.

(3)   Bertrand Russell (1872–1970) is the most celebrated philosopher in twentieth-century Anglo-American philosophy, famous not just as a philosopher but as an influential player in the intellectual life of England and the United States. When Russell in *Human Knowledge: Its Scope and Limits* (1948) discusses the problem of other minds, he embraces a third

attempt to solve the problem. It is referred to as the *argument from analogy*. It goes roughly like this:

I know that I think and experience; in short, that I am minded. I observe that I am similar to others: others have similar bodies and exhibit similar sorts of behavior in similar sorts of situations to me. So, I am entitled to infer that others are minded like me.

On Russell's view, first I am familiar with my own mind because it is immediately evident; then, I justifiably bridge the gap to other minds 'in proportion as their bodily behavior resembles my own'. Another celebrated English speaking philosopher and actually Russell's godfather, J. S. Mill (1806–73) wrote fifty years before the publication of *Human Knowledge*:

> I conclude that other human beings have feelings like me, because, first, they have bodies like me, which I know in my own case, to be the antecedent condition of feelings; and because, secondly, they exhibit the acts, and other outward signs, which in my own case I know by experience to be caused by feelings.[5]

Mill, too, embraced the argument from analogy for other minds. Indeed, the historical popularity of the analogy argument with philosophers has been widespread. However, the consensus among contemporary philosophers is that the analogy argument is weak. Why? Here, briefly, are two influential criticisms.

Parochialism   The analogy argument for other minds may be perfectly natural and appealing when others are like me, but what of cases in which the others are dissimilar in anatomy and behavior? To take an obvious if controversial illustration, if the God of Christianity exists, presumably he is minded. However, presumably he is most unlike us in circumstance, behavior, and body. He might even be without a body (chapter 6 discusses the mind of God). For other examples: Various abnormal humans (e.g. schizophrenics), animals (dogs), and aliens (martians) are also bypassed by the argument from analogy. Each is disanalogous from us in obvious and potentially critical ways; so, neither is readily understood as minded if warrant is restricted to analogy.

Consider two examples from the animal kingdom. Pigeons learn to peck a lighted key to avoid electric shock. A hungry hamster will dig, rear, or scrabble to acquire food. Why? Perhaps the answer, even though I am built like neither pigeon nor hamster, and even though I don't peck or scrabble, is that they believe that these activities will, respectively, avoid shock and secure food. I don't look or act like them; I am neither winged nor prone to peck. So what grounds do I have for saying that they have beliefs and minds? Perhaps the answer involves our individual dissimilarities. I find it hard to grasp why they peck and scrabble without supposing them to believe that such behavior secures goals or ends. Marked differences in body types and behavior patterns, to the point of very little analogy, may block or discourage analogical inference, yet the differences may prod me to picture certain creatures as minded.

Feeble base   The analogy argument represents my warrant for other minds as resting on strictly one case viz. me. However, just because every case of similar behavior, and so on, is accompanied by pain in me does not warrant me in believing that it is accompanied by pain in others. This would be like supposing that all bears are white merely on the basis of observing a single bear (polar bear) or that all people in Scotland are Grahams just on the basis of discovering one Graham from Aberdeen. Paul Churchland writes: 'It may well be wondered whether our robust confidence in the existence of other minds can possibly be accounted for and exhausted by such a feeble argument. Surely, one wants to object, my belief that you are conscious is better founded than *that*.'[6]

It is the great irony of the argument from analogy that it is used to argue that I am not unique, that others are minded, whereas one of its outstanding problems is that merely one case – my unique case perhaps – is insufficient to warrant the conclusion that others are minded. The reason that we should not accept analogy arguments based on one case is that we should not, at least without supplementary argument, assume that our own case is typical. Just as a polar bear is not a typical bear, perhaps being minded is not typical of creatures who look and act like me.

Today most philosophers recognize the failure of the three arguments we have examined. There are not many logical behaviorists; those sympathetic to the humbling disclosure have tried to reformulate the disclosure without presupposing that mental concepts are behavioristic concepts; and those friendly to the argument from analogy have revised the argument so that it is virtually indistinguishable from the inference to the best explanation argument – the fourth argument – we will now examine.

Fourth argument?   Examining three arguments has required patience, especially since neither has produced satisfactory warrant for belief in other minds. It is tempting to abandon patience and to endorse a quick-fix solution to the problem of other minds. Quick-fixes purport to require little or no argument. There are quick-fixes on the philosophical market. Here's one:

> *Warrant by telepathy* (WT): One person can become aware of the thoughts or experiences of another in a direct or telepathic way which does not involve inference or the observation of behavior. One person can immediately experience another's mind by exercising telepathic powers.

WT attempts to settle the question of other minds not by argument or appeal to behavioral evidence but by invoking special power to bridge the gap between self and other. However, WT is infected with difficulties. First, not everyone claims to be blessed with telepathic powers; I certainly do not. But we all wish for warrant in believing in other minds. Second, if people were telepathic this would not so much solve the problem of other minds as relocate it. Suppose I am telepathic. How do I know that what I experience is the mind of another? For instance, suppose I somehow feel your pain. How do I know that it is *your* pain? Arguably, if I feel pain, *my* experience is painful. So what makes it your and not my pain which I experience? Finally, in the history of psychology, claims for telepathic powers have a history of failure, of being replaced by better explanations and more sensible claims. Hence, it is most unlikely that people are telepathic.

The temptation to quick-fix we must admit. Yet we should not yield to it. Philosophy requires patience. So, let us turn to a fourth attempt to solve the problem of other minds. Happily, the fourth argument succeeds. Patience pays with a solution to the problem of other minds.

3.3 How to Solve the Problem of Other Minds

The fourth and currently most favored attempt to solve the problem of other minds is a version of what is known as *inference to the best explanation.*[7] The argument has several versions, each suggesting the same general point. It goes as follows:

I am directly familiar with my own conscious thoughts and experiences; so, I am amply warranted in believing that I am minded. Moreover, there are certain phenomena which I must explain if I am to satisfactorily understand the world. Specifically, I must explain the behavior of other apparent minds (people, animals, and so forth). I see others moan, shelve library books, hammer nails, and peck keys and I need to explain why they say and do these things. I need to account for their behavior. The proposition or hypothesis that others, like me, are minded provides the best explanation of their behavior. Therefore, I am warranted in believing in the existence of other minds.

What can be said for the argument? One of the most powerful warrants for accepting a proposition or hypothesis is that the hypothesis explains something (some datum or phenomenon) better than any alternative hypothesis. For instance, suppose I hold up a piece of wire and ask, 'Why does this wire conduct electricity?' Consider the following two explanations:

A1 Because it's made of copper and copper conducts electricity.
A2 Because I bought it at Sam's Electrical Supply Store and whatever Sam sells conducts electricity.

Even though A2 is plausible as explanation, A1 is a much better explanation than A2. The superiority of A1 to A2 as explanation is good and sufficient reason for believing A1 rather than A2. In the same way, according to the best explanation argument, in observing the behavior of others, we should prefer the best explanation of behavior.

Suppose I point to a man whose hand has just been cut and who is moaning, and ask 'Why is he moaning?' Consider the following two explanations:

A3 Because he is in pain and pain causes moaning.
A4 Because he is a mindless robot and cut hands in mindless robots cause moaning.

Again, we would not hesitate to say that A3 is better explanation than A4. Again, the superiority of A3 to A4 as explanation is good and sufficient reason for holding A3 rather than A4. Thus is born the idea that belief in other minds is warranted by providing the best explanation of behavior. The picture is this. If I consider explanations which do not invoke the idea that others are minded, and compare them with explanation which does, explanation in terms of other minds is best. Since it is best, I am warranted in believing in other minds.

The idea that explanation in terms of other minds is best, is intuitively plausible in the light of cases like Thomas's library dwellers. Picture the dwellers again. They walk adroitly about the library; they place books appropriately on shelves; when they lock themselves in the reading room, they unlock the door before they exit; when they slam the door on their foot they moan; and so on. Suppose we ask why the dwellers behave in these ways. One explanation is that they are mindless robots which have been programmed or designed to act in these ways. Another explanation is that they are minded. They walk adroitly about the library, because they *see* where they are going and *want* not to bump into shelves and walls; they place books appropriately on shelves, because they *wish* to place books where they *know* the books belong; and so forth.

In comparing and contrasting robot and mind explanations, mind-explanation emerges as superior especially once it is realized that robot-explanation will be immensely complicated and difficult to construct. A fan of robot-explanation, such as Thomas, must describe robots in robot terms; he must identify their design or program as well as the origin of the design or program. He must also explain why everyone else but him is mindless although he behaves exactly as they do in the library and possesses an anatomically similar body. The advocate of the other minds explanation faces no such tasks. Other minds explanation is natural and simple; indeed, it is part of common sense. Not only do I explain others' behavior in terms of reference to (their) minds, but I commonly explain my own behavior by reference to my own mental activity. Plus, unlike Thomas, since I believe in other minds, I do not have to explain why I am minded while others are unminded, although they resemble me in other respects.

3.4 Other Minds and the Best Explanation Argument

To many philosophers the best explanation argument is the key to warranted belief in other minds. What are its virtues? I have already mentioned some, but let us look at four main virtues in more organized detail.

(1)   The argument avoids both problems connected with the argument

from analogy. Marked differences between myself and others may discourage analogical inference, but if believing that dissimilar others (animals, aliens, and so forth) are minded best accounts for their behavior, then the differences are not truly important. Others are analogous to me in being minded even if, unlike me, they are winged, schizophrenic, martians who are prone to peck. Likewise, the warrant for belief in other minds depends on its explanatory power and this is not in any way impaired by the fact that there is only one mind (my own) of which I have direct observation. All that matters is the relative explanatory strength of the other minds idea as compared with competing non-minds hypotheses. This is not in any sense to deny the essentially inferential step to other minds, nor to endorse claims about the ease of knowing oneself. Self-knowledge is vexing and difficult. It just is to say that as long as we can better explain another's behavior by attributing mind than by not attributing mind, we are warranted in believing in other minds.

(2)   The argument accounts for the popularity and appeal of the analogical argument. In many situations (say, the fanciful library example) others closely resemble me. They look similar, act similar, and occupy similar circumstances to me. Now it is clear that if they don't possess minds, I must explain how they can emulate or simulate me, as it were, without being minded like me. Why do they act like I do when I am in pain if they themselves are pain free? The task is not just to explain their behavior but to explain their behavior *plus* my uniqueness. Of course this chore is avoided if I hold that they, like me, are minded.

When there are genuine analogies between myself and others, the best explanation argument urges me to understand others in ways analogous to those in which I understand myself. Just as I painfully moan, they painfully moan.

(3)   Our pre-philosophic, common-sense view of mind is that mind causes behavior. Minds are responsible for behavior. I moan because I am in pain. I throw the hammer against the wall because I am angry. I grab an umbrella from the closet because I believe that it will rain.

The fact that we often can successfully predict what others will do or say next, by attributing minds to them, suggests that explanation by attribution of other minds is generally accurate. We can anticipate the future behavior of others by ascribing minds to them. 'He believes it is raining, so he will grab an umbrella from the closet.' 'He will moan because he is in pain.'

(4)   For several years one of the most active areas of psychological science has been the psychology of conceptual development. The psychology of conceptual development is the study of how people acquire and use concepts. One of the most deeply entrenched hypotheses in the psychology of conceptual development is the idea that very young children cannot make sense of others without believing in other minds. The behavior of others is enigmatic to them unless they believe in other minds. Some psychologists even try to identify when children begin to believe in other minds. Alison Gopnik, a psychologist working in this area, writes: 'Clearly, at least from the age of 5, [a child's] notion of belief is not solipsistic.'[8] Gopnik means that a 5-year old conceives of not only herself as minded but others as minded. She does not merely self-ascribe mental concepts; she other-ascribes them.

Other psychologists implicate absence of belief in other minds in various childhood deficiencies and impairments such as autism. Autistic children fail to enter into satisfying relationships with other people. Perhaps, as Alan Leslie speculates in a recent paper, this is because autism tragically strikes at their ability to believe in other minds. Autistic children fail to treat others as having feelings and experiences distinct from their own.[9] Somehow or for some reason, the autistic child does not fully or genuinely believe in other minds.

Evidence from developmental psychology does not directly support the best explanation argument. However, developmental evidence does suggest that the hypothesis of other minds should be virtually irresistible. In childhood as well as adult life, we make sense of others by attributing minds to them. The best explanation argument codifies this practice into an argument that belief in other minds is warranted because of its explanatory power and success.

Imagine what it would be like to believe that others are mindless. When one person spoke to another, there would be no presumption that he was saying anything intelligible or meaningful. No mind would be at work. So if another says, 'I wonder if Thomas was an autistic child?' he hasn't asked a meaningful question. The meaning of the question, and its answer, depend on the fact that when people use the words 'I', 'wonder', and so forth they are minded: they use 'I' *intending to refer* to themselves, 'wonder' *intentionally* connotes wonder, 'child' is *deliberately* deployed to denote a child, and so forth. Mindless speech is indistinguishable from mere noise, from blibble blabble.

Within Thomas's library, if the denizens really are mindless, there would be no reason to assume that the building deserved to be classified as a library or merited holding books. Social institutions like libraries (and universities) and artifacts like books presuppose minds engaged with them. Books are read, not robotically eyeballed. Libraries are places where subjects of thought and experience – minds – study and do research, not empty-headed ambling. In fact, there is no building libraries unless real minds properly design and construct them. Imagine, for example, what it would be like to describe how creatures construct libraries without presupposing that building behavior is under the guidance of minds. The intricate patterns of architectural design and construction activity would seem inscrutable without presupposing minds at work.

Many philosophers have remarked that without believing in other minds it is virtually impossible to identify or describe the behavior of others, let alone explain why behavior occurs. Mind is implicated in intelligent speech, social institutions, creation and use of artifacts and a host of other sorts of activities. Whereas if we believe in other minds, we avoid the difficult task of disbelieving. Speech turns out to be speech (meaningful, not just noise); books turn out to be books (read, not just eyeballed); libraries turn out to be libraries. Belief in other minds is childhood wisdom in knowing the best explanation of otherwise baffling and senseless behavior.

Are there difficulties with the argument? Are there reasons to suspect that it is incorrect? Certainly there are questions which need to be addressed. In the first chapter, I mentioned that philosophy is comprehensive. Unanswered questions spoil comprehensiveness.

One question is what to include in other minds explanation. Does the attribution of mind have assumptions built into it? One assumption which many philosophers say is packed into the idea of mind is that mind is rational. A completely and totally irrational mind – especially one responsible for intelligent behavior – is a contradiction in terms. Another question is whether explanation of behavior in terms of mind deserves to be called a 'theory' (albeit an implicit theory when possessed by children and ordinary folk) which should be tested and confirmed like theories in science. A third question is how to select from among competing other mind explanations of behavior the very best. Andy checks Melville's *Moby Dick* out of the library. Why? Does he want to read about whales? Or does he wish to impress Annie with his taste in literature? Or both? What is the very best explanation among the best? It is beyond the scope of this chapter to discuss these questions. I mention them simply to note that although the best explanation argument is favored among contemporary philosophers, questions need to be addressed in its comprehensive and systematic development.

Absent developments is it possible to quarrel with the undeveloped version of the argument presented above? Is it possible to object to the argument?

At the heart of the best explanation approach is a certain background assumption about explanation: where we have behavior *B*, and explanatory hypotheses or proposals *P* and *P**, we should endorse *P* rather than *P** if *P* offers the best of the two explanations of *B* (and provided that *P* and *P** are otherwise satisfactory or acceptable).[10] To take a simple illustration, where we have another's moaning, and propositions that the moaner is in pain or that the moaner is not in pain, if the proposition that the moaner is in pain better accounts for the moaning, we should infer that the moaner is in pain.

Some philosophers worry that at present we do not know enough about best explanation to use this idea to warrant belief in other minds. The very idea of best explanation, of *P* being better than *P**, to adopt the purple prose of Alvin Plantinga 'is still a black and boundless mystery'.[11]

The worry is potentially ambiguous. It can be interpreted as a worry about two different things. One is whether warrant for belief in other minds should hinge on other minds being best explanation; and the other is whether we know enough about best explanation to say that *any* explanation of *any* phenomenon from electrical conductivity to moaning is best.

On the second interpretation, the worry is misplaced. We know enough about best explanation to know when certain explanations are best even if at the present time we do not comprehensively and systematically understand explanatory bestness. For example, one criterion for best explanation is that the explanation indicates why what is explained could have been expected to occur. This amounts to saying that an explanation is a potential prediction and that the best explanation offers the best potential prediction. After I wrap wire around the battery terminal and it conducts electricity, the conductivity is explained by its being copper; prior to wrapping, the wire could have been predicted to conduct because it is copper. After I moan, my moaning is explained in terms of the sensation of pain. But prior to moaning, the behavior could have been predicted on the basis of pain. 'Graham was in pain, so he did moan.' 'Graham is in pain, so he will moan.'

Although at present we cannot completely and exactly specify the elements of best explanation, nevertheless we know enough about explanation to know, very often, when an explanation is best – best from an available pool of otherwise acceptable explanations. So, for instance, if reference to other minds best predicts, this is one good reason for claiming that explanation by reference to other minds is best.

On the first reading, the worry may be more troublesome. Again, suppose we have behavior B, and explanations P and P^*. Suppose P refers to minds; P^* does not. Suppose P^* refers only to, say, the electrochemistry of the brain. Now suppose the following puzzling phenomenon takes place: P^* seems the *best* explanation. Suppose, for example, that I best predict whether another will moan on the assumption that moaning is caused by another's brain states and not on the assumption that moaning is produced by pain.

If competition is genuine and not bogus, explanation by reference to other minds can in theory be defeated by explanation without reference to minds. If or when this happens (and it may never happen of course), would this mean that we lose warrant for believing in other minds? Yes it would.

Some philosophers find the vulnerability of competition and the risk of lost warrant too dear a price to pay to endorse the best explanation account. They claim that the best explanation argument leads to trouble, for it represents warrant for belief in other minds as hinging on the success of other minds explanation. Whereas, they contend, warrant exists prior to and independent of explanatory success.

To understand this anxiety more clearly, let us illustrate it my means of a brief, concrete historical example.

Nothing shows how to refute an other minds explanation of a particular sort of behavior better than the medical history of Dr Samuel Johnson (1709–84). Johnson was a respected poet, playwright, and biographer. He edited the greatest of all folios of the works of Shakespeare, and composed the first great dictionary of the English language. But throughout his life, Johnson exhibited spasms, tics, jerks, and obsessive mannerisms. According to Johnson's contemporaries, these movements were regarded as the idiosyncracies of his genius. Because Johnson thought and felt oddly, he acted oddly. But over two hundred year's after his death, we may know better. Johnson, it seems, was a victim of Tourette's Syndrome, a neurological movement disorder, which had nothing directly to do with his genius. His spasms were not mind caused ('psychogenic' in technical clinical jargon); instead, they were purposeless, involuntary contractions of his muscles, necessitated, at least according to the best and most popular hypothesis to date, by chemical abnormalities in the brain.

Johnson's fate has a philosophic moral. Once belief in other minds is accepted as the hypothesis which explains behavior, something *may* come along and refute it. In the case of Johnson's tics, evidently it did: reference to Tourette's Syndrome and to understanding the Syndrome in neurochemical rather than psychological terms.[12]

Thus there is risk in holding that belief in other minds is warranted just when attribution of mind best explains behavior. The attribution may be refuted. But what sort of risk is it? Is wholesale defeat of the assumption that others are minded a serious possibility? Is our overall sense that others are minded likely to be defeated by competing non-minds explanation?

Surely not. Consider just one person: Johnson. Reference to Tourette's Syndrome defeats reference to Johnson's genius in explaining his tics. But there is much more to Johnson than tics; there are plays, poetry, dictionaries, and Shakespeare. Suppose it is true that, say, Johnson's tics were produced by chemical disorder. It does not follow from this that we can explain his plays, poetry, and editing of Shakespeare without reference to Johnson's mind – his imagination, sense of language, feeling for Shakespeare. It is grossly unlikely that we can explain Johnson's behavior in writing plays and other creative and intelligent activity without referring to his thought and experience. Chemistry can account for tics; but it barely scratches the surface of creative genius.[13]

True, in certain behavioral instances (such as Johnson's tics) attribution of mind should be challenged and can be eliminated. Non-minds explanation should be preferred to other-minds explanation. In others, however, such as building libraries, writing books, speaking, and so on, reference to mind seems ineliminable. Johnson had his wits about him in writing plays, even if his tics were mindless.

Skepticism about other minds is sometimes attacked for being in the grip of an overly simple or narrow picture of how belief in other minds can be warranted. The idea develops that since access to other minds is indirect, belief in other minds is unwarranted. The best explanation argument breaks the grip of the simple picture. It challenges the skeptic to account for the behavior of others without presupposing the existence of other minds. Impotent skepticism creates no scandal. Explanatory warrant is strong enough to preserve our common-sense conviction in other minds.

NOTES

1   Behaviorism admits of forms and variations other than logical (also known as philosophical) behaviorism or peripheralism. For information on various meanings of 'behaviorism', see A. Byrne, 'Behaviorism', in *A Companion to the Philosophy of Mind*, ed. S. Guttenplan (Blackwell Publishers, Oxford, 1994), pp. 132–40.

2   Ludwig Wittgenstein (1889–1951) was one of the most original and provocative philosophers of the twentieth century. He composed the *Philosophical Investigations* between 1936 and 1948, although it was not published until 1953 – after his death. P. F. Strawson's sympathy for the 'humbling disclosure' argument may be found in his 'Persons' in *Individuals* (Methuen, London, 1964), pp. 87–116.

3   See A. Plantinga, *God and Other Minds* (Cornell University Press, Ithaca, 1967), p. 199.

4   Brentano's notion of the immediately evident is explored in his *Psychology from an Empirical Standpoint* (Open Court, New York, 1946).

5   See J. S. Mill, *An Examination of Sir William Hamilton's Philosophy*, 6th edn (Longman's, Green & Co., New York, 1889), p. 243. As for being Russell's godfather, Russell was an atheist, Mill a deist or agnostic. So 'godfather' signified a social or quasi-familial rather than religious bond.

6   Paul Churchland, *Matter and Consciousness* (MIT Press, Cambridge, Mass., 1984), p. 69.

7   Robert Pargetter's 'The scientific inference to other minds', *Australasian Journal of Philosophy*, 62 (1984), pp. 158–63, is an excellent treatment of the argument to which I am indebted.

8   The quotation is from Alison Gopnik, 'Developing the idea of intentionality: children's theories of mind', *Canadian Journal of Philosophy*, 20 (1990), pp. 108–9.

9   Leslie's reflections on autism and other minds are helpfully summarized in his 'Some implications of pretence for mechanisms underlying the child's

theory of mind', in *Developing Theories of Mind,* eds D. Olson, J. Astington, and P. Harris (Cambridge University Press, Cambridge, 1988), as well as in A. Leslie and D. Roth, 'What autism teaches us about metarepresentation', in *Understanding Other Minds: Perspectives from Autism,* eds S. Baron-Cohen, H. Tager-Flusberg, and D. J. Cohen (Oxford University Press, Oxford, 1993).

10   The topic of best explanation is not without its own internal subtleties, independent of the problem of other minds. For instance, suppose that the only available explanations of a phenomenon are weak or unacceptable, but one is best among the weak. This certainly does not warrant endorsing the best. Thus, to be warranted in accepting the best available, the availables must not be unacceptable. Subtleties of the kind just mentioned lie beyond the scope of this book. Except for the remarks of the next few paragraphs, I bypass them.

11   Plantinga, *God and Other Minds,* p. 269.

12   For information on Johnson's affliction, see Harold L. Klawans, 'The eye of the beholder', in *Toscanini's Fumble and Other Tales of Clinical Neurology* (Contemporary Books, New York, 1988), pp. 87–91.

13   For more detailed discussion of the relationship between mind explanation and non-mind explanation, see chapters 8 and 11.

4

Mind and Belief in Animals

4.1 The Mental Community

Who or what has a mind? Which creatures or beings deserve to be counted as card carrying members of the community of mind? Philosophers answer this question in different ways. Some – 'panpsychists' – go to extremes of tolerance. Everything is minded, including volcanoes, viruses, thermostats and thermometers. Others – 'psychological chauvinists' – go to extremes of intolerance. Nothing but humans have minds. All else is mindless.

I shall assume that the truth lies somewhere in the middle: in neither panpsychism nor chauvinism. Humans do but viruses do not have minds, while various other creatures or beings likewise have minds. But where in the middle? Which creatures or beings? Some philosophers say that God has a mind; others ascribe minds to computers; many of course contend that nonhuman animals have minds; while some philosophers hold each of these positions.

Philosophers are sometimes bewildered when confronted with the possibility of nonhuman minds. There are two sources of bewilderment: (1) the complex variety of mental states and activities in the human case; (2) fear of slipping into crude anthropomorphism. Crude anthropomorphism, the view that nonhumans may be characterized in absolutely literal human psychological terms, is an intellectual dead end.[1]

A little reflection reveals serious flaws in crude anthropomorphism. The flaws are visible when we consider examples like these:

1   Primitive peoples invest trees and other natural objects with human

minds as part of explanation of the objects' behavior. Plants grow because they 'want' sunlight; clouds burst because they are 'angry'. Primitives see human personalities everywhere. Science displaces crude anthropomorphic explanations with superior non-anthropomorphic explanations. Clouds burst because of barometric pressure; plants grow because of sunlight and nutrients in the soil.

2   Young children invest dolls and other toys with human hungers, fears, and tears. As children grow they outgrow these attributions.

3   Some religions invest God with human or human-like traits. In Christianity, for example, God is pictured as a loving, knowing, faithful parent even though he is also supposed to be radically other – perfect, incorporeal, timeless. This tension between the picturing of a human-like God and his radical otherness makes for the intriguing theological project of explaining how God can be both human-like and not human. It is commonly recognized that crude anthropomorphism, speaking of God's jealousy, envy, cowardice, and tears should be avoided; although, it is hoped, other ways of referring to God as, for example, loving and knowing can be given analogical extensions or legitimate meanings when applied to him.

Thoughtful advocates of minds in animals, computers, or God recognize that crude anthropomorphism must be avoided and fear heading into it. Mental terms and concepts must be given, or otherwise possess, extended or merely similar (not identical) meanings if applied to nonhumans. If mental concepts apply to God, computers, or animals, as well as to human persons, they do not apply univocally, with the exact same meaning in each sort of case. The mind, for example, of a perfectly knowing and loving God is not the same sort of mind as the mind of an imperfect human person. So talk of God's mind is not just like talk of your or my mind. If God loves, he doesn't crave kisses.

As for the first source of bewilderment, the immense variety of human mental phenomena makes consideration of nonhuman minds truly complex and difficult. Think of the diverse phenomena of human mental life: perceptual experiences, memories, dreams, beliefs, desires, bodily sensations, decisions, emotions, self-awareness. We have and lead complex mental lives. Do animals share all of it? Some of it? What about computers? It may be thought that computers share some (memory) but not the spicy or dramatic parts (sensations, feelings) or the truly intelligent parts (belief, reason). Or perhaps mental concepts which apply to humans are mere metaphors when applied to computers. Computers really do not remember or believe. It is sheer poetry to speak of computer thought and machine recall.

In face of the bewildering variety of human mental states and activities we must restrict the range of discussion in both this and the next two chapters. In these chapters I will focus primarily on *belief* in nonhumans. I will begin by considering whether animals possess beliefs and related attitudes. Then, in chapter 5, I will turn to beliefs and related attitudes in computers. In chapter 6 I turn to God. The purpose of these discussions is not only to explore the possibility of nonhuman minds but to illuminate the various mental phenomena themselves. Selected themes in recent philosophy of mind will wind their way through the discussion. One of the most important will be Intentionality.

4.2 Optimism about Animal Belief

David Hume (1711–76), the great Scottish philosopher of the eighteenth century, might well be called 'philosophy's majestic skeptic'. Hume was unyielding in the application of skeptical doubts to our most popular notions of causality, mind, selfhood, and divinity.[2] Yet there was at least one notion which Hume could not doubt, one proposition he did not question:

> Next to the ridicule of denying an evident truth, is that of taking much pains to defend it; and no truth appears to me more evident, than that beasts are endowed with thought and reason as well as men. The arguments are in this case so obvious, that they never escape the most stupid and ignorant.[3]

Nonhuman animals, or 'beasts' as Hume called them, have minds. Hume's principal 'obvious' argument went like this. If a person behaves intelligently, we believe that he or she has a mind; so, if an animal behaves intelligently we should believe that it, too, has a mind. Meanwhile, many animals behave intelligently. So, we should believe that they have minds. Hume's examples include 'a dog, that avoids fire and precipices, that shuns strangers, and caresses his master' and 'a bird, that chooses with such care and nicety the place and materials of her nest' where she sits upon her eggs taking precautions of 'the most delicate proportion'.[4]

The details in Hume's reasoning may be expressed as follows. We explain and predict the behavior of fellow human beings who shun fires and protect their young by ascribing states of mind to them; so, we should explain comparable behavior of the dog and bird in the following parallel way. The dog is *fearful* on *seeing* the fire; the bird *wants* to protect her eggs and *believes* that she can do this by building a strong nest and guarding it. Other terms may be used, perhaps less sophisticated psychological concepts should be employed; but we must ascribe mind in some way if we want to account for the animals' behavior, just as we must attribute mind to explain comparable human behavior.

The age of close scientific inspection of animals had not dawned, so when Hume said that animals are minded, he did not intend this as precise designation of where on the ladder of evolution or scale of intelligent behavior to draw the line between creatures with minds and those without. If, for example, we consider how the primitive little flatworm, *Planaria*, behaves, then we probably should avoid attributing mind to it. Planarian behavior seems to lack the intelligence required to reveal a mind at work. Its moving parts are capable only of a narrow range of stereotyped movements and its sensory receptors are so simple that it cannot register the direction from which stimuli come. However cats, dogs, birds, dolphins, chimpanzees, and a host of other sorts of animals qualify by Hume's criterion.

Nor did Hume explicitly delineate the standard by which intelligence in behavior should be defined. Hume seemed to presuppose the unproblematic standard to be, roughly, the capacity for appropriate and flexible responses to a variety of environmental changes or events. Thus if a dog shuns strangers but caresses its master or a bird chooses appropriate elements for a nest, these behaviors are sufficiently intelligent to reveal 'the reasonings of beasts'.[5] Striking additional examples, which Hume might have mentioned had he been familiar with the contemporary animal psychology literature, include accounts of coordinated cooperative hunting behavior among lions and the versatility with which domesticated chimpanzees can learn and employ elements of American Sign Language for the Deaf.[6]

Today most philosophers recognize the truth of Hume's thesis. There are not many who deny that animals are minded. However, there are denials. We will examine in detail one such denial. Then we will extract a critical moral from this examination which helps in understanding animal minds.

4.3 Pessimism about Animal Belief

Writing in the academic journal *Dialectica* in 1982, Donald Davidson recounts the following story due originally to the philosopher Norman Malcolm:

> Suppose your dog is chasing the neighbor's cat. The latter runs full tilt toward the oak tree, but suddenly swerves at the last moment and disappears up a nearby maple. The dog doesn't see this maneuver and on arriving at the oak tree he rears up his hind feet, paws at the trunk as if trying to scale it, and barks excitedly into the branches above. We who observe this whole episode from a window say, 'He thinks that the cat went up the tree'.[7]

However, to believe that the cat it was chasing has gone up a certain oak tree, says Davidson,

> the dog must believe, under some description of the tree, that the cat went up that tree. But what kind of description would suit the dog? For example, can the dog believe of an object that it is a tree? This would seem impossible unless we suppose that the dog has many ... beliefs about trees: that they are growing things, that they need soil and water, that they have leaves or needles, that they burn. There is no fixed list of things someone with the concept of tree must believe, but without many (such) beliefs, there would be no reason to identify a belief as a belief about a tree, much less an oak tree. Similar considerations apply to the dog's supposed thinking about the cat.[8]

Davidson's idea is that the topic of animal belief is not so simple as Hume and others contend. His claim is that only if animals possess many beliefs which are themselves presupposed by the beliefs ascribed to them, do they truly possess the beliefs ascribed. However, animals do not possess the presupposed beliefs, for they are conceptually and cognitively impoverished. Genuine belief, therefore, escapes them.

Suppose, for instance, we say of the dog that it believes that the cat has run up the tree. According to Davidson, the dog can believe such a thing only if it also believes related things such as that trees need soil and water, that they have leaves or needles, and that they burn. However, since the dog does not believe these things, it does not believe that the cat has run up the tree. The dog may act *as if* it believes that the cat has run up the tree. But it does not really believe it. It is a nominal or apparent believer, but it is not a true or genuine believer.

To make Davidson's argument clearer, consider an (imaginary) related human case, due to the philosopher Stephen Stich.[9] Mrs T. has grown old and now suffers from a serious neural disorder evidenced by an unusual memory loss. As a youngster, she was shocked and greatly impressed by news of the assassination of President McKinley. Expectedly, when questioned about McKinley, she says that he was assassinated. However, so serious is her disorder that she seems to recall nothing else about the man or event. If, for example, asked whether McKinley is dead, she replies that she does not know. If asked whether the Vice President took office after the assassination, she asks 'Vice President? What's a vice president?' In brief, she has no, or virtually no, grasp of either assassination or presidency, although she plainly insists that McKinley was assassinated. How are we to understand this?

Does Mrs T. believe that McKinley was assassinated? Is there a state of her mind which deserves to be called *the belief that McKinley was assassinated*? The question provokes two responses, depending upon which criterion or standard is used for the presence (or absence) of a particular belief.

Particular job criterion One criterion for belief presence is that a belief is a mental state or attitude which performs a particular behavioral job. If the behavior occurs, the belief is present; if the behavior does not occur, or does not occur when prompted, the belief is absent. To take a simple illustration, in saying of a person, Smith, that Smith believes that it will rain today, we are attributing to Smith the psychological state which performs the particular job of leading Smith to wear a raincoat. If Smith wears a raincoat, he believes that it will rain today. If, on the other hand, Smith sports a sun visor, he believes that it will be sunny. By the particular job criterion, Mrs T. believes that McKinley was assassinated, for she says 'McKinley was assassinated'. If she disbelieved, she would not assert that he was assassinated.

Network criterion Another criterion or standard for the presence of a belief is that belief is a network state in the mind with links or cross-references to other states and attitudes of mind. A belief is an attitude positioned in a total scheme or network of beliefs and other states of mind. Only if the scheme is present is the belief present. For example, in saying of Smith that Smith believes that it will rain today, we are saying that he also believes such things as that rain is wet, that he should wear a raincoat if he wishes to keep dry, that driving conditions may be hazardous, and so on. If Smith's supposed belief that it will rain today is not part of such a network, then it should not be classified as *the* belief that it will rain today. By the network criterion, Mrs T. fails to believe that McKinley was assassinated because she sincerely confesses not to know whether McKinley is dead. Her understanding of assassination is too conceptually impoverished to permit her alleged McKinley belief to count as the belief that McKinley was assassinated.

An analogy will help in understanding the network criterion. Imagine a baseball game with a full count on the batter. What is the significance of the next pitch? If another 'ball' is thrown, the batter walks freely to first base; if a 'strike' is thrown, however, the batter strikes out. The meaning of the next pitch, whether it walks or strikes out the batter, depends on the pitches before it. Likewise, whether the pitch ends the game (last batter, last inning) or merely retires the batter depends on its location in the game. The identity of the pitch is positional. Its character depends on its position in the scheme or network of the game. By the network criterion, the same is true of belief. Mrs T. has no, or almost no, understanding of assassination, for her alleged belief that McKinley was assassinated is not positioned so that she also believes that he is dead. Whatever (if anything) she believes when she claims he was assassinated, she does not believe that he was assassinated. If a person does not realize that assassination constitutes death, how can he or she believe that someone has been assassinated? Beliefs, like strikes, occur in a total scheme. A belief unconnected with belief in death does not count as belief in assassination. Analogously, strikes do not strike out unless two strikes on the same batter precede them. Perhaps Mrs T. merely recollects the words of an old newspaper headline. Why does she assert 'McKinley was assassinated'? Perhaps she echoes the headline without believing anything whatsoever about McKinley.

The moral to be extracted from the digression about Mrs T. is that Mrs T is just a special instance of the situation of the dog in Malcolm's story. (For convenience now, let's refer to the dog as 'Phaedeux', pronounced 'Fido'). Davidson adopts a network criterion for the presence of belief. The presence of a thought, he says, 'cannot be divorced from its place in the ... network of other thoughts.'[10] He writes: 'Individual beliefs ... owe their identities in part to their position in a large network of further attitudes: the character of a given belief depends

on endless other beliefs.'[11] Davidson contends that the network criterion
leads to nothing less than the complete rejection of animal belief. If we
accept that beliefs must occur in networks, we must reject, Davidson
says, that animals believe.

Consider Phaedeux again. Suppose we entertain the hypothesis that
Phaedeux believes that the cat has run up the tree. What should we
expect Phaedeux to believe of trees if the hypothesis is correct and he
really does believe that the cat has run up the tree? Does he believe that
trees are growing things, that they need soil and water, that they have
leaves or needles? This seems unlikely, says Davidson. For what should
we expect him to believe of water, if he believes that trees need water?
That water is composed of chemicals? That it evaporates? This also
seems unlikely. Failing to have such beliefs, the dog doesn't believe that
the cat has run up the tree. His 'tree beliefs' are not positioned in a
suitable tree-belief network to count as tree beliefs. They are tree beliefs
in name only. Dogs simply are not conceptually sophisticated enough to
believe things which they must believe if they *genuinely* believe that the
cat has run up the tree. Indeed, dogs are not conceptually sophisticated
enough to possess beliefs at all, for the Davidsonian argument may be
repeated with necessary changes for beliefs about cats, bones, and
anything else which dogs allegedly believe. Similarly, it may be reiterated
for any and all nonhuman animals. Our temptation to attribute beliefs to
'beasts' is undermined by their conceptual poverty.

Davidson's argument, then, may be formalized like this:

D1 A creature can have a belief only if the belief is positioned in a
     network of beliefs.
D2 Animals lack belief networks.
D3 Hence, animals lack beliefs.

Does this argument succeed in establishing that animals lack beliefs? It
is, in my judgment at least, the best effort by a philosopher to demonstrate that animals lack beliefs. But there are two sets of ways in which to
criticize it. The second works, although the first fails.

(1) The first challenge D1. One challenge to D1 is to argue that the
notion of a belief network is incapable of precise definition, and that
without precise definition there is no point in insisting that animals must
have networks in order to possess beliefs. What network must one have,
for example, to believe that it will rain today? We cannot say precisely.

Therefore nothing follows about whether animals lack beliefs from the notion of a belief network.

This challenge has a certain superficial plausibility, but just by itself it cannot be used to undermine the network criterion for belief possession. Davidson can plausibly deny that imprecision is a liability in the notion of belief network. There is nothing in his use of the notion which requires exactitude. Consider the following analogy. There can be little doubt about whether certain animals feed, flee, and fight, although there is plenty of room to debate exactly what it means to feed, flee, or fight. Vagueness or imprecision in ideas of feeding, fleeing, and fighting may be inherent but is not damaging to those concepts. Flamingos feed, foxes flee, and watermelons do not fight. Likewise, for Davidson's purpose, imprecision in the concept of belief network is not damaging. It can remain true that beliefs are embedded in networks and that a creature can have a belief only if it is positioned in a network. The notion of network is rough around the edges, but not for that reason poorly suited to argue that animals fail to possess beliefs or that Mrs T. fails to believe that McKinley was assassinated. Vague notions may be used as criteria provided in other respects they are sound.

The principal challenge to D1 has to do with the particular job criterion. One might try to defend this criterion as over and against the network criterion. One might argue that the belief that the cat ran up the tree is present just in case Phaedeux barks at the branches and paws at the trunk. The dog's behaving in such a fashion is the handiwork of believing that the cat is up the tree. Since the job is performed, contrary to Davidson the belief is present.

Alas, the particular job criterion is narrow in the extreme. Do I wear a raincoat just if I believe it will rain today? Whether I wear a raincoat is determined not just by whether I believe that it will rain, but in conjunction with various other attitudes, such as the desire to keep dry, wishes with respect to alternate ways of keeping dry, beliefs about the water-repellant properties of the coat and so on. Furthermore, even if I do not wear a raincoat, I may still believe that it will rain today. Suppose I wish to get soaked. Or suppose I am ignorant of the water-repellant properties of the raincoat and believe that nothing can protect me. Thus my behavior is not a job performed by a particular belief. The job criterion is too restrictive. Beliefs do not perform jobs by their particular selves.

We can appreciate the excessive narrowness in the particular job criterion even with respect to animals. Does Phaedeux paw at the trunk and bark at the branches just because he believes that the cat has run up the tree? Whether he paws and barks seems determined not just by whether he believes that the cat has run up the tree, but by his desire to capture the cat, beliefs about whether barking will scare the cat out of the tree, and so on and so forth. Again, even if Phaedeux does not bark and paw, he still may believe that the cat is up the tree. Suppose he believes that barking and pawing is fruitless. The cat isn't going to climb out of the tree. Phaedeux trots away, though convinced that the cat has run up the tree. Even in the case of animals the particular job criterion is too narrow a standard for the presence of belief.

Most contemporary philosophers of mind favor the network criterion. A typical recent statement is the following. 'What I do is not just a function of a single psychological state but rather of the total psychological "field" at the moment.'[12] The network criterion admits into the picture the way in which surrounding beliefs and other states of mind – networks or fields – influence behavior. If I wear a raincoat, this is not merely because I believe that it will rain but because I want to keep dry and believe that the raincoat is water repellant. The belief that it will rain does not by itself perform the job of leading me to wear the raincoat. Other states of mind are included in the picture. Similarly, the belief that the cat has run up the tree does not alone perform the job of leading Phaedeux to paw and bark. Other states of mind must be mentioned in the story.

(2) In addition to trying to attack D1 and defending the particular job criterion, there is a second line of attack on Davidson's argument for rejecting animal belief. This second line is successful. It attacks D2. It is not unrelated to the charge of vagueness but goes beyond that charge.

Suppose Phaedeux's belief that the cat has run up the tree is somehow connected with other beliefs about both tree and cat. Assume that the network criterion is true. It does not follow that we should insist on the specific complement of beliefs which Davidson requires the dog to possess, that is, that Phaedeux must believe that the tree has leaves or needles, and so on. Belief networks occur along something like a continuous or floating scale. Think of my belief that Horowitz was a better classical pianist than Rubinstein. My competence in answering questions about piano skill is negligible when compared with my colleagues in the music department. Surely, however, I do believe that Horowitz was a better pianist than Rubinstein, and so might they. The musicologists and I share the same belief but in varying ways or different degrees, where the ways or degrees are determined by our conceptual sophistication and the sophistication of our different belief networks. In me the belief that Horowitz was a better pianist than Rubinstein does not rest in the same belief network as it does in the musicologists.

Analogously, Phaedeux may believe that the cat has run up the tree, although he has no notions of the value of soil and water or of whether the tree has leaves or needles and burns. Phaedeux conceives of the tree with his own stock of canine concepts. However we ultimately describe his belief network or conceptual stock, it does not need to be very similar to ours.

Recognizing that belief networks occur in scales amounts to more than appreciating that the network notion is vague. It amounts to permitting two creatures with different networks to share the same beliefs. This does not help Mrs T., but it helps animals, for it shows that Davidson's attempt to undermine the case for animal belief is at best severely strained, at worst fails. Mrs T. isn't helped, because if her 'McKinley assassination' belief is so conceptually impoverished that she does not even know whether the poor fellow is dead, then it is absurd to suggest that she believes that McKinley was assassinated. Her belief is off the assassination scale (no matter how vague the scale is). On the other hand, we may be perfectly justified in ascribing beliefs to animals. Ascribing beliefs to animals, as Hume noted, can help to account for their behavior: Why the pawing? Why this tree? Phaedeux's pawing at this tree is accounted for by his belief that the cat has run up it and desire to catch the cat. To employ the language of chapter 3, when the ascription of beliefs to animals best explains behavior, animals believe.

True, human beliefs may be deeply embedded in complex and sophisticated networks. However, we should not insist on similar networks for animals, just as, I hope, my colleagues in the music department will admit that I believe that Horowitz was a better pianist than Rubinstein without insisting that my network is similar to theirs. I believe that Horowitz was a better pianist than Rubinstein, although I cannot tell an arpeggio from a cadenza. Phaedeux believes that the cat has run up the tree, although he cannot distinguish oak from pine, or burnt leaves from crisp autumn foliage.

It is also worth noting that some animals may fail to have beliefs because they lack belief networks entirely. The flatworm, rigid in its movements, displays no recognition of the direction of stimulation. In a dish of water brightly illuminated at one end and dark at the other, a set of flatworms will eventually assemble in the shade. But what conducts the flatworm into the shade? Beliefs about effective movements, the source of light, the merits of tightly knotted curls as opposed to the occasional loop as it gravitates towards darkness? Hardly. Its meandering and almost random trail as it drifts into the shade is feeble warrant for attributing conceptual stock. Flatworm behavior is too feckless and unintelligent to evidence a network of beliefs. It simply is a neurochemical tropism or reflex.

Neither Mrs T. nor the flatworm draw succor from the network criterion. Meanwhile, Phaedeux is unthreatened by Davidson's attack on animal belief. The dog, I believe, believes.

4.4 The Challenge of Animal Belief

The denial that animals are minded has had advocates in the history of philosophy, although it has not been popular. Davidson is a thinker of importance who supports the denial. Descartes (1596–1650) is another philosopher who denies animal minds. However, as demerits of various denials have surfaced, philosophers have extracted an important challenge to advocates of animal belief from the debate.

The challenge is noted by David Armstrong in his *Belief, Truth, and Knowledge,* and has since been discussed by several philosophers, including John Heil.[13] *If we want to say that animals believe something, we must be able to say what.* It is intellectually irresponsible to suppose that we can explain animal behavior by ascribing beliefs if we cannot say what it is that animals believe. We must be able to identify the content of animal beliefs – the 'what' – if we ascribe beliefs to them.

The challenge of identifying animal beliefs is complicated by three factors. First, if beliefs occur in networks, how do we non-arbitrarily characterize networks of animal beliefs? How do we discover animals' stocks of concepts? If we wish, for example, to attribute to Phaedeux the belief that the cat has run up the tree, which sorts of concepts or beliefs does he have of cats and trees? When Phaedeux fixes his gaze on something across the lawn, 'we may wonder', notes John Heil, 'whether it is best to describe him as seeing Tabby, as seeing a cat, a furry gray animal, or a foe.'[14]

Second, there is a general and related feature of beliefs as well as of other propositional attitudes, such as desires and fears, which stands in the way of any simple or facile response to the challenge. We can describe a particular belief as a belief only if we acknowledge that it is embedded in the believer's attitudinal point of view or conceptual perspective. This feature of belief – point-of-view embeddedness or fusion – is simply the logical recognition of the *aboutness* of belief. The dog's belief that the cat has run up the tree is about the cat and the tree. Your belief that the book you are now reading is an introduction to philosophy of mind is about the book. Of course, just because you see yourself as reading an introduction to philosophy of mind does not mean you also believe that you are reading a best seller, even if the book is (I hope!) a best seller. Likewise, just because Phaedeux believes that the cat has run up the tree does not mean he also believes that Tabby has run up the tree, although the cat is Tabby. From the point of view of you and your belief network, the book is just an introduction to philosophy of mind. Fused to the dog's conceptual stock, Tabby is a nameless cat. Phaedeux does not appreciate that 'Tabby' is her name.

The same goes for desires, wants, and other attitudes with the feature of aboutness. Each is fused to the point of view of the person or creature who possesses the attitude. For instance, suppose Phaedeux wants to catch the cat; then if it is true that

1 The cat is Professor Malcolm's favorite pet,

we do not get the conclusion that

2 Phaedeux wants that he catch Professor Malcolm's favorite pet.

This is because wants, like beliefs, possess aboutness; and, since they possess aboutness, they are fused to a point of view. Just because Phaedeux wants the cat does not mean he wants something which he conceives as 'the professor's pet'. The concepts of professor and pet may not be part of his conceptual stock.

Here is one more example. Suppose you believe that your neighbor's teenage son would make a good museum curator and suppose, unknown to you, he is the Neighborhood Vandal. You don't in believing he would make a good curator also believe that the Neighborhood Vandal would make a good curator, for you don't conceive of the son as the vandal.

From your angle he is simply the generous young man next door, who spends many selfless hours keeping a watchful and protective eye on other people's expensive lawn statuary.

In philosophical jargon, the aboutness of belief and other attitudes is called 'Intentionality'. This is because the attitudes are pointed, as it were, outside themselves. Your belief that the son would make a good curator is about, directed at, or aimed at the son. (The word 'Intentionality' may confuse since it sounds like it identifies something voluntary, as in 'He shot the sailor intentionally'. But Intentionality should not be confused with intentional in the sense of voluntary. 'Intentionality' means aboutness. To avoid confusion I follow a convention introduced by the philosopher Daniel Dennett of beginning the word with an uppercase 'I'.) Meanwhile, the fusion of beliefs and other attitudes to points of view means, in philosophical jargon, that belief ascriptions are 'referentially opaque'. Though boy and vandal are one and the same, believing that the boy would make a good curator is not equivalent to believing that the vandal would make a good curator: you, for example, believe the one but not the other. However, no matter the jargon, a thorn by any other name would still hurt as much. In describing animal belief, the challenge is not just to describe beliefs and networks but beliefs and networks *as* points of view. It is the tree and cat as conceived, seen as, or thought of as, by the dog which must be described, along with the belief network within which the dog's conception of tree and cat is embedded.[15]

The third factor which complicates the challenge of describing animal belief is that animals – nonhuman beasts – are mute. They don't speak or communicate in language. Or at least they don't possess languages with the grammatical devices or communicative sophistication of human language. This means that animals cannot tell us what they believe. We may, if we like, say that Phaedeux's pawing and barking at the tree tells us something; but all we mean by this is that the animal's behavior is best explained by attributing beliefs. And we may, if we like, say that a dolphin who touches a paddle after searching its tank in Sea World Amusement Park tells her trainer that she wants a reward; but all we mean by this is that she expects a reward after touching the paddle and the trainer knows this. However, Phaedeux cannot say 'I believe that the cat has run up the tree'. Nor can he write a memorandum concerning the 'Terrible Truth about Professor Malcolm's Favorite Pet'. Nor can the dolphin protest 'I've performed my trick, so now reward me'. Neither animal can string words together; neither creature can read, write, or speak.

The third factor should not be overestimated. Perhaps the most serious form of overestimation is to insist that without language animals lack beliefs. Thought requires talk. A few philosophers, including Davidson, adopt this line. 'Beliefs', he says, 'demand the gift of tongues.'[16] However if, as Hume argued, belief evidence hinges on intelligent behavior, then it is difficult to see why this should necessitate linguistic ability. Many sorts of speechless animals appear to behave sufficiently intelligently: appropriately, flexibly. So why not classify them as true believers? On the other hand, lack of linguistic ability should not be underestimated. It may be impossible for a creature to conceptualize certain situations or engage in certain belief activity without language.

The German philosopher and mathematician Gottfried Leibniz (1646–1716) surmised that animals are incapable of scientific beliefs and theories because they cannot form long chains of reasoning; and they cannot form long chains of reasoning because they lack linguistic ability – the ability to string words together. Words permit long chains. 'The world changes and ... men become cleverer and find hundreds of new tricks – whereas the deer and hares of our time are not becoming craftier than those of long ago.'[17] Might Phaedeux, for example, possess beliefs about the Lowenheim–Skolem Theorem (a theorem in set theory)? Has he the ability to endorse capitalism over socialism? These seem to be sorts of attitudes which require linguistic mastery and attendant capacities to read books, converse, participate in ideological discussion, and so on.

Indeed, once we admit that animals are incapable of certain sorts of attitudes and activities without language, tantalizing theoretical possibilities emerge. Some philosophers contend that language is critical for expectations about the distant future, or memories of the distant past, or beliefs about the truth value of linguistic statements or utterances. Phaedeux barks at the foot of the tree, but we feel no compulsion to credit him with the belief that the following utterance is true: 'The cat is up the tree'. A belief that an utterance is true obliges Phaedeux to have concepts of true or false utterance. Arguably, such concepts are available only to linguistic creatures. (Caution: This is not to deny that Phaedeux believes that the cat is up the tree. Phaedeux may believe that the cat is up the tree without believing 'The statement "The cat is up the tree" is true'.)

How about the distant future? What can Phaedeux do here and now to evidence the belief that next year his master will move to Siberia? So long as he remains speechless, we may never have the slightest warrant to suppose that he expects that next year his master will move to Siberia. Some thought requires talk even if thought itself is compatible with speechlessness.

Thus to sum up: Animals believe. However, the challenge to those who attribute beliefs to animals is to say what animals believe, given that they cannot tell us, beliefs occur in networks, and networks are permeated with aboutness. To make the task or challenge clearer, consider two cases from the animal psychology literature in which the challenge has been acknowledged and the attempt has been made to meet it.

4.5 Horse and Chimp

Clever Hans, a once famous horse, was exhibited in Berlin at the turn of this century by his trainer and owner, a retired mathematics professor, Herr von Osten.[18] Hans was trained to answer questions by tapping his hoof and shaking his head, and his trainer, von Osten, claimed that Hans was able through tapping and head shaking, and a communication code which von Osten had devised, to demonstrate that he could solve arithmetic problems, read and spell many German words, tell the time and understand the calendar. Von Osten was sincerely convinced that he had a clever horse and although many observers were skeptical and some suspected fraud, no one ever discovered duplicity on the part of von Osten.

However, in 1904 skeptics (foremost Oskar Pfungst, an experimental psychologist) started to search for unconscious and unintentional communication between Hans and his questioner. They noticed that Hans's talents retreated when either Hans could not see the questioner or the questioner himself did not know the answers. As one report puts it: 'Hans's accuracy ... hit zero if the questioner stood behind an opaque screen.'[19] So the skeptics surmised that Hans's talents hinged not on cleverness, but on unintentional subtle motions of questioners in asking Hans questions and observing Hans 'answer'. These included head posture, nostril dilation, and the raising and lowering of eyebrows – movements associated with the involuntary relaxation of tension among questioners when Hans's hoof taps reached the correct numerical value.

Some of these behaviors Hans believed to be 'go' signs, prompting Hans to begin tapping or shaking his head, others he took as 'stop' signs. Hans 'read' the signs; while his non-skeptical belief ascribers, including von Osten, interpreted Hans's behavior as showing that he possessed complex beliefs, including beliefs about arithmetic, German, time, and the calendar.

The skeptics' procedure is one good way to show that one set or network of belief ascriptions should be replaced with another. Essentially it involves demoting or deflating the alleged conceptual sophistication of an animal by demonstrating that a less sophisticated stock of concepts and beliefs suffices to explain its behavior. The skeptics showed that Hans did not conceive of or possess beliefs about arithmetic, German, dates, and times; beliefs about such things were not in his network or conceptual stock. From von Osten's point of view, Hans understood German. But from Hans's own perspective, he simply desired to 'go' when the questioner behaved in one manner, and 'stop' when the questioner behaved in another. He had not learned to recognize German *as* German, dates *as* dates, or arithmetic *as* arithmetic. Although he wasn't dumb, he certainly wasn't clever.

Two features of the Hans case are relevant for our purposes; and then we shall turn to another case. Both concern the challenge of describing animal beliefs. First, just as belief ascription to Hans involved ascribing a network to him, described allegedly from his own point of view, so demoting the ascriptions involved demoting the network, and replacing concepts alleged to be in the animal's stock with less sophisticated concepts. No belief was treated as isolated. Each had to be treated as part of a network: a network of beliefs about arithmetic, time, and German, or (after demotion) a network about 'go' and 'stop'.

One way in which philosophers speak of belief ascription as involving whole networks is by referring to the 'holism of intentional interpretation'.[20] Belief ascription – interpreting the attitudes of another person or subject – is inherently holistic; it ascribes networks. The stop/go ascription is inimical to attributing the sophisticated network necessary for grasping German. The German network breaks down when Hans is viewed as less sophisticated in conceptual stock. Looked at the other way around, we can succeed in ascribing particular sophisticated concepts to a creature only if we presuppose that its conceptual stock is already at least partially sophisticated. If, for example, Hans has beliefs about January 14 *per se*, he must have beliefs about other days in

January, other months, and so on. The holism of intentional interpretation is a by-product of the network criterion of belief. Beliefs are
linked together; hence, belief ascriptions are linked together.

The point I am making in the above two paragraphs is not that when
one belief is replaced or demoted *each* and *every* other belief is discharged
or deflated. Holism or network embedding is not all or nothing. You can
have beliefs about months, without knowing of January. Suppose a
young child is learning of months for the very first time and January has
yet to be mentioned. What I am saying is that, when beliefs are replaced
and demoted, those beliefs with which they are cross-linked are
demoted; the network destabilizes.

A second feature of the Hans case is also relevant for our purposes.
The Hans case reveals the fear expressed at the beginning of the chapter
about crude anthropomorphism, but it also reveals how to respond
reasonably to that fear. Skeptics worried that Hans did not believe what
von Osten claimed, for although von Osten's ability to answer German
questions presupposed that he understood German, Hans's ability to
answer did not necessarily mean that he, too, understood German.
Indeed, the doubters proved that Hans was responding to stop and go
signals, not to German. His trainer's interpretation of Hans was crudely
anthropomorphic.

It is all too easy to slip into crude anthropomorphism without a proper
dose of caution or skepticism. A classic and still useful antidote to crude
anthropomorphism has been offered by Lloyd-Morgan, an animal
researcher and psychologist whose influential textbook, *An Introduction
to Comparative Psychology*, was first published in 1894. 'In no case may
we interpret an action as the outcome of the exercise of a higher psychical
faculty, if it can be interpreted as the outcome of one which stands lower
on the psychological scale.'[21]

This is sometimes referred to as Morgan's Canon. The main idea
behind the Canon is that when animal behavior can be explained by
reference to either sophisticated or unsophisticated belief networks, the
unsophisticated should be preferred. Why? The short answer is that
observing Morgan's Canon helps to resist slippage into crude anthropomorphism. When von Osten ascribed sophisticated beliefs to Hans he
projected his own human intelligence onto the horse. But Morgan's
Canon chides that before endorsing human projection, one must seek to
discover whether a lower or less complex belief network is sufficient to
produce the same behavior. Rudimentary conceptual stocks should

always be preferred over sophisticated, human ones. The Canon fires a warning shot at crude anthropomorphic interpretation.

Let us conclude our discussion of animal beliefs by considering a second case in which the challenge of describing animal beliefs has been understood and addressed.

Partly because chimpanzees have been able to learn elements of American Sign Language for the Deaf and segments (at least) of other similar language systems, there has been a tremendous interest not just in the scientific community but in popular culture in the mental capacities of chimpanzees. One of the most remarkable manifestations of this interest has been the work of the psychologist Gordon Gallup. Here is one of Gallup's projects.

Gallup set out to determine if chimps have a self-concept. The main idea behind possessing a self-concept is that a creature with a self-concept can recognize or classify itself as itself. It has a sense of itself as such. If a chimp possesses a self-concept, then some of its beliefs must be described with a self-referring expression. For instance, 'That object, with that appearance is me.' To test this possibility Gallup conducted a simple experiment. He placed a large mirror next to a chimpanzee's cage, and within a few days the chimp started to use her image in the mirror as a means of exploring parts of her body which she could not see directly (e.g. by picking bits of food from between her teeth).[22] Gallup argued that the chimp seemed to recognize itself as itself and not as another chimpanzee; it seemed to possess a self-concept. If so, the use of the mirror to guide the chimp's behavior should be explained by ascribing to the chimp beliefs with content like 'That food is between my teeth' or 'That creature, with that food between its teeth, is me'.

Gallup's claim would be resisted by certain philosophers. Immanuel Kant (1724–1804), for instance, adopted a demoting attitude towards animal self-concepts. He claimed that although animals notice and respond to conditions of their bodies, they cannot believe that they themselves are in such conditions. They lack concepts of themselves.[23] They may perceive food between their own teeth but not *as* food between their own teeth. Gallup, however, seems to have shown that Kant is wrong and that at least some beasts are equipped with self-concepts, although the jury is still out on this issue.[24] In any case, I wish to make a different point.

I am not concerned with whether chimps actually harbor self-concepts. My point is that Gallup put his hypothesis of animal belief to test. He checked his conjecture by running a controlled experiment. It is through tests (and more generally careful observation) that, ultimately, we should be able to discover animal beliefs and meet the challenge noted by Armstrong. Animal belief is empirically researchable territory. Kant exclaimed, from his library armchair, that animals could not have self-concepts; Gallup said, from his observations, that the question is empirical. We can test the ascription of animal belief and belief networks by casting about for evidence and by designing both field and laboratory experiments to uncover animals' stocks of concepts. Does the chimpanzee believe that food bits are between her teeth? Well, does the chimpanzee behave differently towards her body now that she has looked at herself in the mirror? Does she treat her body differently than she treats the bodies of other chimps? Does she use mirrors for herself but not for others? Almost inevitably behavioral details begin to mount in favor of one set of answers rather than another. Perhaps like the rest of us on a Monday morning she thinks 'My goodness, that chump in the mirror is me'. If so that would be belief and self-concept indeed!

NOTES

1 John A. Fisher wisely argues that much conceptual confusion surrounds the fear of anthropomorphism; see his 'The myth of anthropomorphism', in *Interpretation and Explanation in the Study of Animal Behavior*, eds M. Bekoff and D. Jamieson (Westview, Boulder, 1990), pp. 96–116.

2 This fact about Hume has not been lost on friends of the idea that animals are minded. See Bernard Rollin, 'How animals lost their minds: animal mentation and scientific ideology' in Bekoff and Jamieson, *Interpretation*, p. 375.

3 This quotation is from David Hume, *A Treatise of Human Nature*, ed. L. A. Selby-Bigge (Oxford University Press, Oxford, 1739/1960), p. 176.

4 See Hume, *Treatise*, p. 177.

5 Indeed, Hume does not use the expression 'intelligent behavior' but speaks instead of behavior which reveals the 'reasonings of beasts' and 'that act of mind which we call "belief"'. See Hume, *Treatise*, p. 178.

6 For information, see D. Griffin, *Animal Thinking* (Harvard, Cambridge, Mass., 1984), pp. 85–7; B. Gardner and R. Gardner, 'Teaching sign-language to a chimpanzee', *Science*, 165 (1969), pp. 664–72. The best overview of what is known about the minds of animals is the beautifully

illustrated and engagingly written: James Gould and Carol Gould, *The Animal Mind* (Scientific American Library, Freeman, New York, 1994).

7   The quotation is from Donald Davidson, 'Rational animals', *Dialectica*, 36 (1982), pp. 318–27; reprinted in *Actions and Events*, eds E. LePore and B. McLaughlin (Blackwell Publishers, Oxford, 1985), pp. 473–80. The exact page reference (to LePore and McLaughlin) follows in the next note.

8   Davidson, 'Rational animals', p. 475. Parenthesis added.

9   Stich's discussion of Mrs T. may be found in his *From Folk Psychology to Cognitive Science*, (MIT Press, Cambridge, Mass., 1983), especially pp. 55–6.

10   Davidson, 'Rational animals', p. 475.

11   The quotation is from Davidson's self-descriptive entry in *A Blackwell Companion to the Philosophy of Mind*, ed. S. Guttenplan (Blackwell Publishers, Oxford, 1994), p. 232.

12   The statement is from William Alston, 'Functionalism and theological language', in *Divine Nature and Human Knowledge* (Cornell University Press, Ithaca, 1989), p. 68.

13   See David Armstrong, *Belief, Truth, and Knowledge* (Cambridge University Press, Cambridge, 1973), p. 25; John Heil, *Perception and Cognition* (University of California Press, Berkeley, 1983), pp. 176–215.

14   See Heil, *Perception*, p. 189.

15   There may be room for technical philosophical terminology here. Belief with respect to some object (the boy) is sometimes contrasted with belief with respect to some proposition or fact (that he would make a good curator). The first is called belief *de re* (about the object), the second belief *de dicto* (about the proposition). *De re* beliefs are held with respect to particular things or people, no matter how they are conceived. Using this distinction to offer a conceptual sibling to the previous sentence in the text, in describing animal belief, a challenge is not just to identify what animal beliefs and networks are about (cats and trees, the *res*) but to describe animal concepts ('cat', 'tree', the *dicta*). I do not invoke the *de re/de dicto* distinction in the text because it raises complications which add to those more immediately associated with animal belief. One of these complications is the question of whether *any* creature (person or nonhuman animal) can hold a belief with respect to a particular thing without having some conception of a *relevant* sort about the thing. If not, no belief may qualify as *de re*. For additional discussion of the *de re/de dicto* distinction, see Michael Tye, 'Belief, the metaphysics of', in *A Companion to the Philosophy of Mind*, pp. 140–6.

16   The quote is from Davidson, 'Rational animals', p. 473. See also his 'Thought and talk', in *Mind and Language*, ed. S. Guttenplan (Oxford University Press, Oxford, 1975), pp. 7–23.

17   The quote is from G. W. Leibniz, *New Essays on Human Understanding*, tr. and ed. by P. Remnant and J. Bennett (Cambridge University Press, Cambridge, 1981), p. 51.

18   For an account of the significance of the Hans case for belief ascription to animals, to which I am indebted, see Hugh Wilder, 'Interpretive cognitive ethology', in Bekoff and Jamieson, *Interpretation and Explanation in the Study of Animal Behavior*, pp. 344–68. See also Gould and Gould, *The Animal Mind*, pp. 1–2.

19   Gould and Gould, *The Animal Mind*, p. 2.

20   The quoted expression is from John Haugeland, 'Understanding natural language', in *Foundations of Cognitive Science*, ed. J. L. Garfield (Paragon, New York, 1990), p. 399.

21   The quote is from C. Lloyd-Morgan, *An Introduction to Comparative Psychology* (Walter Scott, London, 1894), p. 53.

22   For an account of Gallup's experimental activity – a bit out of date now, but still informative – see Gordon Gallup, 'Self-recognition in primates', *American Psychologist*, 32 (1977), pp. 329–38. For a recent statement by Gallup, see his 'Self-recognition: research strategies and design', in *Self-Awareness in Animals and Humans*, eds S. Parker, R. Mitchell, and M. Boccia (Cambridge University Press, Cambridge, 1994), pp. 35–50. See also Gould and Gould, *The Animal Mind*, pp. 155–9.

23   Kant's skepticism about animal self-concepts may be found in a letter to Marcus Herz, whose relevant material is cited in Jonathan Bennett, 'Thoughtful brutes', *Proceedings of the American Philosophical Association*, 62 (1988), p. 207.

24   Much depends on what is meant by a self-concept. The more loose the notion, the more likely some animals possess self-concepts. For additional discussion, see R. Epstein, R. P. Lanza, and B. F. Skinner, 'Self-awareness in the pigeon', *Science*, 212 (1980), pp. 695–6; Lawrence C. Davis, 'Self-consciousness in chimps and pigeons', *Philosophical Psychology*, 2 (1989), pp. 249–59; see also Bennett, 'Thoughtful brutes'.

5

Mind and Belief in Computers

According to Plutarch, the ancients were convinced that elephants entertain religious beliefs, since they cleanse themselves in the sea and face the rising sun with trunks lifted in supplication. But so loosely analogous is elephant behavior to religious behavior that Morgan's Canon should be used to demolish the conviction. Attribution of mentality should not turn on loose analogy. On what should it turn?

The present chapter is an attempt to explore a question connected with the attribution of mind. It is a question philosophers have been debating at least since Thomas Hobbes (1588–1679), the foremost British philosopher of the seventeenth century, although historically, it took work on artificial intelligence and the design of sophisticated computer programs to render the question deeply puzzling and problematic. This is the question of whether mechanical artifacts or machines, in particular computers, are minded. Could a computer possess a mind? Could a computer qualify as a true believer?

5.1 Could a Computer Believe?

Could a computer believe? At first sight, the answer seems obvious. No. Computers are made of silicon chips rather than neuroproteins; they house dry inanimate hardware rather than wet living brains. By contrast, humans and animals are alive; they possess wet living brains. One is tempted to say, for example, as Britain's Anthony Kenny remarks, 'computers are not alive, and only living beings can think'.[1] Since computers lack wet living brains, they are mindless.

Fans of the idea that computers could believe charge that folks like Kenny beg the question when they insist that wet living brains are essential for belief. Kenny's 'biochauvinism' assumes what needs to be proven. One counter-argument runs in outline form something like this: If brains are unnecessary for intelligent behavior, and intelligent behavior is sufficient for belief, and computers behave sufficiently intelligently, then even though computers are devoid of fleshy living brains, they believe. They possess minds of their own.

To see all this a bit more clearly, recall the discussion in chapter 4 of David Hume on animals. According to Hume, the mark of mindedness in an animal is the capacity for intelligent behavior – not perhaps of the flatworm but of the bird or dog. Now it is commonplace knowledge that computers behave intelligently: they win chess games, perform numerical calculations, and guide missiles. On this behavioral way of thinking, if computer behavior is sufficiently intelligent, computers have minds. So misgivings about Kenny's allegiance to living brains arise. Could a computer believe? Even though its inanimate brainlessness tempts saying no, its behavior prompts saying yes.

What are the prospects for resolving the debate between biochauvinists like Kenny and more ecumenical attributors? Between those who contend that brain is essential and those who fix on behavior?

Imagine that a creature from another planet lands in your backyard and tells you (in perfect English) that it is going to enroll for courses at Princeton University. Then the creature dresses up like a human (suppose that otherwise it looks most unhuman and that the creature is devoid of anything which we would classify as a brain) and enrolls at Princeton. Within three months it is awarded a Ph.D. in Comparative Literature! What should you say? Should you say that brains are essential for belief or that they are inessential?

I shall call this the Case of the Ivy League Alien. In this case, most of us would think it obvious what we should say: we should say that brains are unnecessary. The alien has a mind of its own even if it lacks a brain.

The Case of the Ivy League Alien is, of course, a fictitious example; but it shows that the biochauvinist's insistence on brains may be unreasonable. The basic idea is this: If an individual's behavior is sufficiently intelligent – if it is, for example, relevantly similar to human behavior of the sort which in us warrants the attribution of belief – then there is good reason to say that it believes, even if it lacks a brain. If a human who enrolls at Princeton and is quickly awarded a Ph.D. believes, then an alien who enrolls and is quickly awarded a Ph.D. also believes. We should not say that the human believes but then deny that the alien believes. Of course, this does not prove that the brain *is* unnecessary. Perhaps brains are needed for behavior of sufficient intelligence to evidence genuine belief. Perhaps there is no way a brainless computer or alien could support what an organic brain supports: rapid progress towards a Ph.D. Or perhaps brains are essential for conscious experience or other psychological processes which may be necessary for belief.

It does not automatically follow that just because we can imagine (or think we can imagine) an ivy league alien, the brain is inessential. All that automatically follows is this: We should disallow claiming *without defense* that brains are necessary. The Case of the Ivy League Alien shows that defense is needed and that, absent defense, evidently a computer could believe if it was capable of sufficiently intelligent behavior.

5.2 Functionalism and Intentionality

Many philosophers are attracted to the idea that beliefs and other propositional attitudes can occur in not just fleshy brains but dry hardware. Different sorts of things – both animate and inanimate – can perceive the rainfall, attend to the red triangle, believe that Descartes is a great philosopher or understand that the French 'Il pleut' means in English 'It is raining'.

What then are beliefs and other attitudes if they should not be identified with brains? Reflecting on the possibility of computer minds, Hilary Putnam, a philosopher whose career began at Princeton and then moved to Harvard, in the 1960s introduced the hypothesis that beliefs and other attitudes possess a certain abstractness relative to their embodiment.[2] Organisms and individuals that are diverse biologically and physically can possess the same attitudes. Or, to put the point another way, two things possessing the same belief can have nothing physically in common in virtue of which they possess that belief. Biochauvinism, according to Putnam, unwisely restricts possible embodiments of attitudes to fleshy brains. Putnam proposed that beliefs and other attitudes should be described independently of how they are materially embodied. They are *multiply realizable*, and should not be identified with any of their realizations.

What is it, then, that attitudes have in common which makes them attitudes? What do all beliefs – the beliefs of people, animals, and computers – possess in virtue of which they count as beliefs?

According to Putnam – the Putnam of the 1960s – attitudes are 'functional' sorts of things. The concept of a belief is a functional concept. Functional concepts are role-identifying concepts. They specify what something does in the course of an operation or activity, without consideration for how that something physically is constituted or composed. The role of a belief rather than its neural embodiment determines its nature or identity.

The conceptual core of Putnam's idea can be captured in a simple example. Suppose two people in similar circumstances both believe that it is raining. What matters in identifying the belief state of each is not their underlying neurophysiological conditions, but the functional relation of their state to such inputs as, say, the rainfall and sound of thunder, other internal states, such as the desire to keep dry, and such behavioral outputs as looking for a raincoat or umbrella. In living creatures the brain must somehow implement the functional role, but it is the role, not the neurophysiology, that makes the attitude a rain belief.

Putnam labelled his theory *functionalism*. He advertised that through functionalism the biochauvinism of limiting attitudes to creatures with living brains can be avoided, and his position was quickly endorsed by philosophers and other cognitive scientists sympathetic to the possibility of computer belief. Functionalism claims that whether a creature or thing possesses beliefs and other attitudes has nothing directly to do with its neurobiological or physical makeup, but concerns whether that makeup – whatever it is – can somehow implement the roles distinctive of beliefs and attitudes. Functionalists hasten to add: If computer hardware can implement the functional roles distinctive of beliefs and attitudes, then we have all the evidence that we need for computer belief. Indeed, according to some functionalists, functionalism constitutes a major breakthrough in the scientific study of intelligent behavior, since it encourages picturing the computer as a model or prototype of intelligence. The nature of artificial intelligence reveals the character of natural (human and animal) intelligence, which consists of fulfilling the functional roles of beliefs and other attitudes. In computers those roles are executed by sophisticated, highly complex computer programs. Many functionalists claim that there are analogues of computer programs in brains in the form of neural codes which cause the brain to run a certain sequence of operations when given a certain kind of input. In Putnam's words: "'Functionalism" views us as *automata*; that is as computers that happen to be made of flesh and blood.'[3]

When outlined as baldly as this, functionalism may appear esoteric, but functionalism, the Putnamian doctrine, actually is a rather intuitive idea. Many concepts in ordinary language are functional concepts. The concepts of clock, money, and radio, for examples, are silent on the physical characteristics of clocks, money, or radios. As long as a physical object or system functions like a clock, money, or radio, it counts as one of these things. There are mechanical clocks, electric clocks, and water clocks; a dollar can be made up of a paper bill, four quarters, or ten dimes. Or consider two radio devices. One uses integrated circuits, the other (an antique model) uses vacuum tubes and coils. There are many differences between them in quality of production and ease of repair, and so on, but they nevertheless permit listening to the same shows and use the same input (radio waves). Functionally (at a certain level of description) they are equivalent. They perform the same roles (permit listening to the same shows) under the same input conditions (receiving the same radio waves). There is no specific physical property that every radio must possess.

Many concepts in ordinary language are functional concepts. According to Putnam, concepts of belief and other propositional attitudes are among them. For example, imagine a person and a computer with robotics so that the computer moves around the environment. When deprived of food, the person moves to the refrigerator, opens the door, and reaches for a loaf of bread; we speak of the person as believing that there is food in the refrigerator. 'Inside' the person is a propositional attitude. It plays the role of accepting certain input (food deprivation) and 'processing' it in such a way that the person reaches for a loaf of bread. If we could get the computer to do the same thing, in response to its 'deprivation', then it would be in a state which plays the same functional role as the belief in the person; it would be in a *functionally equivalent* condition. Then, if functional equivalence makes for attitude possession, just as the person believes that there is food in the refrigerator, the computer believes that there is food in the refrigerator. Furthermore – and here is the functionalist notion of multiple realization – it is no good complaining that the computer is made of silicon chips. Functional roles, if they are embodied, operate in devices or systems independent of their physical constitution. Persons cannot regard themselves as special from a psychological point of view: we cannot consistently maintain that our brains permit us to believe that there is food in the refrigerator, and that there are neurobiological constraints prohibiting computers from harboring this belief. That would be like regarding a dollar bill as special, from an economic point of view. We could not consistently claim (relative to the American economic system) that there are physical constraints prohibiting four quarters from counting as a dollar.

Intuitive or not, functionalism makes some philosophers more than a little skeptical. The notion of functional equivalence has the effect of cutting off attitude possession from the ways in which attitudes are embodied in the brain. It also has the related effect of dissociating behavior from the neurophysical activity which may be responsible for attitude possession. Does the functionalist way of thinking represent a deep insight, or does it express merely an uncritical pro-computer bias? John Searle, a Berkeley philosopher, has repeatedly argued that functional equivalence to attitude possession is insufficient evidence of attitudes. Behavior – even sophisticated program executing behavior – is not enough to warrant attributing beliefs to computers.[4]

Searle urges that we observe a distinction when we consider whether a computer could believe. This is a distinction between 'intrinsic' Intentionality and 'as-if' or 'observer-dependent' Intentionality. Intentionality, it will be recalled by readers of the last chapter, is an essential feature of beliefs and other attitudes. What has Intentionality is *about* something. It is directed towards something. My belief that Descartes is a great philosopher is about Descartes; your fear of flying is about flying; my love of oranges is directed at oranges. Searle's gloss 'intrinsic' refers to Intentionality which *is* (real, honest-to-goodness) Intentionality. It is the Intentionality of genuine belief and true believer. Searle's as-if Intentionality, by contrast, is unreal Intentionality. It is Intentionality in the eye of the beholder which does not truly inhere in the subject beheld; it is the Intentionality of nominal belief, not genuine belief. To some eyes, for instance, water flowing downhill has Intentionality. A primitive cave-dwelling observer in the grips of crude anthropomorphism may ascribe beliefs and other attitudes about the hill to the water. It *tries* to flow downhill and *wants* to get to the bottom. However, of course, the water really does not try, want, or believe. Its Intentionality is in the eye of the cave-dweller. Water Intentionality is as-if Intentionality.

Searle uses the distinction between as-if and intrinsic Intentionality to undermine the functionalist idea that computers could believe just by virtue of behaving in a manner which is equivalent to the intelligent behavior of an animal or human being. His tactic, which we will examine momentarily, is to argue that computers possess only as-if Intentionality. On Searle's way of thinking, they cannot believe. They may simulate belief. However, simulated belief is not belief; belief requires intrinsic Intentionality.

Searle clarifies the distinction between as-if and intrinsic by means of illustrative examples. We will look at his most famous and provocative example, which he uses to try to undermine computer belief, in a moment. First, however, Searle's distinction is so suggestive that it is worth digressing to briefly note one of its aspects.

The reader blessed with a good memory will recall that the third chapter was sparked by skepticism about other minds. A central element in skepticism is the claim that no amount of purely behavioral evidence is sufficient to absolutely prove that another creature possesses a mind. There is always an inferential gap or step between evidence for the presence of belief (mind) and belief (mind) itself. Searle's distinction between as-if and intrinsic Intentionality is rooted in that gap. Central to his distinction is the point that there are no *sure* steps from behavior to mind. For the most part (except for logical behaviorists and disciples of Wittgenstein) those who try to tackle the problem of other minds agree. Even if we maintain (as argued in chapter 3) that belief in other minds is warranted, there is still an *inference*. No behavior, by itself, proves beyond the shadow of doubt the presence of mind. Between behavior and mind there is conceptual space for denying that other minds exist.

There is more that can (and will) be said about Searle's attitude towards the relationship between behavior and mind. But set Searle's views of mind/behavior aside. More important, for our present purpose, is that Searle's distinction between intrinsic and as-if Intentionality enables him to build an argument against computer Intentionality and belief. The argument is designed around an imaginative example, which, for reasons which will soon become obvious, is known as the *Chinese room argument*.

5.3 The Chinese Room Argument

Chess and related activities (e.g. numerical calculation) provide well-studied cases of the intelligent behavior of computers. But chess and such activities may be misleading. They are utterly flat or one-dimensional and, in the words of John Haugeland, 'separable from the rest of life'.[5] Hence, a chess-playing computer is more tool or toy than true believer. Although we may speak of a chess-playing computer as if it has beliefs about the current board positions and possible continuations of the game, for example, this is too restricted and shallow a belief network to qualify a chess-playing computer as a true believer. Consider the following situation. You are playing chess with a chess-playing computer. Suppose you wonder if the computer plays Monopoly as well as chess. Alas, it doesn't. It is limited to chess, unless you load another program. It is as if a chess-playing computer is a brilliant flatworm, locked in stunning stereotype. It can knock a person's socks off in chess, but it sits impotent in the face of Monopoly.

'Yes, it can play chess. But is it minded?' So goes the usual reaction to chess-playing computers. Alan Turing (1912–54), a distinguished logician and father of a lot of the modern theory of computers and computation, had another behavioral test for whether computers are minded. Not chess, but conversation. He proposed, in a paper which appeared in the journal *Mind* in 1950, that if a computer could communicate with a human being in such a way that the human being could not tell the difference between conversing with the computer and with another human being, then it would be arbitrary (mere biochauvinism) to deny that the computer is a believer simply because it is a computer.[6] Turing argued that the capacity for linguistic conversation is a good, strong test for computer belief. Wouldn't it be impressive if a computer could speak a language, say, Chinese, and engage in real dialogue? Its conversational range might manifest a thick and elaborate belief network, a stock of attitudes visible through its 'speech', concerning such topics as chess, Monopoly, games of all sorts – on boards, in love, politics, and life. Who could deny intrinsic Intentionality of an intelligent conversationalist, even though it was brainless?

To challenge the validity of Turing's proposal that computer conversation would demonstrate computer belief, John Searle has constructed an imaginative 'thought experiment' (the example to which I referred earlier). Thought experiments are important analytical devices in the history of philosophy. They have already appeared in this book, in the forms of Mary the Superscientist and The Case of the Ivy League Alien. Classic examples include Plato's Ring of Gyges and Descartes' Evil Demon Argument. A thought experiment consists in hypothesizing certain imaginary assumptions and extracting insights from those assumptions. Plato, for instance, supposes that a person possesses a magical ring the rubbing of which enables him to become invisible and to commit undetected immoralities and misdeeds. By this device Plato explores the view, which he himself abjures, that we follow moral rules merely because we fear punishment and not because we respect morality for itself. The Ring of Gyges is a thought experiment in human moral psychology.

Searle's Chinese room is a thought experiment in computer conversational psychology. It goes roughly as follows.

Assume that we have a computer program that purports to account for how a person or system engages in an Intentionally meaningful conversation in Chinese. The program processes Chinese text, performs some physically formal operations upon it.

Imagine that a man executes the program. Imagine that he is locked in an enclosed room with one entrance slot through which Chinese symbols are sent in and one exit slot through which symbols in the same language are sent out. Imagine that to the man these symbols are utterly meaningless, since he is unfamiliar with Chinese. The symbols appear just as straight and curved lines arranged in various visual patterns. In the center of the room are several baskets containing Chinese symbols of the same general physical type as those which pass through the entrance slot. Then, on a table in front of him is an immensely large and complex manual, written in English (his native language). The manual contains instructions or rules (the computer program) which specify merely by their shapes (and not by their meanings) which symbols to take from the baskets and pass through the exit slot in response to symbols received through the entrance slot. Looking up and following instructions in the huge manual is a long and boring process, but in time the man in the room learns and becomes adept at passing marks through the exit slot.

Imagine in addition, and of course again unknown to the man, that the marks sent in are questions, written in Chinese, and the marks he passes out are answers to those questions. In fact, they are perfectly reasonable answers, so much so that Chinese speakers outside the room are convinced that they are engaging in Chinese conversation with a fellow

Chinese speaker. For example, someone outside hands him symbols that unknown to him mean, 'Who is your favorite philosopher?' and after following the rule book he hands back symbols that, also unknown to him, mean, 'My favorite philosopher is Donald Davidson, though I admire Martin Buber a lot'. The speakers outside the room are impressed.

While unapparent to outside observers, Searle contends, it remains certain that the person in the room does not understand Chinese. He applies instructions, and he understands those instructions, but the sequences of Chinese symbols are gibberish to him. They are mere squiggle-squaggles. Also clear, contends Searle, is that the entire system of the room including the person and its contents is ignorant of Chinese. Nothing here grasps Chinese, except those sending and receiving messages, and those who composed the instruction book. No conversational response of man or system has any real or intrinsic Intentionality, or is about anything, or means anything, except as it is viewed by outside observers interacting with it.

Searle contends that the Chinese room argument hits the mark of undermining computer intrinsic Intentionality, belief and understanding. For the setup, according to Searle, is functionally equivalent to a computer. The person in the room, functioning like the central processor of a computer, manipulates physical symbols ('syntax'); the instruction book is the 'computer program' for manipulating the symbols. The baskets full of symbols are the 'data base'; the small bunches that are handed in are the 'input' and the bunches then handed out are the 'output'. According to Searle the impact of the example is as follows: If the person in the room (or system) does not possess intrinsic Intentionality (does not understand Chinese) solely on the basis of executing a computer program for understanding Chinese, then neither does any computer on the basis of running its program possess intrinsic Intentionality. Manipulating symbols in accordance with rules, which is the essence of computer program execution and transpires in the Chinese room, produces mere as-if Intentionality, as-if belief, as-if Chinese understanding.

Given Searle's conclusion, there cannot be any dispute about whether passing the Turing test is sufficient for computer belief. It is not. Far from being the product of intrinsic Intentionality, computer conversation by itself reveals nothing more than as-if Intentionality and as-if belief.

Searle first presented the Chinese Room in the pages of *Behavioral and Brain Sciences* in 1980, and it has since appeared and been refined in many of his publications. It also has been subjected to a flood of comment, discussion, and criticism, including 26 commentaries to the original article.

Even to critics, much of what Searle says seems both right and important. He is correct in his contention that the thought experiment shows that someone or something can appear to understand without really understanding; or appear to converse without really conversing; or appear to believe without truly believing. In life, we may simulate mental characteristics or abilities we actually do not possess. Behavior can mask ignorance. Also, Searle is on to something true and significant in his thesis that as-if Intentionality differs from intrinsic Intentionality. Few would deny that people differ from water flowing downhill. The distinction between as-if and intrinsic Intentionality may mark the psychological divide which separates water from persons as well as non-believers from believers. Finally, many critics of Searle concede that the Chinese room raises troubles for functionalism. Perhaps the notion of functional equivalence is unhelpful as a means through which to understand intelligence. Or perhaps Turing equivalence, the ability to pass the Turing test, is not one and the same thing as functional equivalence for linguistic understanding. However, although critics agree that the Chinese room raises good points, they deny that Searle succeeds in showing that computers could not believe. Many philosophers and others continue to maintain that computers, in one way or another, could believe.

The most popular anti-Searle, pro-computer belief counter-argument attacks Searle at just this point: it urges that various other technological possibilities, in addition to those exhibited in the Chinese room, are relevant to determining whether a computer could believe. Therefore, the Chinese room does not undermine computer intrinsic Intentionality.

5.4 The Counter-Argument from Possibility

The first counter-argument goes as follows: Perhaps the person in the room (or the system of person plus room) does not understand Chinese, but more sophisticated kinds of computers with programs or design architectures using discoveries about human linguistic intelligence could. What Searle's Chinese room is missing is realistic analogy to intelligent conversational behavior. (Perhaps equivalently: it lacks real functional equivalence to intelligent conversational behavior.) Searle's person in the room is utterly constrained by a book of explicit instructions. He engages in rule-governed dialogue in which conversational questions lead to answers generated by combining symbols in strict accordance with the book; his performance is too stiff and limited to count as intelligent Chinese. If, however, the person simulated more realistic Chinese conversation, then he (or the system of which he is a part) would understand Chinese. Indeed, even if he did not appreciate that he understood Chinese – even if he did not describe himself as a Chinese speaker – he could understand Chinese. For people can understand things which they do not appreciate that they understand. At any rate, as the distance between human conversational behavior and the conversational behavior displayed by the person or person-plus-room or a computer decreases, evidence for intrinsic Intentionality, belief, and linguistic understanding in a computer increases.

The central point in the counter-argument is the contention that Searle's Chinese room is a hollow mock-up of the possibilities of a computer. It wants to defuse the Chinese room before it starts to fire. As Searle sees it, the Chinese room convinces outside observers that the person (or system) understands Chinese, but fans of the counter-argument are unconvinced. For them the behavior of the system is too unlike a normal, human Chinese conversationalist to foil or fool serious investigators. Meanwhile, if programmers or computer scientists could just set in motion an upgraded flexible and dynamic computer, it could produce the sort of linguistic understanding found in human beings. Such a computer could burrow into the soul of intrinsic Intentionality.

Does the counter-argument succeed? The counter-argument succeeds only if computers can be upgraded. But the critic of computer belief and friend of Searle need not admit this. The critic can retort that computers are unlikely to be upgraded. Immensely difficult hurdles must be surmounted, so difficult, that from where we stand, it seems safe to say that computers could not simulate a normal, human conversation. 'No one', says one scientific observer, 'has yet designed computer software or any other complex machine that satisfactorily simulates human ... language.'[7]

We will not dwell on details, for they would take us into the esoteric interior of linguistics and artificial intelligence research. Briefly, however, ponder the upscale standards set by human conversation.

Human speech involves several distinguishable types of abilities and capacities. Foremost is the ability to draw on relevant aspects of the actual world as the conversation changes and dictates. One example – suggested by philosopher John Tienson – will illustrate the nature of the capacity to which I refer.[8]

Recently one of my philosophy students took a group of third graders for a concert at the Birmingham Zoo. They were all familiar with zoos, and some had attended concerts, but none had attended a zoo concert. Yet they were able to blend together their knowledge of zoos with their understanding of concerts. Apart from a few highly restricted mistakes, they managed intelligent ongoing conversation throughout the trip and visit. What's so impressive about this is that speakers never know what is going to be relevant next. The whole direction of conversation can shift from zoos to concerts to concerts-within-zoos to what's-for-lunch to where's-the-toilet, and so on, so that speakers must make sense of topic changes and must appropriately coordinate conversation to changing circumstance and conversational contour.

Because we adjust conversation so fluidly, and topical changes seem so natural and obvious, it may be difficult to appreciate how skillful is ordinary speech. However, as John Tienson has pointed out, no one has a clue about how to get computers to do it. In my own academic department, where a taste for verbal shenanigans and encyclopedic display prevails, it is a rare day that does not witness at least a hundred topical shifts before the closing siren. But none of our verbal jousting and professorial showboating makes conversation immensely difficult. Quite the contrary, topical shifts polish conversational contours, making speech lively, expressive, and engaging.

Consider any computer which tries to simulate merely the third graders at the zoo – not a philosophy department. There are virtually no limits to the zoo and concert knowledge which may be relevant to a potential comment or query at the entry/input slot. If the computer is to match the performance of the students, the program (book of rules) must not only be massive in size and topical scope, but it must enable the machine to respond appropriately and quickly to all sorts of metaphors and ambiguities, which third graders deal with rapidly and adroitly. What makes it especially difficult to simulate normal speech is the unpredictable and often startling way that odd little topics show up and fold in (to borrow one of Tienson's apt metaphors) as relevant:

'The monkeys are listening to the concert,' says the third grader, 'while the lions are staring at the man with the stick.'

Is 'monkey' the mammal, or a pejorative reference to the quality of attentiveness in one's classmates? Are 'lions' noisy students, or the big cats in cages? And how about 'the man with the stick'? Conductor, zoo keeper, or elderly patron with a cane?

To load an instruction book – program a computer – to comment appropriately in such a conversation would be a herculean task. Arguably, there is no realistic prospect that a computer can scale up to match human conversation, even those of third graders. And so long as we are profoundly short of making such a computer, and ignorant of how to program the ability to respond intelligently to unpredictable changes of topic, we cannot afford to be optimistic about computer conversation. Fanciful aspirations like 'Some day a computer will speak like us' mask the enormous problems quickly accommodated by normal human speakers. It may be possible, but it just does not appear likely.

Now of course nothing I have said here comes close to a knockdown argument against computer belief and in favor of Searle. Some advocates of computer belief say that computers with the skill and versatility necessary to simulate speech are on the architectural or technological horizon. Some say that the potential speakers are the so-called massively parallel distributed processing machines or connectionist systems currently being advertised as a major innovation in computer design, rather than the traditional von Neumann style serial or digital computers (on which Searle's room seems modeled).[9] Some claim that connectionist systems will display sufficient intelligence and versatility in behavior to warrant the attribution of computer belief. One day parallel processors will converse in Chinese about concerts at the zoo.

This is a bold prediction. It is based in part on the ability of connectionist systems to behave intelligently, in certain learning tasks at least, without being directed by fixed rules (without executing explicit programs), which is a potentially relevant and promising ability when it comes to linguistic behavior. One of the questions that linguists and other cognitive scientists debate is whether competent use of language requires following complex syntactic or grammatical rules (principles of sentence formation encoded in the brains of language users).[10] If the answer is no, a controversial 'if', connectionist systems may be in a much better position to converse in Chinese than the Chinese room or digital computer.[11]

No matter how the optimistic aspiration turns out to be correct, if it is correct, it would mean that computers have performed a marvellous feat. I, for one, will be only too pleased to concede that computers possess intrinsic Intentionality. In the meantime, however, the barrier of simulating human speech will not be easily surmounted. Similarly, the divide which separates as-if from intrinsic Intentionality will not be easily crossed. So, for now, it seems a plausible if not certain bet that no computer will talk its way into belief, Turing notwithstanding.

I have argued that the first counter-argument rests on a currently dubious or contentious aspiration or hope. It should be noted that Searle responds to the first counter-argument differently. He claims that even an upgraded computer/room, a massive parallel processor, which he dubs 'the Chinese gym', cannot possess intrinsic Intentionality. He takes the force of the Chinese room argument to be independent of advances in computer design. Searle writes:

> We are not talking about a particular stage of computer technology. The argument has nothing to do with the forthcoming, amazing advances in computer science. It has nothing to do with the distinction between serial and parallel processes, or with the size of programs, or the speed of computer operations, or with computers that can interact causally with their environment, or even with the invention of robots.[12]

Searle insists that simulating conversation would be insufficient evidence of intrinsic Intentionality even if it occurs. 'No simulation by itself ever constitutes duplication.'[13] But why? The main reason is Searle's skepticism about the power of *mere* behavior (mere functional equivalence) to provide sufficient evidence of belief. Searle assumes that no facts about behavior warrant attribution of belief without possession, in addition, of 'powers equivalent to the powers of the human brain.'[14] If the behaving subject lacks powers equivalent to the brain, it is mindless.

Powers equivalent to the brain? Is Searle a biochauvinist? A California Kenny? It is tempting to interpret Searle as a biochauvinist. But, in intention at least, he is no biochauvinist. His position is complicated and has evolved in content and clarity over time.[15]

The gist of Searle's appeal to powers of the brain is that real (intrinsic) Intentionality is not a matter of realizing the right functional roles; it is a matter of possessing something which the brain makes possible. This something is conscious experience. It makes no sense, claims Searle, to attribute Intentionality to something (like a computer) which is (presumably) non-conscious or to try to explain behavior in terms of essentially non-conscious Intentional states. Intentional states are real in us because our brain by producing conscious experience makes them real to us.

Now all this is pretty complicated and demanding. No Intentionality without consciousness? What exactly is Searle insisting on? Searle is genuinely worried about where intrinsic Intentionality derives or comes from. He is worried about its source. If attitudes somehow are connected to functional role, but we are persuaded by Searle's Chinese room argument that functional equivalence is insufficient evidence of belief, nothing in the functional role of belief is responsible for a belief's Intentionality. Nothing in the role of a belief compels the admission that the belief is about anything. So what is responsible for the Intentionality of belief? Searle insists that consciousness is important insofar as it provides the only means by which Intentionality is intrinsic and not just in the eye of the beholder. All and only conscious believers are true believers.

The topic of the contribution of conscious experience (and powers of the brain) to Intentionality is a realm of Searlean theory into which, despite its importance to Searle, I shall not presume to try to introduce the reader. Suffice it to say that Searle's view that consciousness is necessary for Intentionality does not fit well with contemporary cognitive science. It runs counter to cognitive scientific orthodoxy (a fact which Searle both appreciates and relishes). A common assumption of many cognitive scientists is that most mental or psychological states are non-conscious and that we can attribute Intentionality to these states without presupposing that they are or can in principle become conscious. To take one quick example, there are so-called blindsighted persons (whom I discuss in the final chapter) who have damage to the brain and cannot consciously see objects in certain portions of their visual field, but they are sensitive to those objects – extracting information about their movement and orientation – as appears on a variety of behavioral tests. This informational sensitivity to various features of objects arguably exhibits Intentionality; it is directed at those objects. It is about their movement and orientation. But it is not accessible to the consciousness of the blindsighted person. Intentionality, writes Dan Lloyd, is 'abundant, teeming, and rarely visible on the surface of consciousness'.[16]

If this is right – if Intentionality does not rely on the actual or potential

presence of conscious experience – then it is unwise of Searle to say that
the Chinese room may be upgraded but still lack Intentionality because
it would lack conscious experience. Better for him to admit that sufficient
upgrading (with or without consciousness) could provide ample evidence
of belief but to argue that computers are unlikely to be upgraded. Better
to argue that linguistic competence is too difficult to simulate. This
focuses the debate over computer belief on the nature and likelihood of
upgrading rather than on allegiance to consciousness and powers of the
brain, an allegiance which risks being indefensibly wedded to conscious
or biological systems.[17]

5.5 The Counter-Argument from Intentional Anti-Realism

The second counter-argument against Searle is much more bold and
dramatic than the first. A small circle of contemporary philosophers of
mind offers a very different reply to Searle's Chinese room argument
than the first counter-argument. The second counter-argument is not
designed, like the first, to evoke the concession that a computer could
possess intrinsic Intentionality. Quite the contrary, the fundamental idea
behind the second counter-argument is that *nothing* possesses intrinsic
Intentionality.

The counter-argument has been proposed by Patricia and Paul
Churchland and Daniel Dennett, three of the most respected figures in
recent philosophy of mind.[18] It goes as follows.

The first counter-argument contains more misunderstanding than
promise. While it can reasonably be claimed that if a computer could
simulate human conversation, it would possess intrinsic Intentionality *if*
humans themselves possess intrinsic Intentionality, humans do not
possess intrinsic Intentionality. Intrinsic Intentionality is wholly elusive,
vague, and mysterious; nothing has intrinsic Intentionality. It does not
exist. Moreover, since intrinsic Intentionality does not exist, all Intentionality merely is as-if. A human being is just as innocent of intrinsic
Intentionality as a computer. Furthermore, since as-if Intentionality is
observer dependent, computer Intentionality and 'belief' is easy to
demonstrate. Even a Chinese room may qualify as an as-if believer, if it
successfully tempts or motivates outside observers into ascribing belief to
it. Granted, Searle's Chinese room is not up to the level of human

conversation. But intrinsic Intentionality does not lie at that level. It lies at no level.

The impetus behind the Churchland–Dennett counter-argument comes from several sources, not just desire to attack Searle. The main source is skepticism about the prospects for incorporating reference to intrinsic Intentionality into the scientific and materialist picture of mind favored by both the Churchlands and Dennett. However, the Churchlands' and Dennett's interpretation of science aside, suppose we take the Churchland–Dennett line seriously. What would be some of the consequences for computer belief?

1   We would no longer have to worry about whether and when computer behavior is sufficiently intelligent to reveal intrinsic Intentionality. Neither would we have to wonder whether conscious experience is necessary for intrinsic Intentionality. This, of course, is one of the main virtues noted by both the Churchlands and Dennett. No Intentionality threshold would separate nominal believers from true believers.

2   We could decide whether computers 'believe' merely by determining whether we are motivated, tempted, or otherwise led into saying that they believe. The Churchland–Dennett line suggests the following simple criterion for determining whether a computer 'believes': If it stumps external observers, it 'believes'. Hence if, for instance, the Chinese room leads external observers who interact with it into saying that the person in the room or system understands Chinese, then the person or system 'understands' Chinese, for understanding is mere as-if or in-the-eyes-of-the-observer understanding.

In spite of, or perhaps because of, its consequences philosophers by and large have rejected the Churchland–Dennett approach. We will look briefly at three reasons for rejection.

(1)   The approach is incompatible with common sense. Ordinarily we suppose that people do, but water does not, believe. The Churchlands and Dennett do not agree with this. For them there is no psychological threshold separating persons from water flowing downhill. On their view, there is no objective psychological difference between persons and water. Of course, water flowing downhill is not viewed by us non cave-

dwelling moderns as believing. But this is not a fact about water, it is a fact about us (observers). It reveals not a threshold between water and people but between our interpretations of water and people. We manage without ascribing beliefs to water; we cannot manage (at least not yet) without ascribing beliefs to ourselves.

Whatever the precise impact of clashing with common sense, there is one thing we can be sure of: we have a lot to lose by running foul of common sense. Our common sense conviction that we believe is deeply entrenched in ordinary life. It plays a major role in our sense of ourselves as morally responsible agents and as parents, lovers, citizens, and friends. People assume themselves to be believers, and the Churchland–Dennett alternative, strictly speaking, abandons that assumption.

(2)   The Churchland–Dennett reply rests on an idea which is difficult to formulate and may even be conceptually incoherent. It isn't clear to what extent the Churchlands and Dennett really offer a 'counter-argument' or 'reply'.

A counter-argument or reply is characterizable by reference to two factors: (a) a particular object or direction of the reply (in this instance, what Churchlands–Dennett talk about), and (b) its thrust or purport (what they say about it). Thus, the second counter-argument is presumably a reply *to* or *about* Searle's Chinese room argument. However, at the same time, the Churchlands and Dennett say that there is no aboutness in anything. The thrust is that nothing – neither computer, nor animal, nor human being, nor speech – possesses intrinsic Intentionality. Well, if nothing possesses intrinsic Intentionality, their counter-argument is not *about* Searle; it is all mere as-if aboutness. Hence, paradoxically, were the Churchland–Dennett reply correct, no reply (even theirs) would be a real reply.

This last point may sound a bit bewildering, so let me give it a slightly different twist in presentation. If we accept the Churchlands' and Dennett's counter-argument against Searle, we lose grounds for saying that counter-arguments are counters to anything. We as outside observers may attribute Intentionality to the counter-argument, or to the Churchlands and Dennett, and certainly we do. But there is no Intentionality in either the counter-argument or its proponents, the Churchlands and Dennett, if the counter-argument is correct. The incoherence or difficulty is this: Once intrinsic Intentionality is eliminated, this sounds dangerously close to saying that the counter-argument itself isn't a counter-argument. Unless some way can be discovered to remedy this problem in formulating the counter-argument, the judgment must be that the counter-argument is defective. Absent aboutness no counter counters.

(3)   The Churchland–Dennett reply seems to fly in the face of psychological facts. These three philosophers labor heartily to defend the uncommonsensical conclusion that nothing has intrinsic Intentionality. But there are good reasons to claim that intrinsic Intentionality does exist. The view that intrinsic Intentionality is *here* – there *are* genuine Intentional states – is called Intentional Realism. Intentional Realism seems like the correct view. Ask yourself, for example, what you visually perceive or consciously experience right now. Perhaps your answer is that you see a page of a book. Perhaps you are preparing a meal in your kitchen while you are reading the book. So, in addition to a page, you visually experience a stove, plates, food, kitchen table, and much else.

Notice that when you seem to yourself to see the page, it appears to have certain properties or to be situated in a certain way. The page appears as shaded, as containing words about the Churchlands and Dennett, and as having a specific location relative to its environment and to yourself. The visual perceptual experience is of a page in a book which itself is on the kitchen table; all of which is in front of you. This includes a great deal of Intentionality, internal (intrinsic) to the experience itself: the experience is *directed* at a book, being on top of a kitchen table, being in front of you, and so on.

Visual experiences of the above sort support the view that some things possess Intentionality intrinsically. Their Intentionality is not (just) in the eye of an external observer; it is in the experiences themselves. Indeed, even when visual experiences are false or mistaken, they carry Intentionality within themselves. Your visual experience of the page has Intentionality even if the page does not exist. Perhaps you are hallucinating or dreaming. Still, the questions 'What do you (seem to) see?' or 'What is your experience about?' would have the same answer. 'A page of a book.' Or suppose we place you in a fake kitchen with cardboard cutouts of a stove, table, and the like. You will still seem to yourself to be reading in a kitchen. Aboutness is in the experience even if you are not in a kitchen.

The Churchland–Dennett counter-argument interprets the Intentionality of visual experience as as-if, and thus seems deficient for this reason. Indeed, it interprets the Intentionality of all experience as as-if, and so seems flawed for that reason. We seem to hear, taste, and smell birds fair and foul in feast and famine. But in each case Churchland–Dennett would say that we have got something wrong, and that our description of experience as *about* such things (or about anything) is in error. Such a claim makes a great many philosophers charge that the Churchland–Dennett line is mistaken.

What do the Churchlands and Dennett call their view? They self-apply various labels, but neither philosopher has fully settled on an 'ism'. (There also are differences between the Churchlands and Dennett.) Since their view contradicts Intentional Realism, some philosophers call it Intentional Anti-Realism. Interpretivism and Instrumentalism are also favored labels in some quarters. The former stresses that Intentionality is in the eye of the beholder or interpreter; the latter emphasizes that the attribution of Intentionality can be instrumental in helping a beholder to understand behavior, even though there is no real Intentionality. If the very first label is adopted we may call the second counter-argument the *counter-argument from Intentional anti-realism.*

Aptly named or not, the second counter-argument appears defective in three places: it violates common sense; it is difficult and perhaps even impossible to formulate; and it seems to fly in the face of experiential facts. At a brief level of analysis, at least, it is flawed.

5.6 Once More: Could a Computer Believe?

Now back to computer belief. Could a computer believe? The following overall answer emerges. A computer could believe if its behavior were sufficiently intelligent. However, there is nothing in well-studied computer behavior (such as chess playing) which is sufficiently intelligent to warrant attributing belief to a computer. So perhaps a computer could believe if it could engage in realistic (i.e. normal human) conversation; in essence this is Turing's Test. However, conversing realistically seems beyond the capacity of present-day computers. Whether it is beyond the capacity of *future* computers isn't obvious, though such computers will have to traverse a room full of conceptual and linguistic obstacles.

One last point before closing this chapter. Both our discussion of animals, in the last chapter, and our discussion of computers, here in this chapter, presuppose a distinction between behavior of sufficient intelligence to reveal or warrant attributing belief and behavior of insufficient intelligence to reveal or warrant attributing belief. On one side of this divide is Phaedeux (the dog of the previous chapter) and the hoped-for computer conversationalist; on the other side sits the flatworm and chess-playing computer. This distinction requires codification. I propose the following division: Behavior which is sufficiently intelligent to reveal belief is *genuinely* intelligent; there is intelligence – a mind – directly responsible for the behavior. Behavior which is insufficiently intelligent to reveal belief is (to borrow an idea from Searle) *at best* as-if intelligent. There is no mind directly responsible for the behavior. In the case of the chess-playing computer, the mind is in the programmer, not within the computer.

I will take no stand here on how the distinction may be precisely delineated or even whether it should be precisely delineated. In the previous chapter, I suggested that part of the difference lies in whether a creature shows flexibility and appropriateness in behavior. By this suggestion I mean to exclude the flatworm, whose behavior is invariably elicited by particular stimuli, but to include children conversing during zoo concerts, who discriminate different kinds of situations and respond appropriately to topical shifts. I leave it to the reader to decide if this is a worthwhile suggestion and how it may be developed. The topic is perplexing. Appeal to notions of flexibility and adaptivity undergirds much recent literature on intelligent connectionist systems and on the possibility of machine intelligence. Is it a sound appeal? One is tempted to exclaim: The adulation of Plutarch's ancients for the religiosity of elephants notwithstanding, perhaps God only knows.

NOTES

1   The quote is from Anthony Kenny, *The God of the Philosophers* (Oxford University Press, Oxford, 1979), p. 123. To be fair to Kenny, it is not absolutely clear just what he thinks of the possibility of computer minds, given other things he says about thought and computers. However, for argumentative purposes I interpret him as a biochauvanist.

2   Putnam's 1960s presentation of the case for abstractness may be found in 'Minds and machines' (first published in 1960), 'The mental life of some machines' (1967), and 'The nature of mental states' (1967). These papers have been conveniently reprinted in Putnam's *Mind, Language, and Reality: Philosophical Papers*, Vol. 2 (Cambridge University Press, Cambridge,

1975), as chapters 18, 20, and 21 respectively. 'The nature of mental states' is also reprinted in *The Nature of Mind*, ed. David Rosenthal (Oxford University Press, New York, 1991); and in *A Historical Introduction to the Philosophy of Mind*, ed. Peter Morton (Broadview Press, Ontario, 1997).

3 The quote is from Putnam's self-description in *A Companion to the Philosophy of Mind*, ed. S. Guttenplan (Blackwell Publishers, Oxford, 1994), p. 507. As he notes in the self-description, Putnam has since recanted functionalism, for reasons discussed in his 'Reflexive reflections', *Erkenntnis*, 22 (1985), pp. 143–53.

4 See John Searle, 'Minds, brains, and programs', *Behavioral and Brain Sciences*, 3 (1980), pp. 417–57 (including peer review); reprinted in Rosenthal, *The Nature of Mind* and Morton, *A Historical Introduction*. See also John Searle, 'Is the brain's mind a computer program?', in *Metaphysics*, eds R. C. Hoy and L. N. Oaklander (Wadsworth, California, 1991), p. 281. This article originally appeared in *Scientific American* (January 1990).

5 Quote is from John Haugeland, 'Understanding natural language', in *Foundations of Cognitive Science*, ed. Jay Garfield (Paragon, New York, 1990), pp. 398–410.

6 Turing discusses his test in 'Computing machinery and intelligence', *Mind*, 59 (1950), pp. 433–60.

7 Lawrence Weiskrantz, *Consciousness Lost and Found* (Oxford, Oxford University Press, 1997), p. 193.

8 See John Tienson, 'An introduction to connectionism', in *Foundations of Cognitive Science*, ed. Jay L. Garfield (Paragon, New York, 1990), p. 385.

9 For information on connectionism and parallel processing, see William Bechtel, 'Connectionism', in *A Companion to the Philosophy of Mind* (Blackwell Publishers, Oxford, 1994), pp. 200–10; William Bechtel and Adele Abrahamsen, *Connectionism and the Mind: An Introduction to Parallel Processing in Networks* (Blackwell Publishers, Oxford, 1990).

10 See N. Chomsky, *Language and Mind* (Harcourt, Brace, Jovanovich, New York, 1968); J. A. Fodor, *The Language of Thought* (Crowell, New York, 1975); W. Bechtel, 'The case for connectionism', *Philosophical Studies*, 71 (1993), pp. 119–54.

11 For additional discussion, see W. Bechtel, 'The case for connectionism'.

12 The quote is from Searle, *Minds, Brains, and Science* (Harvard University Press, Cambridge, Mass., 1984), pp. 36–7.

13 Searle, *Minds*, p. 37.

14 Ibid., p. 41.

15 For Searle's reflections on powers of the brain and Intentionality, see his 'Consciousness, explanatory inversion, and cognitive science', *Behavioral and Brain Sciences*, 13 (1990), pp. 585–642 (including peer review); *The Rediscovery of Mind* (MIT Press, Cambridge, Mass., 1992).

16 See D. Lloyd, 'Loose connections', *Behavioral and Brain Sciences*, 13 (1990), p. 615.

17 I do not mean to deny that consciousness may be essential to linguistic competence in human beings. For example, it may be that a function of consciousness in humans is to generate the sort of flexible and topically relevant linguistic behavior which helps us to converse intelligently. My methodological disagreement with Searle concerns the issue of how to focus the debate over computer belief. Should it be focused on the presence or absence of consciousness? Or should it be focused on the prospect of simulating successful human speech (and behavior more generally)? Searle picks the former focus; I say we should pick the latter focus.

18 See Patricia S. Churchland and Paul M. Churchland, 'Functionalism, qualia, and Intentionality', in *A Neurocomputational Perspective*, ed. Paul M. Churchland (MIT Press, Cambridge, Mass., 1989), pp. 23–46; Daniel C. Dennett, 'Fast thinking', in *The Intentional Stance*, ed. Daniel C. Dennett (MIT Press, Cambridge, Mass., 1987), pp. 323–37.

6

Mind and Belief in God

'God', wrote St Thomas Aquinas, in his magisterial *Summa Theologica*, 'is at the highest point of cognition.' William Alston, a contemporary Christian philosopher, says this:

> As creator, governor, and redeemer of the world God acts in the light of his perfect knowledge to carry out his purposes and intentions, and as an expression of his love for his creation. As is implicit in this last sentence, the divine psychology comes into our religious dealings with God as an essential background to divine action.[1]

In spite of its conceptually rarefied atmosphere, the subject of this chapter is the mind of God.

A common attitude among contemporary philosophers of mind is that our mental concepts – our psychological theories and mental notions – apply only within the observable world of organisms and machines. They do not apply to suprasensible individuals like God. Historically, however, from the time of Augustine (354–430) through such medieval Catholic writers as Aquinas (1225–74), all the way to Leibniz (1646–1716) and Immanuel Kant (1724–1804), considerable philosophical reflection on the mind occurs in the context of speculation about God's mind. A common conviction among such writers and others is that the conceptual core of various mental concepts, such as 'know', 'intend', 'love', can be identified by reflection on whether and how they apply to God. The assumption is that God has a mind *in excellence*.

In this chapter I propose to exhibit the wisdom of that historical conviction. I will examine, albeit briefly, whether two mental concepts apply to God: 'belief' and 'suffering'. The inquiry I make is limited by two sets of assumptions. The first concerns the idea of God.

I assume that, as in the western theistic tradition of St Anselm (1033–1109), the idea of God is the idea of a maximally perfect or greatest possible being with an array of great-making traits or characteristics. Alvin Plantinga describes the notion of God as a being of incomparable greatness as follows:

> He is the first being of the universe, one than whom it is not so much as possible that there be a greater. God's greatness is not just one step – even a big step – further along a scale measuring the greatness of things in general; his greatness is of a different order from that of his creatures.... God's greatness has many facets; preeminent among them are his love, justice, mercy, power, and knowledge.[2]

This perfectionist conception of God is broad enough to permit disagreement concerning the precise nature of his perfection and the scope of divine characteristics. Examination of what mindedness may be for a perfect being is the guiding theme of this chapter's exploration of the mind of God.

The second assumption is that a philosopher needs no theological axe to grind to reflect on the mind of God. Just as philosophers may inspect notions of computer belief and disembodied minds without endorsing propositions like 'Computers possess beliefs' or 'Minds need no embodiment', so they may examine the idea of a divine mind without endorsing claims like 'There is but one God'.

6.1 A Dilemma for St Thomas

Consider the following evils:

- a mother's cannibalism of her own child;
- slow death by starvation;
- Nazi death camps;
- having to choose which of one's children will be disfigured by terrorists.

These events may be too horrible to contemplate. Many people find themselves disbelieving in God because of them. Others pray for divine deliverance.

Does God know about evil? In the *Summa Theologica*, St Thomas asks whether 'evils, deprivations, and defects' ever enter into the mind or thought of God. Does God think about evil? His answer is that God knows about evil 'speculatively', but not 'practically'; that is, he knows of evil's existence, but not of what it is like to do evil or experience suffering. Evils, deprivations and defects are not part of his practice. God knows of the evil and suffering which transpire in our world, but he does not know as, say, Hitler knew evil by performing terrible misdeeds and depriving people of life and limb. And he does not know by experiencing suffering himself, as tragically happened to Hitler's victims.

What prompts Aquinas to ask the question? Why does he wonder whether and how evil enters into the divine mind? Aquinas's question is prompted by a dilemma specifically for the Christian (perfect being) understanding of God. The dilemma concerns the importance to Christianity of God's knowledge, love, and power, and the sort of psychologically impeccable makeup which the God of Christianity is supposed to have. Let's take a few paragraphs to present the dilemma.

According to Christianity, God is perfectly knowing. In technical jargon, he is omniscient. Being perfectly knowing means different things to different Christians, but most of the different meanings coalesce around the following two-part idea: To be perfectly knowing is to be (1) thoroughly free of ignorance (if something is true, God knows it; he is not ignorant of any fact or truth whatsoever) and (2) altogether cognitively sound (he is without error or mistake; he is free of falsehood). You and I, by contrast, are both ignorant and mistaken at least in most matters. I don't know anything about, say, the mating habits of dolphins or atmospheric pressure on Venus; and I am certainly mistaken in many of my beliefs about, say, potash and pottage. So I am imperfectly knowing. I know some things, but I also swim in a vast sea of ignorance and error.

If God is perfectly knowing, presumably he should not be ignorant of dolphins and Venus; and he should harbor no falsehoods about potash and pottage. Likewise, he should know of evil and make no mistake about it. Dolphins transpire in the world; evil does too. God should know about them both. But the question is, how does he know about evil? If evil enters into his mind, how does it enter?

Sadly, you and I know evil all too often by engaging in it. Evil enters our thoughts through intentional misdeed. We lie, cheat, and steal; we behave selfishly and ungenerously towards our fellows. We know what cheating is because we cheat; we know what it means to steal because we steal. An onlooker ignorant of Christianity and related conceptions of God may therefore expect that if God is perfectly knowing, he, too, knows evil by intentional misdeed. He lies, cheats, and steals. God knows what it means to steal because he steals, just as we know what it means to steal because we steal. However, as Aquinas points out, knowledge of evil by doing evil could not be available to the God of Christianity. The God of Christianity is not merely omniscient. He is also perfectly kind and loving. In technical terms, he is omnibenevolent. So, God cannot lie, cheat, or steal. Evil deeds would be unloving, and the very thought of doing evil would be unkind.

Equally sadly, you and I know what suffering means since we suffer. We are afflicted by disease, riddled with doubt and worry, fearful of death, and vulnerable to the whims of madmen (like Hitler). However, the Christian God is not merely omniscient and omnibenevolent, he is also perfectly powerful. In technical jargon, he is omnipotent. So, it seems to many Christians, such as Aquinas, that God is not susceptible to suffering. According to Aquinas, susceptibility to suffering would be a sign of weakness; and the very possibility of weakness ill suits God.

Once perfect love and power are counted as attributes of God, there is reason to deny that God knows the evil which transpires in this world by doing or experiencing evil. On the other hand, denying that God knows evil by doing or experiencing evil risks denying that God knows evil unless another route to knowledge of evil can be found. But what route is available? If God does not know by doing or suffering, how does he know?

Ignoring the details of Aquinas's overall philosophy, Thomas offers a solution to the dilemma of how God can both know evil and yet be perfectly powerful and loving; of how evil, deprivation, and defect can enter into his mind without destroying his divinity. Aquinas's solution is to argue that in addition to knowing by doing or experiencing (practical knowledge), there is knowing by intuiting – by being directly aware. Knowing is then either practical knowing or intuitive ('speculative') knowing. God knows through awareness; he knows by intuiting the evil which transpires in the world. Since God performs and suffers no misdeeds, he remains loving and powerful; and, since he is aware of evil, he also remains altogether knowledgeable. Nothing undermines his goodness or power; nothing escapes his knowledge.

It is tempting to examine Aquinas's solution: his appeal to direct awareness. This would involve exploring several doctrines in his philosophy, including the simplicity of God, God's knowledge of his own essence, the non-discursiveness or non-representationality of divine knowledge, and much else besides. These are complicated and technical ideas which (with one exception which will be discussed shortly) are beyond the scope of this book. My purpose in mentioning Aquinas is not to set the stage for Thomas's theories. I want to extract a different and more general lesson.

There is a general lesson to be learned here, having to do with the mind of God and with psychological concepts which can be applied to him. Because God has a certain stature and nature, because he *is* God, his mind has a special nature or character. Not just any mind concepts befit or suit him. In the case of Christianity, for instance, God is taken to be perfectly knowing, loving, and powerful, so whatever inhabits or enters his mind – whatever he knows or thinks of – must be consistent with his perfection. If Aquinas is right, ascribing practical knowledge of evil to God does not befit him.

Once we recognize the general lesson, examples of concepts of mind which could or could not apply to God reinforce it. I wish to discuss two: the concepts of belief and suffering. I will develop an argument that 'belief' does not apply to God. Then I will briefly sketch an argument that 'suffering' does apply to him, Aquinas notwithstanding. That divine perfection includes experience of suffering may sound heretical, but speculation on the divine mind can admit theological surprises.

6.2 Does God Possess Beliefs?

Should we speak of God as believing? Does God possess beliefs?

Human agents possess beliefs. You do what you believe will satisfy your goals. What of God? He acts, we shall suppose. But does he believe?

The answer depends in part on the nature of belief. There is considerable debate in the philosophic literature over the nature of belief. What is belief? The most common answer, which I shall adopt here, goes something like this: to believe something is mentally to represent it as true. If, for instance, I believe that Descartes is a great philosopher, I represent him to myself as a great philosopher. Equivalently: I take it to be true that Descartes is a great philosopher.

There is a short argument that God does not possess beliefs. It turns on an essential characteristic of belief. The essential characteristic can be summarized in a single sentence: Beliefs are inherently capable of being true or false. I believe, for instance, that my name is George Graham and that I was born in Brooklyn, New York. Both beliefs are true, but they could have been false, if I had a different name and birthplace. They are inherently capable of being true (for they *are* true) or false (they would have been false had the relevant facts been different). Meanwhile, you believe (let's suppose for the sake of example) that I, the author of this book, am a religious zealot. However, the belief is false. I abhor zealotry. Again, the belief is inherently capable of being true (had the fact been different) or false (for it *is* false).

Here, then, is the argument that God does not believe. It goes like this:

God is omniscient. He is perfectly knowing; never in error, never mistaken. So, he is incapable of falsehood. Thus God does not believe. If God believed, he could be mistaken; but he cannot be mistaken, so he does not have beliefs.

Belief (something which can be mistaken) is not the sort of cognitive condition which suits God (who cannot be mistaken). 'Mere belief' has no place in the mind of God. Of course, knowledge suits him: He is – we are supposing – omniscient. However, this cannot be knowledge which involves belief. (Perhaps it is Aquinas's intuitive knowledge and perhaps intuitive knowledge is knowledge somehow without belief. I return to this possibility below.)

The idea that beliefs are inherently capable of being true or false requires defense. It's a tricky idea.[3] At the risk of complicating something which already is complex, what of it? As said, the term 'belief' stands for a certain type of mental representation; namely, beliefs represent things to the subject (believer) as true. Without going into detail, the representationality of belief is connected with its Intentionality. (The notion of Intentionality is familiar from the last chapter on computer belief.) Because a belief is *about* something, it represents it. My belief that Descartes is a great philosopher is about Descartes; it represents him as a great philosopher.

Beliefs are not alone in being representational. Numerous sorts of things can be representational, some mental, some non-mental: a map, a gesture, the dance of a bee, a picture, a desire, and so on. A map may represent Alabama; a gesture hello; a dance the location of honey; a picture Winston Churchill; a desire ice cream. But beliefs are ways in which minds represent. And they are ways in which the mind represents when someone takes something to be true. Beliefs, to deploy an adage, aim at truth.

Of course, whatever aims can miss. Some representations do a better job of representing than others; some correctly represent, others incorrectly represent. My map represents Montgomery as the capital of the State of Alabama; Filbert's map represents Birmingham as the capital. My map is correct; Filbert's is incorrect. Montgomery is the capital; Birmingham is merely the State's largest city. Mine represents; Filbert's misrepresents. In the case of belief, a belief which correctly represents is called 'true'; a belief which incorrectly represents is called 'false'. (Maps which represent are called 'accurate' or 'apt'; maps which misrepresent are 'inaccurate'.) If I believe that Montgomery is the capital of Alabama, this represents the capital correctly, for the capital is Montgomery. The belief is true; the representation 'represents'.

Beliefs are inherently capable of being true or false because beliefs are inherently capable of representing or misrepresenting. They can be correct or incorrect. I can represent something as true when in actual fact (unbeknownst to me) it is false; I can endorse a falsehood. Just in themselves, therefore, beliefs afford no guarantee of truth. They are not inherently correct. Now let's return to the claim that God does not believe.

We now can schematize and detail the argument that God does not possess beliefs as follows:

1 Whatever represents can also misrepresent.
2 Beliefs represent.
3 So, beliefs can also misrepresent.
4 A belief which misrepresents is false.
5 But God is incapable of falsehood and misrepresentation. He is omniscient.
6 So, he does not believe (possess beliefs).

The above argument is not the only argument that God does not believe. Nor is the denial of divine belief some sort of heretical doctrine. A number of Christian philosophers have defended it.[4] True, there are

various ways in which one might try to attack the conclusion of the
argument. I shall consider just one – the most popular.

The most popular attack concerns knowledge. In outline it goes like
this:

A1 If God is omniscient, then he knows whatever can be known.
A2 Knowledge requires belief. To know something is (among other
things) to believe that it is true.
A3 So God believes.

The critical premise in the attack is A2. To possess knowledge, many
philosophers claim, requires belief. Imagine how odd it would be, they
point out, for me to exclaim both that I know that Montgomery is the
capital of Alabama and that I fail to believe this very same proposition.

The second premise is dubious, however. We may be prepared to
grant that *human* knowledge requires belief, without having any good
reason to say that if human knowledge requires belief, divine knowledge
does too. If God is omniscient, perhaps he is omniscient in spite of not
possessing beliefs. Misgivings about the second premise thicken when
we recall that beliefs are representational. Perhaps the divine mind is not
representational. This is what St Thomas seems to have thought, and
something like it may be found in Augustine and Kant. Thomas writes,
again in the *Summa Theologica*, that 'God knows all enunciations that can
be formed ... He knows these not in the way enunciations are known, as
if there were composition or division of enunciations in His intellect, but
He knows each thing ... by understanding its essence ... and whatever
can be added to that.' Aquinas's terminology is obscure. But I take him
to mean that God knows without mentally representing what he knows.
He does not compose and divide his mind: he does not *take* things to be
true. If Aquinas is right, and God's knowledge somehow is nonrepresen-
tational (noncompositional, nondivisional), then the second premise (A2)
in the argument that God believes should be rejected. We should deny
that knowledge requires belief.

My purpose in offering an argument that God does not believe is to
reinforce the general lesson extracted earlier from Aquinas. God's mind
must be characterized in a manner which befits him. *If* because of
omniscience, belief does not befit God, he lacks belief. *If* mental
representation does not suit him, God does not mentally represent.

6.3 Suffering and Love

By way of contrast with the argument that the concept of belief does not apply to God, let's examine a psychological concept which, contrary to Aquinas, arguably does apply to God. Can God suffer?

'Perhaps', says Marilyn Adams in a recent paper, 'the inner life of God includes deep agony as well as ecstatic joy.'[5]

Deep agony? God? On the face of it, it seems incredible to say that God suffers; that he experiences deep agony. It is usually supposed that while human beings are caught up in the experience of suffering, of grief, depression, and sorrow, God's life is altogether unperturbed and serene. He is devoid of passion, unfamiliar with pain, foreign to grief, depression, or sorrow. In the words of Aquinas's *Summa Contra Gentiles*, God's 'intellect must ... be an absolutely unmoved mover'. But Adams gives the mind of God a distinctive twist. There is, on her view, good reason for entertaining the idea that God suffers. God's perfect love comes into play here. God may not be content, she says, to be immutable and impassible, to witness the suffering of his creatures with the cool eye of unperturbed omniscience. He may instead prefer to unite himself to those whom he loves. If he does, then he himself will sympathetically feel their misery and pain. He will be moved: he will suffer.

What is Adams's thought here? What is her line of reasoning? She never quite develops it. But perhaps we can add a few details.[6] Why would God suffer with his creatures? Why would he prefer to give up an unperturbed omniscience?

One answer may be that it is the very nature of love to suffer when its object suffers and that uninterrupted suffering-free serenity is incompatible with love. A person who feels no grief at the death of a friend or child or the rape of his wife is rightly described by us as unloving and uncaring. Similarly, a God who experiences no grief or sorrow over the suffering of his creation also is rightly described as unloving and uncaring. To love another is to sorrow when they sorrow: to live in the solidarity of grieving (and rejoicing) with them. The possibility that God's knowledge of the world gives him no vexation at all, no unhappiness, no sorrow, therefore, is incompatible with the claim that God is perfectly loving. In loving God gives up the immutability and freedom from disturbance he might otherwise possess.[7]

By connecting the divine mind with the idea of loving and suffering, Adams gives the mind of God emotional depth. Instead of a divine subject unfamiliar with longing, everlastingly content, she describes a God who knows what it is like to suffer. Rather than the suffering of his people leaving God untouched, he too undergoes sorrow and disappointment. What we finally think of her suggestion should depend on what we think of other attributes of God and whether the notion of divine suffering systematically fits or coheres with them. In the Christian tradition, for instance, some thinkers contend that God is incorporeal (without embodiment). How does the idea of divine suffering impact on the notion of the purported incorporeality of God? When persons suffer they experience disturbance in their nervous system; some philosophers even claim that neurophysical disturbance is essential for suffering. Well, clearly, if an incorporeal God suffers he is not neurophysiologically disturbed. So is the body truly essential for suffering? Or might God (contrary to some Christian thinkers) actually possess a body, so that when he suffers his body is disturbed? And what sort of body could be God's body? William James remarks in *A Pluralistic Universe*: 'The particular features of *our* body are adaptations to a habitat so different from God's that if God (has) a physical body at all, it must be utterly different from ours in structure.'

Perhaps, as some philosophers speculate, the whole wide world is God's body; hence when he suffers the world is physically disturbed. God is incorporeal in that he lacks a particular body or embodiment. However, he is corporeal in that he is physically realized in everything, everywhere. Does *that* make sense? Perhaps St Paul *literally* meant it when he said (Acts 17:28): 'In him we live and move and have our being.'

A second difficulty with the notion of divine suffering – familiar from discussion of Aquinas on God's knowledge of evil – is perhaps even more challenging. Contrary to Adams, it is an error, some philosophers (Aquinas included) charge, to hold that a perfectly powerful being can suffer. Suffering compromises power. Omnipotence, on this view, involves (in part) freedom from pain and grief. God is omnipotent; thus he does not suffer.

In *Providence and Evil* Peter Geach remarks that when Christians insist that God is omnipotent, they land 'themselves in intractable problems and hopeless confusions'.[8] So Geach, a Christian, admonishes Christians to abandon the notion that God is omnipotent and to substitute the notion that God has less than perfect power.

Perhaps Adams should take Geach's way out. Perhaps she should say that insisting that God both suffers and is omnipotent creates an intractable dilemma. One must choose between suffering and omnipotence. If one chooses suffering one must reject omnipotence. For what could make an omnipotent being suffer? David Blumenfield writes:

> There is no conceivable obstacle to his will. Whatever he wills, he accomplishes. There is nothing which could conceivably thwart him, or interfere with his divine plan. Since he knows this, there is nothing which could provide him with the occasion to feel frustration.[9]

Blumenfield's worry is that if God is omnipotent, there is no conceivable situation in which things fail to go as he wishes. But if this is so, does it not follow that, by being perfectly powerful, God must be free of frustration – disappointment, grief, sorrow?

Much depends on what it means to be omnipotent. What is it to be omnipotent?

An Adamsesque reading of omnipotence may go something like this: In order to be perfectly powerful, it is not necessary to avoid suffering in all possible situations. God is not absolutely impervious to sorrow. In order to be perfectly powerful, it is necessary to avoid suffering *unless avoidance of suffering is incompatible with other divine perfections* (such as omnibenevolence). On this less impassable or more mutable notion of divine omnipotence, God can render himself susceptible to suffering. He can suffer as part of his will, while yet remaining perfectly powerful. And why would God suffer as part of his will? Divine suffering may somehow be the result of creaturely abuse of divinely given free will: of persons turning away from God.[10] Separation from him may cause persons to suffer which, in turn, may cause him to suffer. He no more wants to suffer than he wishes persons to turn away from him. But persons turn away, misusing the freedom which he wants them to possess. And this makes him suffer. The suffering stems from his will insofar as it stems from his love. Omnipotence figures in such suffering, in part, in the following way: Unlike us, perfect power fortifies God when he suffers, so that suffering neither diminishes nor embitters him. He does not sicken, weaken, or perish when he suffers; he does not withdraw or retreat from the source of suffering or withhold his help and support; he does not strip creatures of the freedom to turn away.

In the western theistic tradition the typical theological attitude (or at any rate an attitude encouraged) towards divine perfection is something like the following. God's perfections are not separable. They are fused aspects of divinity, consisting in attributes internally linked with other attributes. So understood, God's power is part of his love which is part of his knowledge, which in turn is part of his power, and so on. Perhaps if God was *merely* omnipotent, he could not suffer. However, he is not merely omnipotent; he is also omnibenevolent. This means that rather than floating mysteriously like some potentate above the world, God's love brings him into communion with his creatures.

We have still to decide whether God is incorporeal and whether an incorporeal being can suffer. We also have not considered whether other divine perfections (such as omniscience) are compatible with suffering. Adams's suggestion offers an interesting if not fully explored alternative to Aquinas's view. Intuitive apprehension or speculative knowledge of suffering may be too spectatorial and removed from the painful fray. Aquinas permits God to know evil but not to know 'what it is like' to experience suffering. Adams implies that Aquinas's approach to God's knowledge of evil may need to be rejected and replaced with the notion that 'God, in His Divine nature, has an immeasurable capacity for both suffering and joy'.[11]

6.4 On Having it All

Can God have it all? Can there be a perfect being with a perfect mind – who immeasurably knows, who immeasurably loves? Some philosophers say no. 'The concept of God', Anthony Kenny writes, 'is an incoherent one.'[12] Kenny's exclamation gives expression to the view that pieces of the idea of the divine mind do not fit together. To Kenny and a number of other philosophers, the perfectionistic concept of divinity is flawed and incoherent. Ultimately, it makes no sense.

Flawed, incoherent, senseless, or just elusive? Towards the beginning of his *Proslogion*, St Anselm offers the following lament: 'Lord, if thou are not there, where shall I see this, being absent? . . . [I am] eager to find thee, and know not thy place.' To Anselm, hidden is the mind of God: too rich and complex for our theories. Any theories.

NOTES

1   William Alston, 'Functionalism and theological language,' in *The Concept of God*, ed. Thomas Morris (Oxford University Press, Oxford, 1987), p. 23.

2   See A. Plantinga, *Does God Have a Nature?* (Marquette University Press, Milwaukee, 1980), p. 1.

3   The claim that beliefs are inherently capable of being false needs qualification in light of potential counter-examples, including 'beliefs' in logical truths, which cannot be false. The topic of how to qualify or precisely formulate the claim is beyond the scope of the present discussion. One move is to deny that belief is the cognitive attitude one takes to logical truths. We *know* logical truths. We don't 'believe' them.

4   See William Alston, 'Does God have beliefs?', in *Divine Nature and Human Language*, ed. W. Alston (Cornell University Press, Ithaca, 1989), pp. 178–93.

5   Marilyn McCord Adams, 'Redemptive suffering: a Christian solution to the problem of evil', in *Rationality, Religious Belief, and Moral Commitment*, ed. Robert Audi and William Wainwright (Cornell University Press, Ithaca, 1986), p. 264.

6   Suggestions along the following lines are found in Nicholas Wolterstorff, 'Suffering love', in *Philosophy and the Christian Faith*, ed. Thomas V. Morris (University of Notre Dame Press, South Bend, Indiana, 1988), pp. 196–237. See also Marilyn Adams, 'Theodicy without blame', *Philosophical Topics*, 16 (1988), pp. 236–7.

7   Do I hear a theological axe grinding? Is the notion that God suffers a veiled endorsement of the Christian doctrine of incarnation? (See M. de Unamuno, *The Tragic Sense of Life*, trans. J. Flitch [Dover, New York, 1954], p. 204.) That God suffers does not require the truth of incarnation. If God is able to become incarnate, he is able to suffer as man. But the thrust of Adams's argument is that a loving God suffers in his divine (not just human) nature, incarnation notwithstanding.

8   Peter Geach, *Providence and Evil* (Cambridge University Press, Cambridge, 1977), p. 4.

9   David Blumenfield, 'Compossibility of the Divine Attributes', in *The Concept of God*, ed. Thomas Morris, p. 207.

10 'For God to create beings capable of loving him', writes Peter Van Inwagen, 'it was necessary for him to take risk: to risk the possibility that the beings he created would freely choose to withhold their love from him.' See P. Van Inwagen, 'The magnitude, duration, and distribution of evil', *Philosophical Topics*, 16 (1988), p. 163.

11 Marilyn Adams, 'Theodicy without blame', p. 237.

12   Anthony Kenny, *The God of the Philosophers* (Oxford University Press, Oxford, 1986), p. 121.

7

Rational Action

No characteristic of mind is more important than its role in bringing about behavior. No behavioral role is more important than bringing about purposive behavior or what philosophers call 'rational action'.

In this chapter I shall offer a definition of rational action, describing what makes action rational, distinguishing rational from irrational action, and briefly examining some issues which typically come up when philosophers discuss rational action, viz., Is weakness of the will unreasonable? Are actions selfish because they are motivated by one's own desires or reasons?

7.1 The Concept of 'Rational Action'

What is rational action? Rational action is behavior done for reasons or purposes of the agent. To take a simple example, suppose it is a hot, steamy summer day in Birmingham, Alabama. You and I have just finished wresting weeds from my favorite patch of backyard okra. I ascend the porch and open the door to my home. I feel absolutely wretched. I want an ice-cold beer – very cold. Suppose, not to be left out in the heat, you, too, wish an ice-cold beer. However, while I walk to the refrigerator, you drive to the supermarket. Why do we travel in different directions? I walk to the fridge because I believe that cold beer is located there, whereas you drive to the market because you believe that, although the fridge is empty, the market stocks cold beer.

Walking to the fridge is something I do for a reason or on purpose:

wishing the beer expected there. It is rational action. Driving to the market is something you do for a reason. So it, too, is rational action.

Rational actions contrast with mere movements or non-rational behavior, activities of the agent or their body which they undergo but which they do not perform for a reason. When I fall or stumble, for example, what happens is not something for which reason is responsible. True, I move when I stumble, but I do not produce the movement. I am not the stumble's agent, but only its anxious and perhaps embarrassed patient. Again, as a young boy when my body grew, its growth was not something brought about by me for a reason. I was not the growth's agent but only, so to speak, its subject or source.

What distinguishes rational action from mere movement or non-rational behavior such as falling and growing? I assume the following partial division: rational action is performed for a reason, whereas mere movement happens because of a cause. Equivalently: Every rational action is explained by reference to the agent's reason for doing it, whereas movements are explained by reference to causes. My stumble – a mere movement – occurs because my foot, say, strikes a rock or sticks in the muddy pavement. The striking or sticking is causally responsible for the stumbling. By contrast, my walking – a rational action – happens for a reason. The reason includes the purpose or goal I seek to attain (a cold beer), and my beliefs about means for attaining it (going to the fridge). The rationality presupposed in explaining rational action is agent-centered or subjective. It turns on whether I take the behavior to be fitting or appropriate means for achieving my purpose given my beliefs and expectations.

If you believe that the fridge is empty, you no doubt believe that it offers zero prospects of containing cold beer. Then, you refrain from walking to the fridge, for there is no reason to walk. Then why do I venture to the fridge? I believe that it contains cold beer. Given my wish and expectation, it is rational (subjectively) for me to go to the fridge.

The distinction between cause and reason, though critical, is not mutually exclusive. Although no mere movement occurs for a reason, actions stem from reasons which causally contribute to action. We may put this by saying that reasons help to causally explain action. For instance, my walk to the fridge springs from my desire for beer, whereas your desire motivates your drive to the market.

Most philosophers favor what may be called a *network* or *holistic* theory of reasons as causes, in which mental events or occurrences mix together to produce an effect. According to network theory, a statement like 'desiring ice-cold beer I walk to the fridge' means that the desire mixes together with my overall state of mind, perhaps including my conscious deliberation or calculation, to contribute to walking. For example, it would be implausible to suggest that I walk to the fridge just because I want beer. A full account of the manner in which reasons help to bring about action would recognize that reasons function in networks of psychological states and perceptual conditions which must prevail if action occurs.[1]

Consider, for instance, the action of flipping a light switch in order to illuminate a dark room. It takes more than reason to flip the switch. For starters, I must perceive the switch; and then monitor, perhaps non-deliberately or sub-personally, the position of my hand and the thrust of my finger, for I should not hit the switch too hard (it may break) or too soft (the electrical circuits may not engage).

Does *any* reason of a person cause or help to bring about action? Certainly not. Just because someone has reason for action does not mean that he will perform or even try to perform the action. Filbert wants a cold beer. Even more, however, he wants to avoid Temperance who is standing by the fridge. So, although Filbert believes that beer is in the fridge, he refrains from walking there.

Likewise, just because a person possesses reason for action and performs the action does not mean that he performs the action for that reason. Consider possessing reason for walking to the fridge and walking, but not for that reason. Albert wants cold beer. However, even more he wants to eat a piece of cake. So, although he believes that beer is in the fridge, and he struts to the fridge, Albert does not act for beer. He cakewalks.

The following three theses are widely held in recent philosophical discussion of rational action and have been employed above:

1   To act rationally is to behave for a reason.
2   Reasons make actions rational or appropriate from the agent's point of view.
3   Reasons help to produce action. They help to causally explain action.

The three theses (especially 3) are not problem-free; but, they will be presupposed in the sections to follow.

7.2 Rationality versus Irrationality

In this section I want to discuss one of the most perplexing philosophic problems connected with the topic of rational action. How should rational action be distinguished from irrational action?

Just as rational action contrasts with mere (non-rational) movement, it also contrasts with irrational action. People no doubt act irrationally. What this means is that we act for reasons, but the reasons themselves may be bad or irrational. When action is performed for bad or irrational reason, the action itself is irrational. Rational action, in contrast with irrational action, is done for good or rational reason.

The basic idea behind irrational action is hard to express without risk of linguistic confusion. The confusion is between (1) 'rational' in the sense of *for a reason* and (2) 'rational' in the sense of *good* reason and thus 'irrational' in the sense of *bad* reason. One and the same action can be both rational (performed for a reason) and irrational (performed for a bad reason).

The two senses of 'rational' surely are not the same. As a young boy, I sometimes feigned illness to escape going to school and taking a tough exam. Unfortunately, because of absences, I fell behind in schoolwork and had to feign still more illnesses to escape more demanding exams. I feigned illness for a reason; so, the feigning was rational. No illness moved me; reason did. But the rationality of the reason should be doubted, since the success of my efforts did not encourage schoolwork. If anything, the practice discouraged me academically. Hence, although feigning was rational in that I feigned for a reason, it was irrational in that I feigned for a bad reason.

Reasons can be bad or irrational from different perspectives and points of view.[2] They can be bad from the agent's point of view, that is, in terms of the agent's subjective conception of the goodness or badness of his or her reasons. Let us call actions performed for subjectively bad reasons *internally* or *subjectively* irrational actions. They can also be bad in terms of external standards or criteria which may or may not be part of the agent's subjective perspective. Let us call actions performed for exter-nally bad reasons *externally* or *objectively* irrational actions.

External or objective irrationality (and rationality) comes in many different forms. In the worst possible cases – instances of severe self-delusion, moral psychosis, mental illness – external irrationality not only expresses failure to act on good reasons, judged by external standards, but it can have tragic personal and social consequences as well. For example, in 1984 the *British Journal of Psychiatry* published an article with the fascinating title of 'Self shooting of phantom head'.[3] The article described the case of a mentally ill man who believed that he had two heads, one of which taunted him with hostile thoughts. He tried to rid himself of the alien head by shooting it off with a revolver. He survived but was seriously wounded, dying two years later of chronic infection caused by the shot. The deed was irrational, externally. However, the man performed the action for a reason. In fact, he acted for subjectively good reason. He believed that he possessed an extra head and wished to terminate its taunting. What more appropriate means to terminate than to destroy? As he said, 'The other head kept trying to dominate my normal head, and I would not let it.'

Why was the man's action externally irrational? The shooting was externally irrational on two grounds. First, it stemmed from a grossly unhealthy or imprudent desire. The desire to shoot ticketed him for personal disaster. Second, it rested on a belief (that he had two heads) which was not merely false but plainly false and should have been plainly false to the man.

Internal or subjective irrationality (and rationality) also comes in different forms. Some subjectively irrational actions stem from beliefs and expectations which the agent in some sense admits are foolish or faulty; others reflect disvalues or unwelcome desires of the agent. To take a simple illustration, Temperance smokes. Indeed, she smokes for a reason; she likes it. But in her own mind this is a bad reason, for she knows that smoking is harmful to her health and she sincerely claims that she values health more than enjoyment. The expected harm undermines the subjective rationality of smoking and makes it, in a certain sense, subjectively irrational for her to smoke.

We need a clear way in which to distinguish linguistically between actions done for reasons (and hence rational) and actions done for bad reasons (and hence irrational). One way is to claim that an action may be both rational and irrational – rational in one sense, irrational in another sense. But this way of speaking is both cumbersome and unclear. Rational *and* irrational? So, I propose speaking of actions which are rational and *unreasonable*, subjectively or externally, as the case may be. Temperance's smoking is both rational and unreasonable, judged from her own point of view. 'Rational' conveys the sense of smokes for a reason; 'unreasonable' identifies the reason as bad.

Note that in calling an action unreasonable, subjectively, we as outsiders are not condemning it. Subjectively bad reasons may be good or bad objectively. The measure of internal badness (or goodness) is agent-centered, not outsider decided.

Objective unreasonableness is another sort of label entirely. Often there is a negative connotation attached to the charge that an action is unreasonable (or irrational) externally. There is room also, however, for debate of a philosophically contentious kind about objective irrationality and rationality. Many theories have been pursued to provide standards for objectively good (or bad) reasons. Some purport to describe a single best objective reason for action – these may be classified as *monist* theories; others claim that different objective reasons are equally good – these may be classified as *pluralist* theories. Some theories of both types are *relativist*, seeking to understand external rationality as a veiled form of subjective rationality by tethering the goodness of a reason to the perspective or interests of the agent. Others are *absolutist* or *interpersonally comparative*, searching for a notion of good reason that can adjudicate between conflicting subjective points of view. Some absolutist theories are religious, pure and devout. Still others are cast in terms of human nature; Aristotle's, for example, turns on notions of which actions if performed will contribute to human happiness and well-being. It is here that the skill of the theorist of objective rationality lies. The road to the best theory of objective rationality is rocky. Contention and difficulty make it difficult to stay on track. Objective rationality, in the words of one traveler, 'remains a contested ideal'.[4]

7.3 Is Weakness of Will Unreasonable?

The ancient texts combed most thoroughly for lessons about the rational and reasonable are, probably, the Old and New Testaments. One of the most intriguing Rationality Tales in the Old Testament is the story of how David, after Saul tried to kill him, sought refuge in Gath, the city from which Goliath had come. According to the version of the story reported in the Book of Samuel, fearful of the reception which he, a onetime enemy, would receive in Gath, especially from its king, Achish, David pretended that he was insane.

So he changed his behavior before them [the Philistines of Gath] and feigned himself mad in their hands, and scrabbled on the doors of the gate, and let his spittle fall down upon his beard. Then said Achish to his servants, 'Lo, you see the man is mad; why then have you brought him to me? Have I need of mad men, that you have brought this fellow to play the madman in my presence?'

David gives us a glimpse of what it means to be a certain type of rational agent: a type much admired by philosophers. This is someone who is strong-willed or 'continent', to use a philosopher's term of art. What is a strong-willed agent? A strong-willed agent is someone who acts in terms of their better conscious judgment, that is, in terms of what they judge to be their best reasons. Even if it seems to outsiders as if they are unrestrained and uncontrolled, they are self-possessed and self-controlled. They are concerned with their reasons for action; they listen to the dictates of their deliberation; and, finally, they hold fast to those dictates. They do what they decide that they should do. In David's case, although his countenance was slovenly, for spittle ran down his face, his behavior ingeniously expressed his strength of will and resolve: to enter the land of the enemy and by feigning madness to seek refuge.

Continence consists in abiding by one's better conscious judgment. If continence is a virtue or admirable feature of rational agency, the corresponding vice may be that of weakness of will or 'incontinence'.[5] A weak-willed or incontinent agent is someone who acts against his or her better conscious judgment; they knowingly fail to abide by the dictates of deliberation. Garden variety examples include: the overeater who is incontinent in acting against his sincere intention to diet, the excessively critical parent who is weak-willed in acting against her conviction that children should be treated with patience and tolerance, and the klepto-maniac who is weak-willed in acting contrary to her resolve to respect other people's property.

Is incontinence subjectively unreasonable? Is one never weak-willed for good (internal) reason but always only for bad reason?

I will argue that in certain situations incontinence may actually be more reasonable than continence, internally. If incontinence is a vice it is a defeasible vice, which means that even if it is usually or typically unreasonable, people can be incontinent for subjectively good reason.

First, let us examine the contrary view that incontinence is sub-jectively unreasonable. An argument that incontinence is subjectively unreasonable finds its roots in Aristotle (384–322 bc), who was (with

Plato) one of the two greatest and most influential of the ancient Greek philosophers. Aristotle says that whereas the 'continent person seems to be the same as one who abides by his rational calculation; ... the incontinent person seems to be the same as the one who abandons it' (*Nichomachean Ethics*, 1145b10–11). The terseness of Aristotle's remark contains a disarmingly subtle argument that incontinence is subjectively unreasonable. The argument may be reconstructed as follows:

> Internally good reasons are reasons consciously judged good by the agent. Incontinent agents knowingly act against reasons which they judge good. Hence, incontinence is subjectively unreasonable.

To take a simple illustration, suppose that Sam sells cars. His boss's business is doing poorly, so he urges Sam to unload some 'lemons'. Lemons are really bad cars and Sam has moral scruples about selling them. He deliberates and decides not to follow his boss's request. However, at the first sign of a customer, Sam abandons his resolve and asks 'Can I interest you in a premium car' – as he points to the worst lemon.

Sam is Aristotle's incontinent agent. Sam deliberates (calculates) and judges 'refraining from selling lemons' as the reasonable thing to do; but Sam then knowingly abandons his calculations and attempts to sell bad cars. For Aristotle Sam's action is unreasonable, subjectively.

Aristotle operates with what may be called a *consistency* with *conscious judgment* model of subjective reasonableness. His idea is that an action is reasonable, subjectively, just when it is consistent with the agent's judgment of the goodness or reasonableness of his reasons. In the case of Sam, if Sam had deliberated again and made a second judgment that he should sell lemons, then his action of selling would have been both continent and reasonable, subjectively.

Aristotle did not regard his argument about the unreasonableness of incontinence as a mere terminological nicety.[6] He stressed that incontinence was a blot against a person's character – 'to be avoided and blameworthy'. Is Aristotle's argument sound? Must incontinent action be unreasonable? Is there no room for reasonable incontinence?

Consider the case of Mark Twain's Huckleberry Finn.[7] In *The Adventures of Huckleberry Finn* Twain tells the tale of a young boy prior to the Civil War in the United States who takes a trip by makeshift raft down the Mississippi River with a runaway slave named Jim. Actually,

Huck and Jim are both runaways: Jim from slavery, Huck from a brutal parent.

Part-way through the trip, feeling what he describes as pangs of conscience for helping Jim escape from his owner, Huck judges that he should turn Jim in at the first opportunity. But when confronted unexpectedly with bounty hunters, Huck's resolve weakens. He lies to protect Jim and blames himself for his weakness.

From an external or objective standpoint, especially from the moral point of view, it is eminently reasonable for Huck to act against his judgment by failing to turn Jim over to the slave hunters. Given the terrible immorality of slavery, Jim ought to remain free. However, such an assessment does not correspond to the reasons which ground Huck's judgment. To Huck, Jim is stolen property and stolen property belongs with its owner. Remember internal rationality is agent-centered. It concerns the agent's own attitudes. Huck knowingly acts against what he consciously judges he has best reason to do and responds to consciously unwelcome reasons leading him to protect Jim.

What would Aristotle say about Huck? Aristotle's emphasis on inconsistency with judgment means that Huck is both incontinent and unreasonable, since he knowingly acts against his own conscious judgment. But the contrary possibility that incontinence can be reasonable gains a powerful foothold in the example of Huck. Reasons figure prominently if not deliberately in his refusal to turn in Jim. Huck sympathizes with Jim's desire for freedom and is aware of Jim's trust and gratitude. And frankly, Huck seems to care much more for these – as he views them – morally irrelevant considerations than he does for moral rules about property.

Twain puts Huck's point of view after refusing to turn Jim over in prose:

> Well, then, says I, what's the use you learning to do right, when its troublesome to do right and ain't no trouble to do wrong, and the wages is just the same? I was stuck. I couldn't answer that. So I reckoned I wouldn't bother no more about it, but after this always do whichever come handiest at the time.

How should we interpret Huck? Arguably, we should say that Huck is reasonable, internally or subjectively, in being weak-willed or knowingly acting against his 'better' judgment. This is because his judgment is out of kilter with his subjectively best reasons. What are those reasons? They are the reasons which matter most to him even though they do not ground his conscious assessment or calculations prior to being confronted with the slave hunters.

Aristotle imagines a standard of internal rationality imposed by the agent in calculation and deliberation. But agents' points of view are multi-dimensional, complex, and sometimes ambiguous. Sometimes, especially in cases of self-doubt or failures of self-knowledge, the so-called 'better' judgment is incompatible with what matters most to a person; it arises from less than the internally best reasons. On this broader conception of internal rationality – which I call *fidelity to the agent's overall internal perspective* – none of us makes all and only those calculations of better which in fact *are* (subjectively) better and which faithfully reflect our total point of view. If behavior runs against the grain of one's most inclusive or personally important reasons, then, admittedly, it is unreasonable (internally) to knowingly act in such a fashion. However, if behavior runs merely against the grain of one's own self-assessment, then this may be reasonable if the assessment fails to reflect subjectively more important considerations.

On the analysis which pictures internal rationality in terms of fidelity to overall internal perspective, Huck's refusal is reasonable. More generally, it can be reasonable to be weak-willed.

The point I am making may be refined with a distinction and sharpened on another example. Talking of the goodness/reasonableness or badness/unreasonableness of an action or reason from the agent's internal perspective is ambiguous. It may suggest two things, which I shall call the 'judgmentalist' and 'holist' approaches to the matter.

The judgmentalist approach takes as its premise that an action to be reasonable (internally) must be judged reasonable by the agent. It concentrates on the agent's calculation. The holist approach, in contrast, factors the agent's judgment as just one among many factors in discovering whether an action is reasonable from the agent's point of view. It focuses instead on the richness, complexity, and often unconscious elements in an agent's perspective. It acknowledges that people sometimes know themselves (their own reasons) too insufficiently to identify their better reasons.

On the judgmentalist approach, Huck's failure to return Jim is unreasonable, internally. But what of the holist approach? Interpreted as an action which fits with what means most to Huck, it is hard to deny its reasonableness.

Let us consider another example. A promising young pianist's hands are injured in a motorcycle accident. Unless she allows the hands to heal she will no longer play piano. She knows this, and resolves that she remain off her motorcycle for two months while the hands heal. Within a few weeks of formulating her resolve, however, in response to an invitation to participate in a cycle race, she rides the cycle fully realizing that the ride contravenes her judgment.

To start with, note that she is not following her judgment or decision. She is incontinent. But does it follow that she races for bad reason, internally? As noted by many writers on weakness of will, there is something unfortunate when a decision is abandoned. On balance, it renders deliberation irrelevant. But must we say that her action is unreasonable – subjectively? Riding in the race may, after all, express her deepest desires in an appropriate way. True, she risks a promising musical career; but, if one takes her overall point of view into account, and not just her judgment or self-assessment, cycling may mean more to her than music. Perhaps racing is a triumph of spontaneous enjoyment over a faulty judgment about a career she neither likes nor finds rewarding.

By distinguishing or disambiguating, as above, between the 'better' judgment which the agent makes – the conscious evaluation of reasons made by the agent – and reason's overall internal standing, we can allow for a broad range of incontinent though internally reasonable actions. All internal factors must receive their due place if we are to call an action unreasonable from the agent's point of view.

One philosopher who perceptively and subtly appreciates that internal rationality should be interpreted in terms of an agent's overall internal perspective is Robert Audi. Audi writes:

It should be expected that where an action accords with those overall grounds ... better than does a ... judgment it contravenes, the action may be rational despite its incontinence. Here, incontinent action, far from a failure to do what is better or best, may be the best option, and may eventually be seen by the agent to be so.[8]

Of course, questions remain. If weakness of will is not always a vice, should it be reinforced and cultivated? Certainly not. Aristotle was correct to warn that incontinence must be uncharacteristic of rational agents, for habitual incontinence reflects impaired powers of deliberation and resolve. Aristotle quotes the proverb, 'If water chokes us, what must we drink to wash it down?' By this he means that if people are habitually incontinent, then they cannot be persuaded by reason to be guided by reason. Their chronic lack of resolution will prevent them from acting even when their judgment is reasonable in their own holistically subjective terms.

What of situations in which the incontinent action is not the best option from the agent's point of view but a very bad option? Is that unreasonable? Certainly yes. Consider a seat-belt case. Suppose a person, say, Ned, judges the aggregate benefits of buckling up to outweigh the costs and inconvenience; he decides all things considered to buckle up. Suppose also that this decision accords with Ned's total subjective point of view. Ned is no Huck or cyclist whose judgment is out of kilter with personally salient values, but someone who properly understands himself including what he most wants. However, on entering a car his resolve fails him. The modest comfort of not buckling up softens his will.

Given Ned's overall perspective, one must pronounce that his incontinent action is unreasonable, internally. Ned has a lot to cherish: a power of deliberation, knowledge of his deepest values and concerns, and a judgment which springs from that self-knowledge. But sometimes personal assets fail to function as assets. In some cases they compete with motivational liabilities, and the assets lose. People act incontinently *and* unreasonably – in their own subjective terms.

7.4 Is Unselfish Action Impossible?

Thomas Hobbes said that 'of all voluntary acts, the object is to every man his own good.'[9] According to traditional interpretation, by this and other remarks Hobbes meant to claim that there is just one kind of reason ('object') which moves agents to act: selfish reason, i.e. promotion of the agent's own welfare or well-being. People act to promote the welfare of others only when they believe that there is something good in it for themselves. Unselfishness is motivationally inert.

The doctrine that all human rational action (Hobbes's 'voluntary acts') is selfishly motivated and driven by selfish reasons is known as *psychological egoism*. The contrary doctrine that some human action is unselfishly motivated and driven by desire to promote the welfare or well-being of others is known as *psychological altruism*.

I cannot settle the question of whether Hobbes truly was an advocate of psychological egoism.[10] I wish to consider whether egoism is true. Is unselfish action impossible? Are the only reasons for which agents act selfish?

Notice how egoism presupposes a partition of reasons for action into two types: selfish or egoistic reasons and unselfish or altruistic reasons. A selfish reason concerns the agent's welfare and well-being, where this does not imply the welfare or well-being of others. An unselfish reason concerns another's welfare or well-being, where this does not imply the welfare or well-being of oneself.

It may be replied that *obviously* people act for unselfish reasons. A mother jumps in front of a car to save her child's life; Mother Teresa nursed the poor in the slums of Calcutta. However, egoism's counter-reply is that the only thing that is obvious is that people *seem* to act for unselfish reasons. Meanwhile, things are not always as they seem. If egoism is correct, 'unselfish' actions really are selfish actions; 'altruistic' behavior is psychologically egoistic behavior in disguise. For instance, many people believe that Mother Teresa's reason for helping the poor was to make them better off; she was altruistic. However, if psychological egoism is correct, the nun's altruism was neither central nor genuine. When Mother Teresa helped the poor, she did so because her own well-being was advanced. Her helping behavior sprang from egoistic motives.

Suppose that Albert notices that Filbert has jammed his finger in the refrigerator door. Assume the egoist dichotomy between selfish and unselfish reasons. Filbert acts for selfish reason if he tries to remove his own finger from the door; whereas Albert apparently acts for unselfish reason when he helps Filbert to remove the finger. However, egoists deny that apparent unselfish actions really are unselfish; they take an agent's reasons to be a direct function of selfish reasons. So, for the egoist, acting to help another requires personal compensation. An agent is moved to protect or promote another's well-being only in case the agent expects to receive significant benefit in return (or he may fear losing significant benefit, such as companionship).

Consider the finger in the door. If Albert fails to help Filbert, Filbert may then neglect Albert when Albert needs assistance. The benefit to Albert in helping is that it may deliver Filbert's help if the tables/doors are turned.

Of course, judged from the perspective of psychological egoism, egoistic helpers are vulnerable when they assist. If Albert's helping Filbert is their single encounter, and they do not exchange services in a mutually beneficial way, Albert may be better off to refrain from helping Filbert. Doing for Filbert will do nothing for Albert; it may even harm him. However, this is only to allow that agents can harbor mistaken expectations. Social life is often unpredictable. Albert may help Filbert, expecting, subconsciously perhaps, that Filbert will help him in return; but Filbert's help may never arrive. This does not fault egoism so much as express human fragility and fallibility.

Is egoism warranted? Is psychological egoism supported by good argument?

The debate over psychological egoism is enormously complicated. I cannot here provide a full discussion of the issues. What interests me here is just one protracted worry about egoism. Producing a good argument for egoism is not as simple or easy as some people think. There are several popular but bad arguments for egoism.

Let's look briefly at three. In order to hasten discussion I shall coin names for each argument.

The ownership argument

This argument rests on the most obvious feature of reasons – *who* has them. It goes as follows: All actions originate in reasons of the agent. When I act, I act on my reasons; when you act, you act on your reasons. Because my actions stem from *my* reasons, I am selfishly motivated. Because your actions stem from *your* reasons, you are selfishly motivated. Psychological egoism is insured by the ownership of reasons.

The ownership argument is flawed. It assumes that simply because a person acts on his or her own reasons, the reasons (and actions) are selfish. But this just does not follow. If Mother Teresa sincerely desired to help others (say, not for her sake, but theirs), the desire was *her* desire, but it wasn't selfish. If, by contrast, Mother Teresa desired to help others for her own sake (say, so that she would go to heaven) and not theirs, the desire was both her desire and selfish.

The fact that actions originate in reasons of the person means merely that reasons are not free-floating entities. Reasons are possessed by real agents. Reasons are things *had*. Whether they are also selfish is another question entirely.

To illuminate the critical point consider the following analogy. I have a hand; you have a hand. I grasp things with *my* hand; you grasp things with *your* hand. Suppose *prehensile egoism* is the (bizarre) doctrine that whatever we grasp is ours. How might we defend this position? With what argument? Here's one: The ownership of grasping hands determines the ownership of whatever is grasped. So, if I grasp something with my hands, it's mine. If you grasp something with your hands, it's yours. But this argument is obviously woefully flawed. Just because I grasp something does not mean that it is mine. I can grasp things which belong to you. You can grasp things which belong to me. (If not, stealing would be definitionally impossible!) Hand ownership does not insure prehensile egoism.

So, likewise, the simple fact that I act on my reasons does not mean that my actions are selfish. To be selfish the reasons themselves (independently of being mine) must be selfish. Two other popular arguments for psychological egoism purport to establish that reasons themselves – those which move people to act – are selfish, and by virtue of features other than ownership.

The satisfaction argument

A reason for action, as noted earlier in the chapter, is a psychological attitude of an agent that explains *why* the agent acted as they did. Thus, in answer to the question, 'Why did Mother Teresa work with the poor in the slums of Calcutta (rather than, say, with the rich in Marblehead, Massachusetts)?' we may cite as her reasons her wants or desires for the poor; her expectations, hopes, fears; and so on.

According to the satisfaction argument for psychological egoism, the reasons which actually motivate people – the reasons which move people – are selfish. Why? It has already been noted that one can have reasons for action that do not move or motivate. However, when a person is moved by a reason this can be for one purpose only. Prior to action they are dissatisfied; they act so as to be satisfied. Satisfaction is selfish; so, people act for selfish reasons. To take a quick illustration, Mother Teresa's apparent objective in helping the poor was to promote their welfare, but ultimately she helped them because she expected that she herself would be discontent if she failed to help and satisfied only if she helped. By contrast, helping the rich of Marblehead would not bring her satisfaction. She may have had reasons to help the rich (perhaps an elderly nephew lived in Marblehead), but the problem there is that she would derive no *personal* satisfaction from helping the rich, neither can such personally unmoving reasons be used to explain why Mother Teresa acted as she did in Calcutta.

The satisfaction argument is subtle. It is also doubly flawed. In the first place, do people act only for personal satisfaction? David Hume, in *An Inquiry Concerning the Principles of Morals*, wrote: 'There is some benevolence, however small, infused into our bosom; some spark of friendship for human kind; some particle of the dove kneaded into our frame, along with the elements of the wolf and serpent.' Hume meant to say that people sometimes act even when they realize in advance that they will not be satisfied. They help others with no hope of satisfaction. They are moved by the 'dove' in themselves. A mother jumps in front of a moving car to save her child knowing that she herself will be killed.

In the second place, egoism misunderstands the nature of satisfaction. Satisfaction is not inherently selfish. People may act for unselfish satisfaction.

This is a crucial, elusive, and perhaps paradoxical point. There are confusing ambiguities in the concept of satisfaction. The main ambiguity is between being satisfied *in* another's satisfaction and being satisfied *independent* of another's satisfaction. You should not be called 'selfish' just because you derive satisfaction in helping others. Mother Teresa found satisfaction in nursing the poor. If she helped for fame, fortune, or heaven, or to evoke their reciprocal help should tables turn, her satisfaction was selfish. But if she helped because of sincere interest in their well-being, her satisfaction was unselfish. The saintly nun was satisfied in their satisfaction.

A romantic way to make the same point is to consider what Harvard's Robert Nozick calls 'love's bond'.[11] According to Nozick a love bond exists between you and someone you love when your own satisfaction (or dissatisfaction) is derived from theirs. When you learn that something negative happens to the person you love, therein something negative also happens to you; you are dissatisfied in their dissatisfaction. When something positive happens to the person you love, therein something positive happens to you; you are satisfied in their satisfaction.

Consider one example. Your lover has lost his tuition money for college classes in the current semester. He is disappointed and unhappy and this leaves you dissatisfied. So you loan him money to attend class. Learning of your action, would we wish to describe it as selfish? Surely not. Selfish for what? For *his* college education? How would Nozick help us to describe the situation? Nozick would say that egoism misunderstands love's bond. The egoist pictures people as closed figures whose boundaries are self-centered; but love shapes or alters your boundaries to include the person you love. You center on them. If the other is dissatisfied by losing his money, so (at least to some extent) are you. The removal of your own dissatisfaction is inseparably linked to the removal of theirs.

The core of the love relationship is how lovers take satisfaction in each other's satisfaction, how they respond with their partner. The core of egoism is how people use other people, how they get the other to respond to them. In love, your satisfaction consists in the other's satisfaction. By contrast, for egoism your satisfaction consists in what the other does for you if and when you satisfy them. The 'love' of egoism is reciprocal tit for tat; the love of love's bond is conjoined satisfaction.

Love's conjoined satisfaction is 'selfish' only in a very attenuated sense. The 'self' of the lover has been expanded; it is no longer an ego but two selves. Because another person is included, love's bond hardly deserves to be classified as selfish. True, the strength of the bond may psychologically grade off into egoism with a vanishing degree of commitment between the lovers themselves. Hume's dove may take flight in a bitter wind. But it behooves us in order not to be tempted to embrace psychological egoism, to admit to the capacity for love's bond within ourselves. The bond is satisfying, if not always lasting. Being taken in by a false doctrine like egoism should be neither satisfying nor lasting.

The baby faced argument

An argument which I shall call 'baby faced' goes as follows: Children enter the world with nothing but selfish needs and desires; acts motivated by needs for food, warmth, and nurture are the first acts performed by the infant. Selfish reasons remain the only reasons for action, although their scope broadens to include desires for fame, fortune, power, and social position.

Suppose we concede, for the sake of argument, that baby's first reasons are selfish. This is a controversial concession for two reasons. First, some psychologists contend that there are unselfish desires for which there is evolutionary selection in young children. Indeed, Charles Darwin, in chapter 4 of *The Descent of Man*, supports the idea that people are natively unselfish by noting that various nonhuman animals are capable of altruism. Second, describing an infant or young child as selfish may be far fetched since the very young do not mentally harbor a self/other distinction. Newborns do not conceive of themselves as one among 'other minds'. But let's make the concession and not question its infantile assumptions. May we still deny that selfish reasons remain the only reasons for action? Must Mother Teresa act within the imprint of her childhood selfishness?

Imagine that Filbert begins life as an egoist. He cares just for himself. But also imagine that he is often placed in situations in which he must help others to receive personal benefit. Might not the link or paired association between his benefit and the good of others change the character of his reasons? Whereas helping others at first occurs just because it helps Filbert, as a consequence of conditioned or paired association with benefiting himself Filbert comes to value the good of others independent of his own benefit. The means (benefit to others) becomes an end-in-itself: something he wishes for its own sake.[12]

To take a simple illustration, suppose that Baby Filbert wants above all to be fed, and that he believes that he must please his mother to be fed. But as years pass, bringing pleasure to his mother slides apart from the desire to be fed. Teenage Filbert looks into her eyes and feels guilty for not bringing pleasure to her, although his stomach is full.

The possibility of developing into altruists is psychologically natural and plausible.[13] Complex are the ways in which reasons develop over time. In general, one type of reason can be the sole motive at one stage of development, only to be displaced by other types at later stages. An analogy should help here: At thirteen years of age Filbert smokes cigarettes because of pressure from his peers, many of whom smoke and urge him to smoke. However, at forty-seven years old, peer pressure points in the opposite direction to stop smoking; yet Filbert still smokes. Whatever the new sorts of reasons (e.g. the desire to reduce anxiety, nicotine enjoyment), the old reasons are impotent. Reasons at one stage need not remain reasons at another stage. Likewise, a person might be an egoist in infancy or childhood, but an altruist in mid-life. When a child perhaps I helped others just to help myself, but now I help others for its own sake.

The dubious assumption behind the baby faced argument is that the reasons of childhood persist uncontested through the seasons of adulthood. The inference from being selfish as an infant to being selfish as an adult is unwarranted.

The above three popular arguments for egoism are nowhere near as powerful as first they may appear. As for positive warrant for altruism, there are a significant number of actions, both heroic and mundane, which seem to be motivated by unselfish reasons. Perhaps the amount of self-sacrifice is great; death is risked. Or there is significant personal unhappiness expected by the agent. Mahatma Gandhi, Desmond Tutu, the anonymous rescuers of Jews during the Holocaust, of Kuwaitis during Iraq's occupation, and of blacks during slavery in the southern United States; the list goes on.

Perhaps it is unusual for altruism to be deeply rooted in a human being; perhaps most people are predominantly egoistic, sacrificing for family and friends but rarely or never for strangers. It may even be that persons are inconsistent, exposing themselves to great risk for others in some situations, but failing to offer even minimally inconvenient help in other similar situations. However, even inconsistent altruism and predominant egoism imply that some actions are unselfish.

To briefly sum up: Readers should be aware that this chapter does little more than skim the surface of many critical topics connected with rational action. But certain conclusions can be drawn even on the basis of our brief discussion. We need not accept the gloomy picture of rational action as selfish; we need not accept the intellectualized picture of abandoned resolve as unreasonable. Rationality is not steering one's way through life, focused on self, settled in judgment. Rational agents can follow a zigzag path, earlier walking to the fridge, now mounting a motorcycle, later risking life and limb for a child's safety or success.

NOTES

1 The network may include a certain amount of elbow room or indeterminacy, if, for example, persons possess the freedom involved in free choice. See chapter 9 for discussion.

2 They can also be irrational (and rational) in different degrees, measuring up to bad (and good) to a different extent.

3 D. Ames, 'Self shooting of phantom head', *British Journal of Psychiatry*, 145 (1984), pp. 193–4.

4 S. Nathanson, *The Ideal of Rationality: A Defense, within Reason* (Open Court, Chicago, 1994), p. x.

5 In talking of continence and incontinence, I trust readers will not be misled

by visions of enuresis. I want to make clear which fish I am trying to fry: 'incontinence' and 'continence' are technical terms of philosopher's art.

6   My interpretation of Aristotle is controversial. Aristotle is sometimes read as addressing whether incontinence has any reason behind it, good or bad. I read him as presupposing that incontinence has reason behind it – that is, agents act incontinently for a reason. What I take him to address is the following question: Supposing incontinence occurs for a reason, must the reason be bad internally?

7   The first edition of *The Adventures of Huckleberry Finn* was published in London in 1884. I am indebted in what follows to Jonathan Bennett, 'The conscience of Huckleberry Finn', *Philosophy*, 49 (1974), pp. 123–34; Alison McIntyre, 'Is akratic action always irrational?', in *Identity, Character, and Morality*, eds Owen Flanagan and A. O. Rorty (MIT Press, Cambridge, Mass., 1990), pp. 379–400.

8   Robert Audi, 'Weakness of will and rational action', *Australasian Journal of Philosophy*, 68 (1990), p. 279.

9   Thomas Hobbes, *Leviathan* (Clarendon Press, Oxford, 1909), ch. 15.

10 For discussion of whether Hobbes was a psychological egoist, which also includes clear and useful reflections on egoism, see Gregory S. Kavka, *Hobbesian Moral and Political Theory* (Princeton University Press, Princeton, 1986).

11 Robert Nozick, *The Examined Life* (Simon & Schuster, New York), pp. 68–86.

12 See Elliott Sober, 'What is psychological egoism?', *Behavior and Philosophy*, 17 (1989), p. 98.

13 See Michael Hoffman, 'Developmental synthesis of affect and cognition and its implications for altruistic motivation', *Developmental Psychology*, 11 (1975), pp. 607–22.

8

Does Mind Depend Upon Brain?

Spare no words: mind depends upon brain. Thanks largely to neuro-science, which is the branch of physical science concerned with the brain, we know a great deal about how damage or trauma to the brain can cripple or damage the mind. We know that impaired mathematical calculation is associated with damage to the posterior sectors of the left hemisphere and that the ability to read can be selectively impaired by cerebral lesions. We know of dozens of behavior and emotion controlling chemicals (lithium, chlorpromazine, cocaine, and so on) and of the susceptibility of consciousness to caffeine, anesthetics, and alcohol. We know, too, that degeneration of nerve tissue will cause senile dementia and other impairments of one's capacity for memory, including facts so plain and ordinary as recognition of one's husband, wife, or home.

But what *exactly* is the dependence of mind on brain? How intimately does mind hinge upon brain? The dependence of mind upon brain, obvious in general though it is, is not clear in its specific character or nature. What sort of dependence is it?

8.1 Materialism

The theory of Materialism or Physicalism – which can be traced back at least to Thomas Hobbes in the seventeenth century – is the most popular contemporary view among philosophers of the nature or character of mind–brain dependence.[1] Materialism can be summarized in three theses:

(1)   *The Physical Constitution Thesis*   Mind is an entity, or is fully constituted by entities, of the physical kind. States and processes of mind are nothing more than physical states and processes. Specifically, in the case of human persons and other vertebrates, the mind is the brain (and central nervous system). Mental states or processes (for example, believing that ice is cold, or being sad) are neurochemical–neurobiological states or processes.

This first thesis is typically presented as a highly confirmed empirical or scientific hypothesis. Paul Churchland writes:

> If we approach *homo sapiens* from the perspective of natural history and the physical sciences, we can tell a coherent story of his constitution ... which encompasses ... biology, physiology, and materialistic neurotheory.[2]

In a classic 1954 paper entitled 'Sensations and brain processes', J. J. C. Smart writes:

> It seems to me that science is increasingly giving us a viewpoint whereby organisms are able to be seen as physicochemical mechanisms.... [They are] nothing but ... complex arrangements of physical constituents.[3]

Michael Tye remarks:

> Given what we now know about how the brain works, about the billions of neurons interacting with one another in response to the electrical messages they receive, it seems very implausible to suppose that there is no wholly physical story. It also goes against the history of science.[4]

The next two theses stem in various ways from the physical constitution thesis. They are implicit in the remarks of Churchland, Smart, and Tye just noted.

(2)   *The Explanation Thesis*   Human and animal behavior is best – fully and most deeply – explained by something physical: not, to be sure, in the seventeenth- and eighteenth-century sense of cogs and pulleys, but in the more contemporary sense of neurochemistry and neurobiology. Rational or intelligent action is the upshot of processes or activities physically internal to the brain. All behavior of the human body is in principle fully causally explainable in neuroscientific terms.

(3)   *The Exclusion Thesis*   Human beings are excluded from possessing

non-physical powers or properties. We are not incorporeal souls and can exist as no immaterial spirits. As the materialist D. M. Armstrong says in his book *A Materialist Theory of Mind*, 'Man is nothing put a material object having none but physical properties'.

Materialism advocates a maximally intimate dependence of mind upon brain. Indeed, strictly speaking, in the materialist scheme of things the relation between mind and brain actually is stronger or narrower than 'mere' dependence. One *thing* (mind) is not dependent upon *another* thing (brain). Given the constitution thesis, mind somehow just *is* brain.

Materialism is a complex doctrine and comes in many forms with many names. Materialists differ over the precise scope of mind–brain constitution, the nature of the explanatory relation between rational action and brain processes, and the force of various exclusions. Some of these disagreements seem so deep and highly divisive as to suggest a fundamental lack of consensus at the heart of materialist philosophy. But beneath the differences that divide materialists is a single unifying commitment, a commitment sufficient to classify one and all as materialists. In one way or another materialists share in the broad constitution thesis tradition of what may be called the 'physical constituent' or 'physical identity' approach to mentality. Their conception of mind is of something which is nothing more than brain. The examination of what constitution of mind by brain means or requires has been the major preoccupation of materialist thinking. Hearty differences which have emerged concerning the explanation and exclusion theses to a large extent turn on differences over how best to articulate the constitutional commitment.

What are materialism's virtues? Materialists claim four main virtues for their doctrine.

The first is an *economy* or *simplicity* achieved by asserting that anything mental or intelligent can be explained by something which is material or physical. We do not have to account for human and animal behavior by referring separately to mind and brain. We can and should refer only to brain.

Economy or simplicity is a feature whose nature and merit may be hard to grasp. What is simplicity? What does it mean to say that simplicity is a virtue? The nub of the first answer is that a theory or doctrine is simple or economical just when it fits neatly with things which we already know. By contrast, when theories fail to fit neatly with background knowledge, they are complex and uneconomical. This is because adjustments must be made in our beliefs to make them fit. Then, assuming that neatness of fit with background knowledge is virtuous, if simplicity means neat fit, simplicity is a virtue.

The idea behind simplicity or neatness of fit is abstract, but it is also important, as may be suggested by the following illustrations. Learning, we know, involves lasting chemical changes in the brain; the materialist holds that such chemical changes are most neatly (simply) explained by presupposing that the psychological processes involved in learning are themselves physical/chemical processes. Some animals (e.g. dolphins), we know, are psychologically more complex than others (e.g. rabbits). The materialist proposes that this is most economically explained by identifying psychological complexity with neurological complexity. Mind is nothing more than brain. Since the dolphin brain is more complex than the rabbit brain, the mind of the dolphin is more complex than the mind of the rabbit.

The second virtue of materialism is its *unified conception of the world.* Behind materialism lies a conception of nature as consisting of objects and processes at different levels of organization and sophistication. A promising if partial description is that animals are made of organs, which are made of cells, which are made of molecules, which are made of atoms. The behavior of these levels are described in terms of different concepts and terminology: those describing animal behavior, cell behavior, and so on. Materialism downwardly unifies the different levels of organization. It understands the behavior of higher levels of organization (e.g. those of animals) in terms of lower level units (e.g. the biochemistry of the brain). Such downward unification is part of what it means to say that materialism is 'physically constitutional' in commitment. Materialism reduces the mind to neural components. It assumes that the mind *has* neural components.

The third virtue is that materialism *expels superstition* from our understanding of human behavior. Let's look briefly at one example: Witches.

Religious madness (or what today psychologists call 'religious hysteria') is a fairly common affliction among humans, and in earlier centuries its victims were often described as cases of devil possession, in which Satan himself occupied the mind of the hysteric.[5] The opening page of what perhaps is the first autobiography in the English language – transcribed because the woman, Margery Kempe, was illiterate – presents an account of a woman born around 1373 whose contemporaries thought her possessed by the devil.

> Because of the dread she had of damnation on the one hand, and [Satan's] sharp reproving of her on the other, this creature went out of her mind and was amazingly disturbed and tormented with spirits for half a year, eight weeks and odd days.

A materialist can point to the success of modern brain-centered theories of mental illness which have helped to eliminate reference to witches and possessed people from our understanding of religious hysteria. Today, instead of diabolical possession, Margery Kempe would likely be diagnosed as suffering from an organic deficiency or chemical disorder in her central nervous system. For instance, one of the most telling signs of demonic possession was thought to be spontaneous and erratic bodily movements: bumps and jerks believed associated with invasion by Satan's spirit. A significant finding in brain-centered psychological science was the demonstration in the mid-1960s that movement disorders (spontaneous bumps and jerks) result from a loss of a neurotransmitter substance (dopamine) in the brain. Modern theories of movement disorder have dismissed reference to immaterial spirits from serious psychology.

Materialism exorcises witch-hunts. It substitutes material neurons for spiritual demons.[6]

The fourth and final if less dramatic virtue of materialism is that it positions the mind so that it can be *studied by physical science*. Materialism puts the study of mind within the scope of physical science. This means that, where mind is concerned, the study of mind is no different from the study of brain. Mental or psychological science is not autonomous. It does not have its own methods and its own standards of truth and validity. It has the same methods and standards as physical science and in particular as neuroscience. Thus, we can and should use what we know about the brain from sciences such as neurobiology and neurochemistry to understand mental states and processes.

8.2 Is Materialism Correct?

Materialism has been enormously attractive to philosophers. Paul Teller sums up popular attitudes when we writes: 'Most of us take ourselves to be hard headed materialists: Everything, we take it, is at bottom physical.⁷ However, materialism is not without problems and puzzles. The appeal of materialism should not obscure its difficult or objectionable features. Indeed, the history of materialism consists largely of attempts to rebut objections by clarifying and reformulating the claims and virtues of the doctrine. Consider an historically influential case.

The access objection

A common objection to materialism, which I shall call *the access objection*, holds that mind cannot be brain because we know mind – our conscious minds – and brain in different ways. We have what is termed 'direct' access or 'immediate' knowledge of our minds, but we find out about our brains only indirectly if at all. Since we have direct access to our minds but lack direct knowledge of brains, mind and brain cannot be one and the same.

Suppose, for example, a neurophysiologist comes up with a complete physical–chemical description of the pain system of the brain. An illiterate peasant may well be able to describe his pains without knowing of their physical–chemical description. He may, like the man described in the last chapter, even believe himself to possess two heads, without any failure in ability to make true claims about his pains.

The access objection relies on an implicit premise. The premise is that if mind somehow is brain, then the knowledge or information which each person has of their mind should be the same in kind or expressed in the same way as the knowledge they have of their brain. Defenders of materialism, like U. T. Place and J. J. C. Smart in the 1950s, reject this premise.⁸ They point out that one and the same thing or condition can be known or accessed in different ways. I can know something in one way even though I know nothing of it another way.

There is a basic reason why I can know something in one way although I know nothing about it another way. Knowledge is aspectual. Consider a famous example from Frege (1848–1925): I may know the planet Venus as the Morning Star without knowing it as the Evening Star, although they are the same entity (Venus). Appearing in the morning is one of its aspects; appearing in the evening is another. In knowing Venus under the first aspect I know it as the Morning Star; in failing to know it under the second I fail to know it as the Evening Star.

Other examples are obvious and numerous. Mark Twain and Samuel

Clemens are one and the same person; but many people know the author of *The Adventures of Huckleberry Finn* as Mark Twain without knowing him as Samuel Clemens. Water is two parts hydrogen and one part oxygen. This is the case even though illiterate peasants who are very good at identifying water may know nothing of chemistry. If materialism is true, we should be able to give a general account of pain in physical–chemical terms. However, even when this project is complete there could still be people who do not describe pain in material terms. They may know when they are in pain without knowing whether pain is physical. They may describe their pain as, for example, sharp and stabbing without describing it as a neurochemical condition.

The reply of Place and Smart exploits the fact that knowledge is aspectual. (Equivalently: Knowledge is knowledge 'under a description'.) I can know of Twain without describing him as Clemens. I can know my mind without recognizing that I know my brain. As we will discover in the next section, criticisms of materialism do not stop with the objection that brain access differs from mind access; but the proposition that knowledge is aspectual and related propositions have been fixtures of every version of materialism developed since Place and Smart. They are invoked to fend off many anti-materialist criticisms. Consider one more example.

The example is sometimes referred to as 'Descartes' first argument for Dualism' and is due to René Descartes (1596–1650).[9] It goes roughly as follows:

I can conceive of myself as lacking a brain, but I cannot conceive of myself as lacking a mind. If I try to doubt that I have a mind, I will discover myself with thoughts like 'I doubt I have a mind', and so must admit that I have a mind – for the activity of doubting is mental. Hence, brain and mind must be distinct.

Here is a second application of the idea of the aspectual character of access to mind. The psychological concept 'conceive' like the concept 'know' is aspectual. Descartes says that he cannot conceive of himself as lacking a mind but can conceive of himself as brainless. However, from this it does not follow that mind and brain are distinct. Just because 'two' things are conceived of in different ways does not mean that they really are two things.

Consider by way of analogy the mythic tale in ancient Greece of a man named Oedipus condemned by the gods to marry his mother. Oedipus of course did not want to marry his mother. If you asked him if he wished to marry his mother, he might have said something like this: 'The very idea disgusts me. I find it inconceivable that I will marry my mother.'

Despite inconceivability, Oedipus met a woman by the name of Jocasta whom be wished to marry; and, without learning until after the marriage that Jocasta was his mother, Oedipus married her. If you asked Oedipus before marriage if he wished to marry Jocasta, he might have said something like this: 'The very idea pleases me. I find it eminently conceivable.'

Now consider the following argument placed on the tongue of Oedipus: 'I can conceive of myself as marrying Jocasta, but I cannot conceive of myself as marrying my mother; so, Jocasta must be different from my mother.'

Obviously something is wrong with the argument because Oedipus's wife (Jocasta) *is* his mother. The crucial mistake is failing to appreciate that conceiving like knowing is aspectual. Consequently, just because Oedipus cannot conceive of his mother as his wife but can conceive of Jocasta as his wife does not mean that Jocasta is not his mother. Analogously: If I can conceive of myself as brainless but cannot conceive of myself as mindless, it does not follow that brain and mind are distinct.

One might quarrel with applications of the materialist appeal to aspectuality, but the main idea behind appeal to aspectuality is highly plausible. Unless we have other reasons to attribute distinctness to mind and brain, the mere fact that we know or conceive of them in different terms does not mean that they are distinct things. They can be one and the same; one can be nothing more than the other. But are they?

8.3 Brentano's Thesis

Many states of mind, both conscious and non-conscious, are characterized by *aboutness* or what Franz Brentano (1838–1917) called the *intentional in-existence of objects* and what we have called earlier in the book Intentionality. Brentano also said that Intentionality distinguishes the mental from the physical. He held the thesis – which I shall call *Brentano's thesis* – that aboutness is exclusively a feature of mental phenomena. No physical phenomenon possesses anything similar. Intentionality is not physically constituted.

How aboutness or Intentionality distinguishes the mental from the physical may be understood by the illustration of a mental attitude like believing. Take, for instance, six-year old Carl and his belief that his Uncle Roderick is bald.

Believing is a mental activity that is about an object or state of affairs. In Carl's case, the belief that his uncle is bald is about the uncle. One could say that it aims or is directed at its object. It mentally points towards Roderick.

Why is mental aiming or pointing different from physical aiming, as when Carl's toy dart gun accidentally points in the direction of Roderick? Why is mental aiming or aboutness nothing physical? There are three differences:

(1) One difference is that physically the dart gun points at Roderick only if Roderick really exists. If there is no Roderick, there is no pointing at Roderick. By contrast, Carl can entertain beliefs about Roderick even if Roderick doesn't exist and never did or will exist, but just is a figment of Carl's youthful imagination.

(2) Even when belief aims at something which does exist, mental aiming or aboutness still is distinct from physical processes or relationships. Mental aiming possesses a specificity or aspectuality which physical aiming lacks.

Suppose the following propositions are true:

Carl's dart gun points at his Uncle Roderick.
Uncle Roderick graduated from Yale.

It follows,

Carl's dart gun points at a Yale graduate.

On the other hand, suppose the following propositions are true:

Carl believes that his Uncle Roderick is bald.
Uncle Roderick graduated from Yale.

It does not follow,

Carl believes that his bald headed uncle is a Yale graduate.

Why? This conclusion does not follow because Carl may not realize that Roderick attended college. Suppose Carl knows Roderick only as his bald uncle, not under the aspect or description of being a college graduate.

The physical process of aiming is not aspectual. If the dart gun points at Roderick, it does not point at Roderick as bald or as having graduated from Yale; it points at Roderick *period* – whether he is bald, from Yale, or whatever. By contrast, Intentionality or aboutness is aspectual. Carl entertains beliefs about Roderick under this or that aspect rather than another; not Roderick whatever he is, but Roderick as bald, as his uncle, and so on.

The same point can be made with a small stone. Suppose Roderick is standing under a cliff wall and a stone drops off the cliff and lands on his head. When the stone traces a trajectory to Roderick, it does not fall on him *as* bald or *as* Carl's uncle or as anything else. It falls on him no matter his aspects. Even if Roderick were nephew-less and hairy, the stone would still have struck him. But when Carl entertains a belief about his uncle, this belief may very well specify Roderick only under the aspect of being bald. The stone hits Roderick *period*; whereas Carl's belief 'strikes' Roderick just insofar as the boy thinks of the man as bald.

(3)   A third and related feature of Intentionality is that whatever is Intentional can misrepresent or misinterpret. Intentional phenomena represent something (their objects) as being a certain way. For instance, Carl's belief that Uncle Roderick is bald is not just a mental state with an object. It also has Roderick characterized in some manner, for instance, as his uncle and as bald.

The representational character of Intentional phenomena helps to explain why there can be false beliefs. False beliefs misrepresent. Suppose Carl believes that his uncle graduated from Columbia. Carl misrepresents Roderick. It is false that Roderick is a Columbia graduate.

The physical process of pointing or aiming cannot misrepresent. If the dart gun points (just) at Roderick, who is a Yale graduate, then the dart gun does not point at someone who graduated from Columbia. Meanwhile, Carl can (falsely) believe that Roderick graduated from Columbia, even if Roderick does not fit the description.

The third point is only a stone's drop away from another example.

When the stone falls in the direction of Roderick, there is a physical relationship between Roderick and the stone. The stone has a Roderick trajectory. In falling towards Roderick it could strike a Columbia graduate only if Roderick himself graduated from that New York university. But Carl can entertain a belief about Roderick's graduating from Columbia even if Roderick has never stepped off the Yale campus.

Taken together, the above distinctions form an impressive argument for Brentano's thesis that Intentionality is a unique phenomenon and that nothing which is both mental and possesses aboutness is physical. Brentano certainly seems to have proven that there are mental phenomena which are not physical and that mind (with aboutness) is not brain (without aboutness).

8.4 Intentionality and Materialism

Brentano's thesis constitutes one of the most serious fault lines in materialism. It threatens to crack open the doctrine. In order to patch up the doctrine, some materialists argue that contrary to Brentano physical states or processes can possess Intentionality. D. M. Armstrong, for instance, explicitly admits that Intentionality is a pervasive and critical feature of the mental and he says that the materialist theory of mind must account for it. 'No materialist can claim that intentionality is a unique, unanalysable property of mental processes and still be consistent with his materialism. A materialist is forced to attempt an *analysis* of intentionality.'[10]

A materialist analysis of Intentionality would account for aboutness in material terms. It would specify Intentionality in non-Intentional terms (i.e. in terms which do not presuppose Intentionality). It would show that even though a process (such as brain activity) is physical it can possess aboutness. Let us briefly look at two candidate materialist analyses of aboutness/Intentionality. One is in terms of resemblance; the other is in terms of causality.

The resemblance analysis

An old idea, dating back to Aristotle and found also in David Hume (1711–76), is that one thing is about something else when it *resembles* it.

A map, for example, is about a city if it resembles or is like the city. In the case of mind it has been claimed that the mind is about objects or states of affairs when it contains images or pictures of those objects or states of affairs. A materialist form of this view (neither Aristotle nor Hume were materialists) holds that the assumed images or pictures are physical or material – perhaps geometrical patterns of electrical activity in the brain. So, for instance, believing that Uncle Roderick is bald means having a physical picture or pattern in the brain which resembles the believed Roderick. The pattern projects onto Roderick: it matches or maps onto the uncle in some physically specifiable way. Therein the pattern is about Roderick.

The resemblance analysis works only if resemblance really can achieve or constitute aboutness. But the anti-materialist should not admit this, for resemblance is radically different from aboutness. Whereas resemblance is 'symmetrical', aboutness is 'asymmetrical'. For instance, a picture of Uncle Roderick resembles Roderick as much as Roderick resembles the picture but Roderick is not about the picture. Aboutness moves in one direction: from the picture to Roderick – in essence, that's asymmetry. By contrast resemblance moves forth and back: from the picture to Roderick and from Roderick to the picture – in essence, that's symmetry. Hence, even if physical resemblances of objects are housed in the brain, one difficulty with appealing to resemblance to account for Intentionality is that the mere fact that two things resemble each other does not mean that one is about the other.

A second difficulty with the resemblance analysis is that aboutness can occur in the absence of resemblance. The word 'George' refers to me, but it does not resemble me in any interesting way at all. It certainly does not look like me. Since aboutness can occur in the absence of resemblance, aboutness cannot be understood in terms of resemblance.

A third and final troublesome feature of the resemblance analysis turns on the assumption that there are physical pictures or patterns in the brain which resemble things outside the brain. What does *that* mean? The brain is helter-skelter with neurological activity. In devising a materialist criterion of brain pictures, the task is to specify precisely which features or configurations of brain activity constitute a picture, leaving the remainder as pictorially irrelevant. For instance, in the case of Carl's belief about Roderick, what specifies the outline of the face, the constellation of eyes, mouth, and bald head? At what level of abstraction or embedded detail do brain processes resemble Roderick? We need a materialist criterion for resemblance which interprets the human brain as the seat for resemblances of objects. But no one – neither scientist nor philosopher – has a clear idea of how to develop the criterion. The point is more complicated than it may look. It is worth pause.

In recent years the following hypothesis has become popular in cognitive science and neuroscience: Cognitively significant information about different features of a stimulus are processed sub-consciously in specialized areas of the brain.[11] Each area is more or less independently responsible for the analysis of different facets of a perceptual scene. In visual perception, for example, information about the orientation, movement, and color of a stimulus is coded in specialized cortical areas or neural 'modules'. Spatially separated visual information processing intrigues neuroscientists for a number of reasons, not the least of which is that somehow (in a manner not yet known) this distributed cortical activity combines to form a unified conscious perceptual experience, in which one and the same stimulus is seen as having orientation, motion, and color. I visually experience a yellow tennis ball moving left to right *as* a yellow ball moving left to right. I do not see it as *something* spherical, *something* yellow, and *something* moving left to right. I see it as one thing, not three. Processing also intrigues because we now possess a technology with which to noninvasively (without surgery) explore just where it may take place. This technology is known as 'neuroimaging' or 'brain imaging'.

Neuroimages depict various events, such as blood flow, in the brain during and ostensibly associated with perceptual and cognitive activity. The techniques include (among others) PET (positron emission tomography) and fMRI (functional magnetic resonance imaging). The representations or depictions are sometimes referred to as scans. So a series of PET scans may depict increased blood flow in areas of cortex during perception of a visual stimulus.

Despite the power of PET and fMRI to pictorially reveal the functional anatomy of the human brain and neural activity, we do not gain from this technology pictures of patterns in the brain which resemble the objects (e.g. moving tennis balls) that a subject may perceive and which, by virtue of that resemblance, possess Intentionality.[12] We find patterns but not aboutness-bestowing pictures.

To illustrate and help to clarify the point consider the following fact. It is easier, in many circumstances, to recognize a moving object than a stationery one. When a butterfly is motionless along a lawn, it may be hard to spot. However, if it moves, we may perceive it immediately. How so? The answer, in part, seems to be that some brain cells respond selectively to the motion of an object as well as to different patterns of motion. Patterns of movement activate those cells (which when a stimulus is stationery are more or less inactive) and boost the likelihood that a person will notice a moving stimulus. The patterns of activation are ultimately responsible for events depicted in neuroimaging and other neuroscientific investigatory techniques. However, the patterns do not resemble – along any dimension or in any manner sufficient to constitute the Intentionality of the mental – objects or features of the environment to which their neural constituents are attuned. To put it crudely, a colorful moth may move across a rug, but a colorful mothlike neuron does not spin across a brain. Pictures *of* brain activity do not depict pictures *in* brain activity.

When the above argument against appeal to patterns of brain activity as constitutive of Intentionality is advanced, it is often met with the observation 'But the patterns are *caused* by objects or features of the world'. Aboutness, some say, is the upshot of a causal process, the presence or absence of any sort of resemblance notwithstanding. Consider, for example, the state in a frog's brain which registers when a.fly crosses its field of vision. The state may not resemble the fly. But it is caused by the fly. Perhaps therein the state is about the fly. Perhaps aboutness can be analyzed in causal terms.

The causal analysis

Few materialists are attracted to the resemblance analysis. Most favor a causal analysis. The causal analysis has been championed by Jerry Fodor, Fred Dretske, and several other philosophers.[13] There is no shortage of versions of the causal analysis and some offer links with biology and other natural sciences, including the neuroscientific theory (to which I just alluded) of subconscious information processing and patterns of neural activity, as arguments in their favor. Some use the related languages of co-variation and counter-factual dependence rather than concepts of causation. Some introduce notions of proto-Intentionality ('Intentionality' supposedly of a less robust sort than Brentano Intentionality) and try to construct a physicalistic analysis of Intentionality from a causal or co-variational analyses of proto-Intentionality.

'Creation', wrote Immanuel Kant, 'is not the work of a moment.' The attempt to create causal and kindred analyses of Intentionality has been one of the most active enterprises within the theory of Intentionality in recent years. But we can attend to it only a moment and for this reason we must keep things simple.

In crudest form, according to the causal analysis something physically internal to the brain is about some object when the object causes that internal activity. For instance, believing that Uncle Roderick is bald means being in a brain state or process produced by Roderick and his bald pate. Since Roderick's baldness causes the brain activity, the activity is about the uncle.

One virtue of using the concept of causality in analysis of aboutness is that causality respects the asymmetry of aboutness. Causality – like aboutness (and unlike resemblance) – is asymmetrical. If A causes B, B does not cause A. If flipping the light switch causes the illumination of the room, the illumination does not cause the flip. Analogously: just because X is about Y does not mean that Y is about X. Just because Carl's belief is about his uncle, does not mean that his uncle is about Carl's belief.

The importance of respecting asymmetry fades, however, when we focus on difficulties for the causal analysis. What about the features of aboutness mentioned by Brentano? Let's look at two.

The causal analysis does not account for objects of mental phenomena ([1] above) which really do not exist, since a nonexisting object or state of affairs cannot cause anything. If Roderick does not exist, there is no Roderick-cause for Carl to entertain beliefs about Roderick.

Misrepresentation ([3] above) also is left out. Suppose that bald-headed Roderick is causally responsible for a photograph of himself. The photo was taken of Roderick. He is the causal spring of the picture. According to the causal analysis, the picture is of him because it is caused by him. But suppose that the image somehow appears as not bald but hairy. Suppose it misrepresents Roderick. Perhaps shadows fell upon him which to the uninformed viewer's eyes appear as hair on Roderick's head. Note that if misrepresentation just is a causal process it would be impossible for the photo to misrepresent. This is because the photo would still represent bald Roderick, since bald Roderick causes the 'hairy' image in the photograph.

Causally speaking, the 'hairy' photo represents Roderick equally to the 'bald' photo because bald Roderick is responsible for both photos. Likewise, a (false) belief that Roderick is hairy represents Roderick as much or as well as the (true) belief that Roderick is bald, once again, if bald Roderick is the causal source of both beliefs and if representation consists in causality. In representational terms, however, the hairy photo or belief does not represent Roderick equally to the bald. Strictly speaking, 'hairy' misrepresents. So, although Roderick is causally responsible for both 'bald' and 'hairy' photos or beliefs, 'bald' represents, 'hairy' misrepresents. Causality does not account for the difference between them.

The most serious unfulfilled project for the materialist causal analysis of aboutness is to provide a satisfactory account of misrepresentation. In whatever detail materialists formulate the account, the objection can always be raised: It does not explain the difference between representation and misrepresentation: between true belief and false belief: between accurate photo and inaccurate photo. To illustrate, let us quickly consider the plight of the most popular variation in the causal analysis, which has been adopted in response to the misrepresentation criticism.

Some causal theorists try to counter-reply to the charge that appeal to causality cannot account for misrepresentation by distinguishing two major causal axes along which representation/misrepresentation can occur. They take as their primary target the idea that misrepresentation does not have the same cause as representation. Misrepresentation occurs along an improper or wayward axis, whereas representation occurs along a proper axis. So, for example, a photo depicting (or belief about) Roderick as hairy is not caused by Roderick properly. Had Roderick been properly photographed (e.g. without shadows) his depiction would be bald. Analogously, roughly speaking, a brain state represents some entity or state of affairs when the entity or state of affairs properly causes the brain state; it misrepresents if causation is wayward or improper.

Appeal to propriety or waywardness works only if proper and improper causes can be distinguished in a theoretically neutral manner, i.e. in a manner which does not presuppose the very notion of Intentionality which the analysis is designed to illuminate. This proves immensely difficult. It makes no sense, for example, to say that an improper (misrepresenting) cause of a Roderick photo is one with shadows upon Roderick's head. Suppose we know that Roderick is bald and has been photographed in shadows. Those with such background knowledge might see the photograph taken under such 'wayward' conditions as accurately depicting Roderick as bald. Meanwhile, those without background knowledge might see the photo as that of a hairy man.

There is no principled manner in which to exclude background knowledge – background Intentionality – from the interpretation of a representation. An 'improper' cause can produce a proper representation for someone who extrapolates the right interpretation. (By the same token, a 'proper' cause can elicit an improper representation for someone who extrapolates the wrong interpretation.) For this and related and more complicated reasons, the distinction between proper and improper causality is like a talented prizefighter, perpetually bobbing and weaving. It forms an elusive target. No sooner does the causal theorist fix on how to define the distinction, when the target shifts and has to be sought in another direction.

When it is attacked as severely as this, the causal theory seems doomed. So why are materialists attracted to it? I should mention that one reason why causality provides an appealing account of aboutness for the materialist is that materialists take causality to be part of the sticks and stones – or better: cement and glue – of the physical world: to be part of the material processes of the world. If causation is physical and aboutness can be analyzed in terms of causation, then aboutness, at bottom, is physical.

Another reason is that objects or stimuli in the physical world often make causal contributions to Intentional states or conditions. What things are seen, felt, or heard in visual, tactile, and auditory perception is determined in part by causal contributions which seen, felt, or heard objects make to relevant perceptual experiences. When, for example, I see the motion of a butterfly *as* the motion of a butterfly, that movement is part of the causal chain leading to visual experience of a butterfly in flight. Such causal contributions tempt saying that the Intentionality of (at least) perceptual experience can be understood in causal terms. However, acknowledging that causality figures in perceptual experience does not add up to an argument that perceptual aboutness just is causal, for not every causal contributor – no matter how 'proper' – to a visual experience is perceived in the experience. Activity in spatially distributed areas of my brain forms essential parts of the causal chain leading to my visual experience of the butterfly in motion, but I don't thereby perceive the brain activity. I see *that* the butterfly moves, not *that* cortical modules are sensitive to the flutter of its wings. Causal contribution is one thing; Intentionality another.

Where does all this leave us? I am reminded of a character in John

Barth's *The End of the Road*. Here, he says, is the story of his life – he finds it difficult to decide, to choose, to commit:

> Instantly a host of arguments against applying for a job ... presented themselves for my use, and as instantly a corresponding number of refutations lined up opposite them, one for one, so that the question of my application was held static like the rope marker in a tug-o'-war where the opposing teams are perfectly matched.

Are the opposing teams – materialism-by-Smart and anti-materialism-by-Brentano – perfectly matched? Whether an appropriately materialist account of Intentionality can be provided is hotly debated. But, from our current perspective, the prospects of a materialist account of Intentionality look weak. Brentano seems to be pulling more rope. I suggest we draw the following conclusion: Materialism must defeat the Brentano thesis with an account of Intentionality in physical terms. Absent offering the account, the doctrine should be resisted.

8.5 Supervenience and Melancholia *or* Why Did Robert Schumann Starve Himself to Death?

To all informed ears Robert Schumann (1809–56) is one of the finest composers of classical music of the mid-nineteenth century. The great Romantic composer Johannes Brahms, who had visited Schumann two weeks before his death, believed it, and his wife, the accomplished pianist Clara Wieck, predicated her marriage on its assumption. Schumann, however, characterized himself as haunted by 'loathsome dreams' and frequent feelings of dread. In his prime, he was victim of dramatic mood swings. For instance, after Clara's concert tour in Russia in 1844, he was abysmally depressed and admitted to being envious of her success. He developed phobias about being poisoned and became withdrawn.

On 27 February 1854, Schumann threw himself into the Rhine River. One biographer describes the scene as follows:

> Just past noon ... a hulking figure suddenly emerged from a house on Bilkerstrasse and turned left on the cobbled street. Although it was a cold, rainy day in Dusseldorf, the man wore only a thin robe and slippers. His face was pasty, his eyes were downcast, and he was sobbing. Walking unsteadily, as if on tiptoe, he headed for the Rhine River, only four blocks

away. There, on the Rathaus Ufer overlooking the west bank he stopped. A narrow pontoon bridge led to the other side, and to get across it one had to pass a tollgate. Absentmindedly he searched in his pocket for money. Finding none, he smiled apologetically and offered his silk handkerchief as a token fee. Then, before anyone could stop him, he rushed down the incline leading to the bridge, ran part way across, paused briefly, and threw himself headlong into the icy torrent.[14]

On rescue, Schumann confessed to being shamed and humiliated by his suicide attempt: 'O Clara, I am not worth your love'. He insisted on being placed in a lunatic asylum. After more than two years in the asylum he again tried to take his life. This time he succeeded: he starved himself to death. He died, alone, on 29 July 1856.[15]

How is this sad event to be explained? Why did Schumann starve himself to death?

Imagine that in Schumann's case or situation you get to play Resident Asylum Psychiatrist and try to discover why he starved himself to death. To organize your search for the explanation you distinguish between two sets of facts which pertain to Schumann. The first you call mental or Mind facts; and the second you call neurophysiological or Brain facts. The point of this pattern of organization will become clear when we examine a candidate instance of explanation.

The Mind set of facts includes the following: Schumann was clinically depressed. He was, to use Robert Burton's seventeenth-century but still apt term, severely 'melancholic'.[16]

The Brain set of facts includes the following: Schumann had depleted biogenic amines. These are special chemicals in the brain which help transmit nerve impulses across the gaps (synapses) between nerve cells (neurons).[17]

It is possible to both vary and complement the Mind facts and Brain facts. As resident psychiatrist you might add fine-grained brainy detail concerning such things as molecular structure, location, synthesis, reuptake, and breakdown of biogenic amines. And you could complement the Brain facts by, for example, describing in neurophysiological detail how things were at some much earlier time before Schumann's suicide. The complementary details might look something like this:

Susceptibility to depleted biogenic amines is a genetic inheritance. The following factors in such depletion are heritable traits: abnormalities of biogenic amine metabolism, disturbances of cortisol circadian rhythms, and, finally, deficiencies in the brain–thyroid axis. Several lines of evidence converge in Schumann's case on saying that he inherited such traits and thus his susceptibility to depletion. Depleted biogenic amines were widespread among his family. During maturation these fundamental biological factors interwove with specific neurotransmitter depletion brought about by heightened neuronal excitability; and in Schumann they caused the neurochemical condition of depleted biogenic amines.

Susceptibility and other esoteric complementary neural details aside, however, the central question is: How are the two sets of Brain and Mind facts related? How do Brain and Mind facts fit together to form a unified explanation of Schumann's suicide?

(1) One response is that they do not fit together. Brain facts have absolutely nothing to do with Mind facts. Brain and mind are wholly independent. As far as mind is concerned the brain just is a stone.

This response of course is outlandishly ill-advised. If there is an absolute misfit between brain and mind, then we should expect mind to be invulnerable to direct control or pathology by damage to the brain. In fact, however, as mentioned in the paragraph which started this chapter, just the opposite is true. Consider, for example, not depression, Schumann's malady, but apoplexy or stroke. The mental consequences of apoplexy can include aphasia (loss of understanding of language), amnesia (loss of memory), and agnosia (loss of perceptual powers). From the case of apoplexy and many others it follows that there is a close relation between Mind facts and Brain facts; brain imparts a special vulnerability to mind.

But how intimate? How tight the fit? How vulnerable?

(2) Materialists argue for the most tight fit. Materialism combines both sets of facts into one set: Mind facts somehow are constituted by Brain facts. Materialists physically identify mind with brain. Thus the following hypothesis may be offered by a materialist:

The Mind fact of severe depression consists in the Brain fact of depleted biogenic amines. To be severely depressed is to have depleted biogenic amines.

It is no easy task to winnow through competing explanations of Schumann's suicide. However, suppose you eventually come to endorse the following explanatory sketch couched in Mind fact terms:

Schumann committed suicide because he was severely depressed. A self-destructive response in depression was not alien to Schumann. He had attempted suicide in 1854.

According to materialism, supposing severe depression is depleted biogenic amines, this would mean that you should also endorse the following explanation of Schumann's suicide, which is expressed in terms of Brain facts:

Schumann committed suicide because he had depleted biogenic amines. In other words: 'Schumann committed suicide because he was severely depressed' just means 'because he had depleted biogenic amines'.

However, the materialist explanation is also (assuming Brentano's thesis) in its own way poorly advised. The materialist locates depression altogether physically in the brain. However, Intentionality permeates many sorts of depression. Intentionality occurs, for example, in Schumann's depression. The central constituents in Schumann's mental illness include such aboutness states as his jealousy over Clara's success as a pianist, his desire for recognition as a composer, his feeling of personal worthlessness, his despondency over his failed suicide attempt, and so forth. All such states possess Intentionality. Matters are far from final; but it certainly appears that the current inability of materialists to provide a physical analysis of aboutness means that attitudes such as those of Schumann are not physical states or conditions. Schumann's depression harbored characteristics his neurochemicals lacked. So there is no neat materialist fit between Mind and Brain Schumann facts. Schumann's depression should not be viewed as a neurochemical deficiency. The explanation of his suicide, therefore, cannot occur strictly within the confines of materialism.

(3)   However, aren't Mind facts vulnerable to Brain facts? Perhaps Mind facts are vulnerable to Brain facts without being exhaustively constituted by or identical to them. This is the view of a number of philosophers who have described the relationship between mind and

brain as one of mind/brain *supervenience*.[18] The primary idea behind mind/brain supervenience can be stated quite simply by means of an illustrative thought-experiment.

Suppose we (or God or Mother Nature) create an exact neurophysical replica of Robert Schumann exactly like him cell for cell, molecule for molecule, biogenic amine for biogenic amine. For a mnemonic think of the replica as Replica Schumann. Given that Robert and Replica are exactly alike neurophysically, will the respective Schumanns also share their psychological life? Will Replica be depressed and commit suicide?

If you answer yes, then you should be sympathetic with the concept of mind/brain supervenience. The core idea behind mind/brain supervenience is that there is (and can be) no psychological difference between two persons (or the same person at different times) unless there is a neurophysical difference between them. Robert Schumann, therefore, cannot be said to be depressed unless his replica is depressed. This is because the replica is perfectly like him neurophysically.

The mind/brain supervenience idea can be generalized by means of the following description using the notions of Brain and Mind facts employed above. Briefly, Mind facts are said to *supervene* on Brain facts, and Brain facts are said to constitute the supervenience *base* of Mind facts, just in the sense that any two persons who share all the same Brain facts cannot diverge with respect to any Mind facts. Only if the Brain facts differ can the Mind facts differ. In short, the brain somehow systematically anchors the mind. It is the 'embodiment' or 'realization' of mind.

What, then, of the third or supervenience way of understanding the connection between Mind and Brain facts? Construed as an admonition to respect physical similarities and differences between people, it is difficult to challenge. But supervenience is capable of many different interpretations and has raised questions in the minds of philosophers.

Some puzzlement over supervenience is explanatory in nature. If mind supervenes on brain, then does reference to brain suffice to explain behavior? If and when we discover the supervenience base of Schumann's depression, do we thereby explain his suicide? In addition, in acknowledging supervenience bases, aren't we presupposing the truth of materialism? If the supervenience base of Schumann's depression is depleted biogenic amines, aren't we saying that the depression itself is biogenic amine deficiency?

Consider the query about materialism first. Things would certainly be neat for materialism if minds have brainy supervenience bases, for then, it may seem, even if Brentano's problem could not be solved, materialism might be defended by defending supervenience. However, advocacy of supervenience is not sufficient to make one a materialist. A philosopher can advocate supervenience without advocating materialism.

If mind/brain supervenience holds, materialism can be false. Consider the following analogy. Imagine that you own a recording of Schumann's *Carnaval*, Opus 9. (*Carnaval* is one of his most successful compositions for the piano.) Suppose that this recording truly is beautiful. To adapt the words of one informed admirer of Schumann's piano music, the recording is 'exuberant, poetic, introspective, grand, and intimate in turn'.[19] Suppose also that beauty/*Carnaval* material supervenience holds. That is, suppose that facts about the beauty of the recording (facts about, for example, its exuberance and intimacy) supervene on facts about its material makeup, so that any recording which is just like yours in all physical respects must of necessity be a beautiful *Carnaval* recording.

No matter how we ultimately analyze the notion of beautiful recording, it seems clear that the beauty of the recording cannot be identified with its material makeup. Other recordings, some made on CD, some on magnetic tape, still others on LP records, might be equally beautiful *Carnaval* recordings. There are many, perhaps endlessly many, ways to make a beautiful recording of the piece. Thus arises the possibility that even if the beauty of the recording supervenes on physical features, the beauty itself should not be equated with those features. The beauty conceptually surpasses the material base on which it may supervene. It is capable of multiple realizations or embodiments, which cannot be anticipated or classified without reference to the beauty or features of beauty which they realize.

Now reconsider mind/brain supervenience. An analogous point obtains for mind/brain supervenience. However we ultimately understand depression, there may be many, perhaps endlessly many, ways to make a depressed person: some with depleted amines; others with disordered neurochemicals of other sorts. Thus arises the possibility that even if Schumann's depression supervenes on amine deficiency, depression itself should not be equated with the deficiency. Depression conceptually surpasses the material base on which it may supervene. Indeed, in the words of three scientific researchers on depression: 'Depression cannot be equated with imbalance in one or another class of neurotransmitters, endocrine messengers, or disordered electrolyte metabolism.'[20]

Hence, supervenience is compatible with non-materialism. Supervenience does not presuppose materialism. But what of the explanatory question above about supervenience? Our explanatory question about supervenience was this: If supervenience holds, does reference to brain suffice to explain behavior?

8.6 Explanation and Mind/Brain Supervenience

A number of friends of supervenience claim that if mind supervenes on brain, then this means that all psychological phenomena or facts are best – most fully – explained by theories of their neurophysiological supervenience, i.e. by reference to Brain facts. Supposing mind/brain supervenience, Schumann's suicide is sufficiently accounted for just by reference to Brain facts such as amine depletion. We can and should dispense with explanation by reference to Mind facts. Mind facts, to adapt and modify a remark of psychologists Stephen Kosslyn and Oliver Koenig in another context, are what Brain facts do – explanatorily.[21]

I cannot here provide a systematic discussion of this bold and complex explanatory claim. Yet, in the end, I believe, along with a number of other philosophers, that the claim is unjustified.[22] The concept of supervenience may be useful for a lot of purposes, but explanation is not necessarily one of them. This is because reference to supervenience bases cannot handle numerous questions we need to ask about the mental phenomena to be explained. The power or ability to answer questions is a hallmark of good explanation.[23] There are numerous questions about Schumann's suicide for which supervenience explanation is a failure and for which reference to Mind facts is required.

Consider the diverse phenomena surrounding the suicide: Schumann suffered from severe, recurring depressive episodes throughout his life. Often he was sleepless, hopeless, and agitated. Imaginary voices would tell him he was worthless and that his compositions were dreadful. Both his parents were occasionally severely depressed. A sister had committed suicide. His social behavior alternated between isolation and intimacy. Schumann's marriage was beset with financial problems, the responsibilities of many children, and the conflicts between his compositional career and his wife's ambitions as a pianist. Schumann was emotionally and quite occasionally financially dependent on his wife. A persistent source of stress was Clara's father, who strongly disliked Schumann and had become in the words of one biographer 'his bitter enemy'.[24] The list of troubles goes on.

Schumann was a genius but also a mess. I am reminded of a remark of Carl Jung: 'Great gifts are the fairest, and often the most dangerous fruits on the tree of humanity. They hang on the weakest branches, which easily break.' Schumann's branch broke.

What sense can be made of the surrounding facts about Schumann? Are some of them explanatorily relevant to his suicide? And how can we know?

A common tactic for criticizing explanatory hypotheses is to brand hypotheses as 'superficial' and 'unrevealing'. The suggestion that Schumann's suicide was caused by depleted amines – by the alleged supervenience base of his depression – would be attacked as a shallow explanation, which touches on merely a fragment of the questions which should be asked of his suicide, and then only superficially. Individually it has little explanatory impact.

Consider, by way of illustration, two questions asked of the suicide:

Q1 Why did Schumann starve himself rather than commit suicide some other way?

Q2 Why did Schumann starve himself after two years in the asylum rather than at some earlier time – say soon after admission?

Obviously the supervenience base for depression most likely did not fix the manner of suicide, for whereas in 1854 Schumann threw himself into the Rhine, in 1856 he starved himself to death. If we assume that his amines were depleted in both cases, his mode of attempt differed. So, something other than deficiency must help to account for the suicide. If so, what? Nor does such a base answer why Schumann resorted to self-starvation in 1856 rather than earlier, when his neurochemicals were perhaps equally or even more seriously depleted. The purported relevant supervenience base is unable to answer key questions about the event. So it is explanatorily deficient.

To make the inadequacy even clearer, consider by comparison how reference to Mind facts helps to answer those two questions.

A1 Schumann committed suicide through starvation rather than by other means because he knew he was closely guarded by asylum staff and death by starvation was the only form of suicide the staff could not prevent.

A2 Schumann starved himself in 1856 rather than earlier because prolonged isolation in the asylum made him believe that he would never recover his status as a composer or musician, and confirmed his deepest fear that he was insane. The asylum became, with time, the exact opposite of everything which Schumann hoped for when he volunteered for admission, which, in brief, was a cure for his depression and a restoration of his creative powers. Hence it took the passage of time to evoke the desire for suicide even if the passage did not markedly increase the depression or deplete its neurochemical base.

Given the illuminating and apparently necessary assistance which reference to Mind facts provides in accounting for the suicide, it is difficult to imagine that any explanation couched exclusively in supervenience terms would be superior to an account which includes reference to Mind facts. True, the criticism of supervenience as best explanation might be deflected if it is argued that Mind facts such as Schumann's knowledge of asylum life and desire for suicide also have supervenience bases and that invoking those bases as well as the bases of other relevant surrounding Mind facts can explain the suicide. But surrounding supervenience bases are likely to be horrendously variable and complicated. As we expand the supervenience base from local biographical facts such as the depression of 1856 to more global and still more multiply realizable facts such as family psychological history, knowledge of asylum life, and so on, we will soon get something much more complicated and elusive than we gambled for or anticipated: a perplexing and bewildering galaxy of Brain facts effectively useless for purposes of accounting for the suicide.

It is no wonder, therefore, that explanation exclusively in terms of brainy supervenience does not figure much in contemporary psychological theorizing about depression and many other mood disorders and mental illnesses. Some explanations are of the supervenience sort but most are not. Most are 'mixed' or Brain fact/Mind fact explanations. Many authorities have drawn attention to the complexities involved in trying to establish an explanatory framework for understanding depression. They have argued that depression is best accounted for in terms of

Mind facts, including facts about the family history and environment of the depressed person, supplemented but surely not displaced by reference to Brain facts.[25]

Note that the conclusion that supervenience is explanatorily inadequate does not mean that reference to supervenience is totally irrelevant for explanation. Supervenience facts may be germane to some questions without being relevant to all questions. For instance, they might suggest neurochemical treatments for conditions like depression. Once the identification of a supervenience base is made, the hypothesis that naturally suggests itself is this: zero in on the base to block or dampen the depression. This may be accomplished by drugs like fluoxetine (trade name Prozac) which alter neurochemical levels. True, matters could be, and likely are, tremendously complicated. Likely no single drug neatly parcels out to block just the depression without having other and possibly unwanted side-effects.[26] One reason for this is that one and the same Brain fact may serve as the supervenience base for many Mind facts and play a role in supporting other and perhaps even antagonistic mental states. However, the point being urged here is that, supposing supervenience bases for mind, supervenience facts can be germane to various questions even if they are not relevant to all questions.

Supervenience has come to play an increasingly influential role in the philosophy of mind, reaching its height of appeal in the thesis that supervenience explanations should displace Mind fact explanations. I am reminded of a line from Shakespeare: 'I'll put a girdle round about the earth' (*A Midsummer Night's Dream*, Act II, Sc 1). Supervenience puts the girdle of brain round about mind. On the other hand, it seems that reference just to supervenience bases is inadequate to answer many questions about behavior and mental phenomena. These questions require reference to mind.

To return for a postscript and moral to Schumann. Clara viewed the body of her emaciated husband within an hour of his death: 'I stood by his corpse.... And as I knelt at his bed ... it seemed as if a magnificent spirit was hovering over me – ah, if only he had taken me along.'[27] To Clara her husband's death was a sad mystery; she knew only that she wished to be with him.

It may be all too easy for the champion of supervenience to pronounce that the brain is all that is relevant to the psychological twists and turns of a person like Schumann. However, Brain facts hardly exhaust the mind of this or any other man or woman. Careful inspection of the conceptual and explanatory complexities involved in supervenience offers a different diagnosis. 'There are more things in heaven and earth, Horatio, Than are dreamt of in your philosophy' (*Hamlet*, Act 1, Sc 5).

NOTES

1   On materialism's popularity, see William Bechtel, *Philosophy of Mind: An Overview for Cognitive Science* (Erlbaum, New Jersey, 1988), p. 94.
2   Paul Churchland, 'Eliminative materialism and propositional attitudes', *Journal of Philosophy*, 78 (1981), p. 75.
3   J. J. C. Smart, 'Sensations and brain processes', in *The Philosophy of Mind*, ed. V. C. Chapell (Prentice-Hall, Englewood Cliffs, New Jersey, 1956), p. 161. Reprinted from *The Philosophical Review* (1959).
4   M. Tye, *Ten Problems of Consciousness* (MIT Press, Cambridge, Mass., 1995), p. 57.
5   For discussion, see Herschel Prins, *Bizarre Behaviours: Boundaries of Psychiatric Disorder* (Routledge, Chapman & Hall, London, 1990), pp. 23–41.
6   One does not have to be a materialist to exorcise superstition. One could merely be a naturalist in the following philosophical sense. Naturalism involves understanding the mind in scientifically acceptable terms, though not necessarily in physically scientifically acceptable terms. Materialism is a version of naturalism.
7   Paul Teller, 'A poor man's guide to supervenience and determination', *Southern Journal of Philosophy*, 22, Supplement (1983), p. 147.
8   U. T. Place, 'Is consciousness a brain process?', *The British Journal of Psychology*, 47 (1956), pp. 42–51; J. J. C. Smart, 'Sensations and brain processes'.
9   See, for instance, Elliott Sober, *Core Questions of Philosophy* (Macmillan, New York, 1991), Lecture 18; Owen Flanagan, *The Science of Mind*, 2nd edn (MIT Press, Cambridge, Mass., 1991). I owe the example of Oedipus (to follow) to Sober. To keep things simple, I formulate Descartes' argument differently than does Sober (and most commentators on Descartes). Sober's formulation is in terms of the concept of propertyhood and the principle of the indiscernibility of identicals; mine is in terms of the notion of conceiving-as. There are important differences in these formulations, but discussing them would take us too far afield in this context.
10 D. M. Armstrong, *A Materialist Theory of Mind* (Routledge & Kegan Paul, London, 1968), p. 57.

11 For representative discussion, see Mark Bear, Barry Connors, and Michael Paradiso, *Neuroscience: Exploring the Brain* (Williams & Wilkins, Baltimore, 1996), pp. 264–6; Susan Greenfield, *The Human Brain* (Basic Books, New York, 1997), pp. 41–53.

12 Just *what* we find is a matter of heated debate within the cognitive neuroscientific community. The most popular answer is that we find where information processing of different sorts takes place. A second and related answer is that brain imaging techniques allow theories of the components of cognition to be tested in new ways. See J. Sergent, 'Brain-imaging of cognitive functions', *Trends in Neuroscience*, 17 (1994), pp. 221–37; M. Posner and M. Raichle, 'Precis of *Images of Mind*', *Behavioral and Brain Sciences*, 18, (1995), pp. 327–83 (including peer commentary).

13 Jerry Fodor, *Psychosemantics: The Problem of Meaning in the Philosophy of Mind* (MIT Press, Cambridge, Mass., 1987); *A Theory of Content* (MIT Press, Cambridge, Mass., 1990); Fred Dretske, *Knowledge and the Flow of Information* (MIT Press, Cambridge, Mass., 1981); *Explaining Behavior: Reasons in A World of Causes* (MIT Press, Cambridge, Mass., 1988).

14 Peter Ostwald, *Schumann: The Inner Voices of a Musical Genius* (Northeastern University Press, Boston, 1985), p. 1.

15 For evidence that Schumann committed suicide and by self-starvation, see Ostwald, *Schumann*. It is not, of course, essential to any philosophic points I make in these next two sections of the chapter that Schumann really did commit suicide. The example of Schumann is merely a means to illustrate various notions (such as supervenience). Other real or imaginary examples could be used.

16 Robert Burton, *The Anatomy of Melancholy* (Vintage, New York, 1621/1977).

17 Why include facts about amines among the brain facts which might be explanatorily relevant to Schumann's suicide? The answer is because one of the most popular neurochemical explanations of depression attributes depression to biogenic amine deficiency. See, for example, David Rosenhan and Martin Seligman, *Abnormal Psychology* (Norton, New York, 1984), pp. 323ff. Just such an explanation will be examined later in the chapter.

18 For information on concepts of supervenience and mind-brain supervenience, see Teller, 'A poor man's guide'; J. Kim, 'Concepts of supervenience', *Philosophy and Phenomenological Research*, 65 (1984), pp. 153–76; J. Kim, 'Supervenience', in *A Companion to the Philosophy of Mind*, ed. S. Guttenplan (Blackwell Publishers, Oxford, 1994), pp. 575–83.

19 Harold C. Schonberg, *The Lives of the Great Composers*, 3rd edn (Norton, New York, 1997), p. 180.

20 Peter Whybrow, Hagop Akiskal, and William McKinney, *Mood Disorders: Toward a New Psychobiology* (Plenum, New York, 1984), p. 195.

21 See Stephen M. Kosslyn and Oliver Koenig, *Wet Mind: The New Cognitive Neuroscience* (Macmillan, New York, 1992), p. 432.

22 Frank Jackson and Philip Pettit, 'Causation in the philosophy of mind', *Philosophy and Phenomenological Research*, Vol. L, Supplement (Fall 1990), pp. 195–214; and Harold Kincaid, 'Supervenience and explanation', *Synthese*, 77 (1988), pp. 251–81.

23 See C. B. Cross, 'Explanation and the theory of questions', *Erkenntnis*, 34 (1991), pp. 237–60. Cross refers to an interesting discussion by W. M. Runyan of an incident in the life of Vincent Van Gogh, which, like incidents in Schumann's life, raises multiple questions about the explanatory relevance of Mind facts. See W. M. Runyan, 'Why did Van Gogh cut off his ear?: The problem of alternative explanations in psychobiography', *Journal of Personality and Social Psychology*, 40 (1981), pp. 1070–7.

24 See Ostwald, *Schumann*, p. 306; see also Roy Porter, *A Social History of Madness: The World Through the Eyes of the Insane* (Weidenfeld & Nicolson, New York, 1987), pp. 65–71; Schonberg, *Lives*, p. 174.

25 See Whybrow et al., *Mood Disorders*.

26 See J. F. W. Deakin, 'The clinical relevance of animal models of depression', in *Behavioural Models in Psychopharmacology*, ed. Paul Wilner (Cambridge University Press, Cambridge, 1991), p. 157. See also Bear, Conners, and Paradiso, *Neuroscience: Exploring the Brain*, pp. 402–30, especially pp. 426–8.

27 Quoted in Ostwald, *Schumann*, p. 293.

9

Inside Persons

9.1 A Question of Gender

What is it like to be a person of the opposite sex? Presumably, there is something it is like to be a man and something it is like to be a woman. But can a woman understand the inner life of a man or a man that of a woman? What it is like to be a woman may be at least partially closed off to me: to know a woman's pain, pleasure, happiness, misery – certainly her sensations in childbirth. For I am a man.

Among the various thought experiments and fantasies available in science fiction, one of the most captivating concerns an account of what a society of human androgynies might be like. (An androgyne is a sexually intermediate or indeterminate individual.) In *The Left Hand of Darkness* (1969) Ursula Le Guin describes a cold planet named Winter, which has been inhabited by a race of persons who are androgynous. Once monthly each person – otherwise neither male nor female – enters 'kemmer', a biological period in which s/he becomes sexually fertile and aroused as either a male or female. Lovers, for example, may enter kemmer at the same time, but neither will know in advance whether s/he will become male or female, although one will emerge male, the other female. Any person may either beget ('father') or bear ('mother') a child, and many individuals do both, although at different periods in life.

Le Guin describes the androgynous world of the planet as follows:

There is no unconsenting sex, no rape. As with most mammals other than man, coitus can be performed only by mutual invitation and consent.... There is no division of humanity into strong and weak halves, protective/

protected, dominant/submissive, owner/chattel, active/passive. In fact the whole tendency to dualism that pervades human thinking may be found to be lessened, or changed, on Winter.

Le Guin's attempt to describe a social world around essentially genderless people and to identify the experiential benefits to both 'men' and 'women' alike which would attach to such a world is described by one commentator as representing 'the fulfillment of an ancient human dream: the dream of bridging the gap which separates male and female experience, confining each of us to just half of the human experience.'[1]

In a world of kemmering, people would still bear distinct personalities, but they would know what it is like to be male as well as what it is like to be female. Or at least they would know what certain experiences are like from male and female subjective points of view. Even if persons turned out to be stereotypically masculine or feminine in interests, nothing would follow about one being unable to grasp, capture, or directly experience female or male pains, pleasures, experiences, or sensations. The persons in Le Guin's imaginary world would grasp much better than people do in our world the inner feelings of both men and women.

9.2 What Is It Like to Be a Person?

Suppose you could 'super-kemmer', as it were, and experience life just as a person – a pure person – abstracted from all the particularities of your own situation, not just the particularities of sex and gender. Is there a general way experience appears which all individual persons share beneath, as Owen Flanagan puts it, 'the noise and clatter of their own particularities'?[2]

The move from genderlessness to generality would be a move from understanding male and female experience to understanding some still more universal way of experiencing things: not what it is like to be a man, woman, African philosopher, Irish hockey player, twenty or ninety year old but what it is like to be a person. If there is something it is like to be a person, it is something for each and every reader of this book – and the author too – no matter what otherwise distinguishes and divides us.

In this section of the chapter, we will look at two candidate components in what it is like to be a person. The main idea behind each candidate is that it is supposed to be universal in the inner life of persons. Individuals stripped of either or both components are subtracted in personhood. They are stripped of the sorts of thoughts, feelings, sensations, and attitudes otherwise deeply ingrained in our own – your own, my own – sense of ourselves as persons. Psychologically stripped individuals may partially share in the inner life of personhood, if their deficits are partial, but they are precluded from fully participating in that life.

1 Memory

Is there a general way experience seems to persons? The first truly great British empiricist, John Locke (1632–1704), thought there is. Locke argued that the inner life of persons feels continuous; a person's subjective sense of identity, of direction, of their own intelligence, happiness, and misery are all grounded in the person's autobiographical memory or the connections they take themselves to have to their past. Locke puts the point as follows: 'As far as consciousness can be extended backwards to any past action or thought, so far reaches the . . . person.'[3] From an inner point of view, a person is who they remember themselves being.

Oliver Sacks, a neuropsychologist, in 'The Lost Mariner' in *The Man Who Mistook His Wife for a Hat* (1987), tells the tale of Jimmie R., who lost his autobiographical memory to Korsakoff's disease.[4] (The classical Korsakoff's syndrome is a destruction of memory caused by alcoholism.) Whatever was said or done to Jimmie was likely to be forgotten in a few moments time. Sacks asks, 'What sort of world, what sort of self, can be preserved in a man who has lost the greater part of his memory and, with this, his past, and his moorings in time?' (p. 23). Jimmie impressed Sacks as, 'isolated in a single moment of being . . . [a] man without a past (or future), stuck in a constantly changing, meaningless moment' (p. 29).

Jimmie's story, and those of others like him, reveal how within persons the continuities of autobiographical memory are necessary for a wide variety of thoughts and experiences. The necessity can be made vivid by considering, by way of illustration, a connection between intending and acting.

A person intends an action only if the person wants himself to perform the action. For someone to intend to, say, play chess, they must want that they themselves play chess. Sacks takes it as given that Jimmie's connections between intending and acting were severed. He could form plans or intentions but of only a few moments duration. Carrying out complex intentions and tasks was beyond him; he would forget his goals. 'He was superb at calculations, but only if they could be done at lightening speed' (p. 27). If there were many steps, and too much time involved, he forgot what he intended, and where he was in the process. His intelligent behavior was fragmented and dislocated. Chess, for instance, was beyond him. It was beyond him not because he was unintelligent; he was bright. It was beyond him because in chess there is an ongoing need to remember one's previous intentions, moves, strategies, and wants. Stripped of that memory one is stripped of capacity for the game.

Guilt and pride were also impossible for Jimmie. For someone to feel guilty for, say, stealing a piece of cake or to take pride in accomplishing a task, say, writing a poem, one must remember the theft and the task. Guilt and pride are bound by contentful autobiographical memories, whereas Jimmie lived in an often surprising succession of unrecollected impressions and events. 'Clearly, passionately, he wanted something to do; he wanted to do, to be, to feel – and could not; he wanted sense, he wanted purpose' (p. 37). Jimmie wanted purpose, but his present could not provide purpose without reference to the past.

If Locke is right, autobiographical memory is an essential and universal element in the inner life of persons. Without the continuity and connectedness that memory makes possible, a distinctively personal life, in any but the most truncated sense, is not possible. In cases like Jimmie's, victims of Korsakoff's syndrome, acute schizophrenia, advanced Alzheimer's disease, and others like them when individuals cannot extend their consciousness from one moment to the next, cannot consciously integrate personal past with present, people are 'condemned to a sort of . . . froth, a meaningless fluttering on the surface of life' (p. 39). Living on the surface, individuals are occluded from the inner life, the 'what it is like' of personhood. Theirs is a life without aspiration, without remembered achievement, without the backward stretch of recoverable hope.

2 The conviction of freedom

Locke is not alone in believing that there are universal elements in personal experience. (I will return to Locke's emphasis on memory much later in the chapter in discussing happiness.) In *Minds, Brains, and*

Science (1984), John Searle argues that a 'conviction of freedom' is built into what it is like to be a person. By 'conviction of freedom' Searle means, 'each thing we do carries the conviction ... that we could be doing something else right here and now, that is, all other conditions remaining the same.'[5] The conviction is the belief that one has *dual power*, that is, the ability to choose or do something or to choose or do something else (including refrain).[6] Searle writes:

> Reflect ... on the character of the experiences you have as you engage in normal, everyday, ordinary ... actions. You will sense the possibility of alternative courses of action built into those experiences. Raise your arm or walk across the room or take a drink of water, and you will see that at any point in the experience you have a sense of alternative courses of action open to you.[7]

New York University's Thomas Nagel makes a similar point when he writes: 'From the inside, when we act, alternative possibilities seem to lie open before us: to turn to the right or left, to order this dish or that, to vote for one candidate or the other – and one of the possibilities is made actual by what we do.'[8]

The thesis that intentional action includes a subjective sense of freedom or dual power may be illustrated by means of an imaginary example. The example involves two prototypical antecedents of conscious intentional action: deliberation and decision.

Suppose Beth, a college student, is deliberating whether to pay her tuition fees. She weighs the reasons on both sides. For instance, on one side, she remembers that the college did not permit her to take the course she needed in physics; the course over-enrolled. She remembers that she could not park her car near the dormitory where she lived. She recognizes that she has not yet picked a major and worries whether she truly belongs in college without a major. On the other side, Beth remembers that the philosophy course in which ultimately she did enroll (when physics closed) was unexpectedly enjoyable. She recollects with enthusiasm the instructor's explanation of the concept of kemmer. She suspects that finding a major is less important than getting a good general education; and she recalls that some of her happiest moments have been in college. So, after considering pros and cons, she finally makes up her mind. She decides, all things considered, to pay her tuition. If Beth is a conscientious ('continent') agent, she will then pay her tuition.

In trying to decide whether to pay it is important to note that Beth believes that she can either pay or not pay. She believes she possesses dual power. If we revise the story so that she believes that her cash reserves are empty and that she cannot secure money, then she could not properly decide whether to pay. To see herself deciding it must seem to her as if it is up to her how she decides. The buck stops (tuition starts) here because her power of alternative choice and action subjectively originates here.

Searle and Nagel are not alone in claiming that the inner life of persons contains a conviction of freedom and that in acting persons believe themselves to possess dual power. It is one of the primary ideas which has fueled traditional debate over the issue of *freedom of will* or *free choice*. To possess free will or the power of free choice is – in the minds of many philosophers – to possess dual power: the power to decide one way or the other. Failure to possess such power spells absence of free will. Searle and Nagel, however, are almost alone among philosophers who write on free will to say candidly that the conviction although essential or unavoidable is also unreasonable or unwarranted.[9] No genuine decision or action can take place without the conviction but, alas, no person truly is entitled to it.

Nagel's candor ultimately is more opaque than Searle's. So I will focus on the reasoning behind Searle's claim.

According to Searle we cannot abandon the conviction of freedom since 'that conviction is built into every normal, conscious intelligent action'.[10] To be an agent is to seem to oneself 'dually' powerful. Why then assert that the conviction is unreasonable or unwarranted? Searle claims that the conviction is unreasonable because it is inconsistent with what we know from science. Science's 'conception of . . . reality simply does not allow for . . . freedom'.[11]

9.3 Freedom and Explanation

Science does not allow for freedom? Searle assumes that if the conviction of freedom is warranted it must be consistent with science. If dual power is incompatible with science, then the conviction is unreasonable and must be abandoned.

It is instructive to distinguish two ways in which the conviction of freedom may be inconsistent or incompatible with science. It may be inconsistent either locally or globally. Local inconsistency means that a particular agent is mistaken that they possess dual power, given what science says or implies about them and people of their type. To be incompatible globally means that any agent is mistaken in the conviction, given what science says about human behavior *period*.

Consider Arthur, an advanced alcoholic. Suppose for the sake of argument that medical science shows that alcoholism is a disease.[12] The classic disease concept of alcoholism includes the following element: 'Those afflicted with the disease eventually progress to uncontrolled drinking because the disease produces a distinctive disability: loss of dual power in the matter of drinking.'

Arthur enters a bar and wonders whether to order a drink. If Searle is right, and Arthur is otherwise normal, he will seem to himself to have the (dual) power to order or to not order. Suppose he weighs reasons on both sides. For instance, he remembers the pleasant drink he had earlier in the day, and he feels acute discomfort associated with not drinking. On the other side, he is beginning to notice negative personal and social consequences of heavy drinking: the depletion of his bank account, the strain on his marriage, insomnia, and fatigue. After weighing reasons, he makes a choice. He decides, all things considered, to drink.

Now the question arises does Arthur truly possess dual power in ordering. The locally relevant facts in the case – that he is an advanced alcoholic and that alcoholism is a disease – mean that although Arthur *feels* 'dually' powerful, he is not. According to science, he is in the grip of a disease. He lacks the ability to refrain.

Supposition of Arthur's disease means that Arthur is unfree, although he feels free. The scientific facts about alcoholism are locally incompatible with his freedom of choice in deciding whether to order. However, not everyone, fortunately, suffers from alcoholism or is beset with disease-like disability. So local incompatibility is not the source of Searle's claim that the conviction of freedom is unwarranted.

Searle's charge that the conviction is unreasonable has a different source. Global incompatibility is the source. On Searle's view of science, no one – neither alcoholic, nor you, nor me – possesses dual power in any situation. Each and every one of our decisions and actions is unfree.

Why is each and every one of our decisions and actions unfree? If we consider science, what is there in science that excludes dual power?

According to Searle, an assumption underlies science which is globally incompatible with the claim that persons possess dual power. Searle never states the assumption explicitly, but it lies behind his argument as well as behind many other philosophers' writings on free will. This is the assumption, which I shall call the *externalist explanation assumption*, that each and every decision and action has a sufficient cause or explanation altogether outside itself. We decide to act in the manner that we do because our decisions and actions follow the heels of conditions which rest ultimately outside those decisions and actions.

Advocates of the externalist explanation assumption develop the assumption in different ways, depending upon what is presumed contained in the notion of explanation or cause being outside the event or decision explained. Two kinds of externality or 'outsideness' may be distinguished. The first kind, which I shall call *sub-personal* or *vertical* externality, has two salient features: (1) it denies that persons have ultimate control over their choices or actions; and (2) it asserts that explanation of behavior can and must be given in sub-personal neuroscientific or (to use the language of the last chapter) Brain-fact terms. An advocate of sub-personal externality may endorse a version of the thesis discussed in the previous chapter that behavior is best explained by reference to brainy supervenience bases of mental states. Searle is attracted to sub-personal externalist explanation. Actions, he says, 'are entirely a matter of neurons and neuron firings at synapses'.[13] However, the previous chapter by raising doubts about the explanatory scope of supervenience suggests that sub-personal externalist explanation of psychological phenomena (decision, action) should be resisted.

In any case there is another kind of explanatory externalism, *horizontal* or *backtracking* externalism, which possesses (1), lacks (2), but asserts (3) that events in an agent's past suffice to explain the person's choices and actions and hence they are wholly outside the decision itself. In order to accommodate the previous chapter's misgivings about neuroscientific explanation, I shall couch Searle's claim that science is incompatible with dual power in backtracking externalist terms.

Imagine that you and I enroll as medical students. For me, in light of my heretofore disappointing academic career, enrolling is a fragile gamble. I have not been a good student; but, somehow, perhaps through my parents' political connections, I am admitted and enroll. For you, in light of your stunning record of academic success, it is a natural step. You graduated near the top of our college class.

Suppose I take my first exam, do poorly, and decide to give up. You take your first exam, do equally poorly, but decide to persist. The question is: Why do I decide to give up, whereas you choose to persist?

Consider a sample scientific explanation which is couched in back-tracking externalist terms. In 1975 Martin Seligman, a professor of psychology at the University of Pennsylvania, conducted scientific inquiries into the sources of quitting and persistence, and reported these in a book with the fascinating title of *Helplessness: On Depression, Development, and Death.* Although Seligman's theory, the so-called learned helplessness model of depression, has had to be refined and reformulated, it remains, more than twenty years later, a primary contender for the title of Best Explanation of Quitting and Persistence in the scientific literature.[14] The gist of Seligman's explanation of the difference between the two sorts of decisions and behavior goes like this:

> Imagine someone (like me, above) with a history of failure; when such a person receives disappointment in spite of their efforts, the person learns that it is pointless to persevere. Impediments are perceived as insurmountable barriers to success. Such a person learns to be help-less. By contrast, imagine someone (you above) with a history of success; when such a person achieves positive results because of their efforts, they learn that it is purposeful to persevere. Impediments stimulate effort. Such a person learns to be industrious.

Within the learned helplessness model, the following explanation may be offered of why I gave up and you persisted:

> I have learned to be helpless. You have learned to be industrious. Failure on my first exam reinforced my history of academic dis-appointment and my expectation that nothing I can do is likely to bring success. Failure on your first exam inspired your effort. You believe that future success still is under your control despite a temporary setback.

My point in mentioning Seligman's model is not to suggest that it is correct or to assert that frustrated history is helpless destiny. I want to make a different point. The point is that the model explains certain decisions in terms of circumstances wholly outside the decisions them-selves. The decisions are accounted for by backtracking: by explanatory reference to past events and personal history. Moreover, Seligman's model illustrates Searle's contention that science leaves no elbow room for dual power, not just for alcoholics, but even for medical students.

9.4 The Dilemma of Free Will

If decisions are explained in terms of circumstances wholly outside or before themselves, then agents lack dual power. This is the conclusion of the so-called consequence argument defended in the free will literature by Peter Van Inwagen and others.[15] The main idea behind the consequence argument goes like this:

1 If persons possess dual power, then we can decide to do something or decide to do something else (such as refrain).
2 If science sufficiently explains decisions and actions in terms of circumstances or events wholly before their occurrence, then we possess dual power only if we can control those past events. Only if we can change the past do we have the power to choose differently now.
3 However, we cannot change the past. What is done cannot be undone. Indeed, ultimately, the past stretches through childhood and before birth. And we certainly cannot change events before birth.
4 Therefore, if science sufficiently explains our decisions in terms of wholly prior events, we do not possess dual power.

As Van Inwagen puts it, 'what went on before we were born' is not up to us, 'therefore the consequences of those things (including our present acts) are not up to us.'[16]

The consequence argument is based on the notion that dual power is incompatible with the assumption that decision and action are sufficiently explained by wholly past circumstances. What is a sufficient explanation? Simply put, a sufficient explanation shows that what is explained is necessitated; under the circumstances (including the laws of nature) it could not have been otherwise. Thus, to take a brief nonhuman illustration, if the breaking of a dam sufficiently explains the flooding of the valley, and the dam breaks, then the valley must be flooded. We can't correctly say that the dam broke but the valley could have been spared. The break suffices.

It is also important for the consequence argument that the events cited in a sufficient explanation occur wholly in the past. We may wish that the flood could have been avoided. However, if sufficient explanation rests in the burst dam, then the flood could have been avoided only if the dam did not burst. Hence, to avoid the flood, one would have to travel backwards in time, which presumably is impossible, and somehow prevent the break.

The consequence argument hinges on prior occurrences which suffice for explanation. Past breaks determine current floods.

What about the human case? Is failing the first test sufficient to make a person quit medical school? Not necessarily: it depends on personal history. According to the learned helplessness model, it depends on whether I have a record of disappointment and frustration. If I have a disappointing history, then the history explains why I gave up after the first exam. We can't correctly say that I failed the test but could have persisted. Giving up follows the determining heels of history.

Of course, I may feel in deciding to give up as if the future contains the possibility of persistence, and that, despite my past record, I have the (dual) power to give up or to persist. However, since history is past, and suffices to quit, then I could persist only if the personal history were otherwise.

The consequence argument makes it easy to see why Searle asserts that science is inconsistent with dual power. Science, for Searle, is committed to explanatory externalism and explanatory externalism is incompatible with dual power.

Explanatory externalism (sub-personal or backtracking) is capable of different variations or formulations. Some are versions of what philosophers call *strict determinism* or *absolute necessitation*; others are not. An externalism is strictly deterministic or absolutely necessitarian if it is committed to a highly rigid form of scientific explanation, according to which events are and must be explained by reference to ironclad and exceptionless natural or physical laws. Searle is not committed to determinism of the strict sort, which is fortunate because in some areas of contemporary science, like quantum mechanics, the occurrence of relevant events cannot be explained by exceptionless laws. Some more pliant form of determinism, perhaps of a statistical sort, fits Searle's picture. Such determinism, says Searle, 'seems to be consistent with the way the world in fact proceeds'.[17]

Specific versions of determinism and explanatory externalism aside,

Searle (and Nagel, too) leaves us in a nasty dilemma. The dilemma is as follows. According to Searle, when we act – consciously, deliberately – we believe we possess dual power. We carry the conviction 'that we could be doing something else right here and now . . . all conditions remaining the same.'[18] However, this belief in freedom or dual power is an embarrassing scientifically misbegotten falsehood. Something we cannot abandon when we act (the conviction of freedom or dual power), we should abandon (because it conflicts with science). 'Science', say Searle, 'allows no place for freedom of the will.'[19] Searle lodges us between the proverbial rock and hard place.

It is instructive to note that the Searlean dilemma arises only if (a) the externalist explanation assumption is sound or (b) we must decide and act with a conviction of dual power. If either the assumption of explanatory externalism is unsound or we can decide and act without believing ourselves dually powerful, then we can escape the dilemma.

Some philosophers sympathetic to free will reject (a). They argue that at least some decisions or actions cannot be sufficiently explained by reference to circumstances altogether outside themselves. Explanatory externalism is incorrect. Explanation of decision and action is possible, but externalist explanation is not comprehensive. This contrary view may be dubbed explanatory *internalism*. The basic idea is this: At least some choices and actions partly are self-explaining or have sufficient explanations partly within themselves. We possess ultimate control over some of our decisions and actions. That we possess ultimate control over some of our decisions and actions does not entail that we are able to decide and act in causal isolation; internal control is partial. One common theme in internalist arguments is that ultimate control is limited and structured by the background abilities, history, and environment of the free or dually powerful person.[20]

Other philosophers antipathetic to free will reject (b). They argue that people can and perhaps do decide and act without believing themselves dually powerful. A prototypical decision, on this view, is one in which I weigh pros and cons but suppress any assumption that my decision is up to me; perhaps I picture myself as ignorant of the ultimate sources of my behavior. I may allow that subjectively alternate possibilities seem dependent upon me. I believe, however, that this impression is woefully incorrect. The present is determined; the future is outside my control.

Much about the topic of freedom of will can be learned by systematically comparing and contrasting the cases for rejecting (a) or (b). We have neither time nor conceptual resources to conduct a systematic comparison and contrast here. So, let us learn what we can from a quick and unsystematic discussion. I will return, in a manner, to Searle's free will dilemma later.

9.5 Folk Psychology, Freedom, and Compatibilism

In framing a discussion of whether (a) or (b) should be rejected, I want to consider a distinction introduced into the philosophical literature by Wilfred Sellars (1912–89), one of the most systematic philosophers of the twentieth century.[21] Sellars draws a distinction which has become standard in philosophic writings on personhood. This is the distinction between the world as it *manifestly appears* and the world as conceived in the *scientific image*. Roughly, the manifest image is the world of ordinary experience; the world as conceived by ordinary folk. It is the world of such familiar objects as tables and chairs. It is the world that contains all the qualities and sensations we experience: of color, size, motion, taste, pleasure, pain, and so on. The scientific image is the world of scientific entities – atoms, protons, electrons, velocity, force, and so on; the world of theoretical scientists and especially of physicists.

In comparing and contrasting the two images, some characteristics of the manifest image survive in the scientific image. Others, however, find or seem to find no place in science. Size and motion, for example, survive. Colors and chairs, for instance, do not. Red chairs play a certain role in everyday life; they are for sitting and ornamenting perhaps with yellow pillows. However, all the stuff we call 'chairs' really is – to Sellars' physical scientists – clouds of colorless molecules. Granny's rocker is bits of matter off which light bounces. The red color of her chair is replaced in the scientific image by frequencies of light waves, for instance, and channels of retinal stimulation.

There is at best limited agreement among philosophers as to just what the manifest image says or implies about persons, but a common theme in recent discussions is that the manifest image includes a psychological theory of persons. It includes a 'story' of what personhood is and of how and why persons decide and act.[22] Arguably, at the center of this theory or story, sometimes called *common sense* or *folk* psychology, is the assumption that people are both free and rational agents. To be a person and to decide and act is to possess the power of free decision and action.

It is also to possess the ability to exercise this power in a non-arbitrary or reasonable manner.[23]

What does rational agency involve? Rational agents make rational decisions and perform rational actions. As readers of the seventh chapter may recall, to the extent that an action (or decision) is rational it occurs for reasons of the agent. Rational actions contribute to the purposes and goals for which the person decides and acts. To take two simple illustrations, Beth's decision to pay tuition fees contributes to her goal of a college education. Your persistence in medical school contributes to your purpose to become a doctor.

Folk psychology is a controversial tale. Philosophers are divided on whether folk psychology is sacrosanct or should and can be replaced by scientific psychology – the psychology of the scientific image. An *eliminative materialist* approach to folk psychology rejects everything about folk psychology. Eliminative materialism says that the manifest image of persons can and should be flouted; not just the idea that persons possess dual power, but the idea that persons act for reasons.[24]

Most philosophers of mind, however, disagree with eliminativists that science can and should replace folk psychology. They contend that 'folk psychology is here to stay' and that it can be integrated with science, although each and every aspect of folk psychology may not be retained in the final integrationist picture.[25] On the matter of freedom, there are two main models or conceptions of the integration of folk psychology with science. On the first model, which I shall call the *anti-dual power model*, the assumption that persons possess dual power must be jettisoned or replaced. Persons undergo beliefs and desires and make rational decisions, but these are explained by reference to outside events. The most detailed and popular version of the anti-dual power model is *compatibilism*. Compatibilism dissociates two notions which otherwise are associated (and have been associated here): freedom and dual power. A type of freedom of decision and action, compatibilism insists, is compatible with both the denial of dual power and the assertion of explanatory externalism.

The pivotal project for compatibilism is to make freedom of an agent-relevant type square with explanatory externalism (determinism of the externalist sort). Versions of compatibilism are varied. Frequently a compatibilist model begins with a denial of dual power, the assertion of explanatory externalism, and then follows this with the identification of a causal factor (compatible with the ultimate external control of decisions and actions) which serves as the basis of compatibilist freedom. Often this proposed factor is rationality: the capacity of persons to decide and to act rationally. Think of Beth. 'Beth freely paid her tuition fees' does not mean, on the compatibilist model, that she could have refrained. It means, according to a popular version of compatibilism, that she acted rationally. In her own mind she had better reason to pay than to not pay. So, in paying she decided and acted 'freely', compatibly with external control of decision and action.

A second *dual-power* (incompatibilist) model or conception wants Beth to have the stronger and dually powerful 'It was up to her whether she paid.' 'Beth could have not paid instead.'

Some philosophers are convinced that when we get down to our own deepest sense of ourselves as agents, there is nowhere deeper to probe than the conviction of dual power. Self-denial or suppression of this conviction by advocating compatibilism is a kind of conceptual blindness or bogus self-comprehension. One such philosopher is Searle. 'Compatibilism', says Searle, 'denies the substance of free will while maintaining its verbal shell.'[26]

In choosing whether to favor an anti-dual power and perhaps compatibilist model or a dual power model of the integration of folk psychology with science, which model should we embrace? There is, alas, weakness in both models.

The dual power model has difficulty trying to explain how a decision which ultimately is not controlled by external events can avoid being inexplicable *period*. Rejecting externalist explanation of decision and action seems tantamount to rejecting explanation of decision and action. However, the anti-dual power model has trouble describing how I can legitimately view myself as an agent without taking myself to possess dual power. The presence of dual power should be a puzzle to us; the absence of dual power is a displacement of us. Let me explain.

Suppose I decided to give up medical school. As a reflective rational agent I am supposed to be able to explain why I made the decision by citing my reasons. But if the choice was free and I possessed dual power, I could equally have chosen to persist. If I had been rational in persisting, I am also supposed to be able to explain why I persisted by citing reasons for persisting. Either way, as rational agent my reasons for choosing are supposed to explain my choosing. Free choice is not just dual power; it is dual rational power. If I am free, I am rationally free. Free decisions are supposed to be reasonable either way.

However, a question needs to be asked. Doesn't the presence of dual power leave the particular choice 'hopelessly under-determined'? Why did I give up rather than persist, if I was able rationally to do either? Without externalism there seems no way to explain why I decided one way rather than an alternative way which was equally and rationally open to me. If I am able to explain why I gave up by citing my reasons for giving up, but would have been able to explain why I persisted by citing my reasons for persisting, then why did I quit rather than persist? Deciding one way rather than the other seems to be something for which there is no explanation, at least no explanation by reference to internal considerations (reasons). Asked why I stopped rather than persisted, it seems I can only say 'I just did'.

'I just did' is not the only explanation available if I embrace explanatory externalism and deny the presence of dual power. By couching explanation of choice in terms of past events the event can be explained. Why did I give up rather than persist? True, I had reasons for giving up as well as for persisting. However, I was moved by reasons for giving up rather than for persisting because of my history: I am a product of learned helplessness. Had I been a product of learned hopefulness or industriousness, I would have been moved by reasons for persisting and persisted instead. Of course, externalist explanation renders unwarranted the claim that my choice was free (in the incompatibilist sense of expressing dual power). My decision is no longer assignable to me as its ultimate origin or source, but instead is a link in a history which suffices for the decision. Externalism – as noted in the consequence argument – eliminates freedom as dual power.

The anti-dual power model may look appealing. But alongside its apparent explanatory benefits, the model harbors an important weakness. It is an extraordinarily unagentic, impersonal portrayal of human decision and action.

An agent *does* something; he or she deliberates, decides, and acts. That which is not an agent does nothing; it is patient (perhaps acted upon). Thus, for example, we talk of rain falling, but it would be more scientifically accurate to say that past events (e.g. rising barometric pressure) bring about rain. Rain is not the agent of falling; it does not *do* anything. By contrast, when Beth pays her tuition fees, that is something she does; she acts. She is not acted upon.

Suppose we look from an anti-dual power/externalist point of view at Beth's decision to pay her tuition fees. We imagine the entire flow of

Beth's history available before us. We see that right at the edge of that flow sits Beth, in the student accounting office, debating whether to pay tuition fees. We also see, although Beth does not grasp this yet, that circumstances wholly other than the decision suffice for her decision. If she believes, with a conviction of freedom, that she has dual power, she is mistaken. The image of herself as able to pay or to not pay is a conceptual mirage. She cannot change the past; she cannot change what she is fated to decide. 'Deciding' is something that happens to her, not something she does. Just as barometric pressure makes rain fall, past circumstances make Beth pay her fees. The decision is all sparkle, glitter, and noise; her past does all the necessary work.[27]

The anti-dual power model appears to throw the baby (decision, agency, action, individual person) out with the bathwater (incompatibilist free will, dual power). Thomas Nagel sums up the weakness with the model as follows: 'Something peculiar happens when we view action from an ... external standpoint. Some of its most important features seem to vanish under the ... gaze. Actions seem no longer assignable to individual agents as sources, but become instead components of the flux of events in the world of which the agent is a part.'[28]

Each of these models – dual power and anti-dual power – has advocates arguing in favor of its picture of the integration of folk psychological commitments with science. If the scientific worldview is not deterministic, for example, then, at a maximum, specific details of decision and action may underwrite the dual power model of internalist explanation of some decision and action. Decision may be structured but not fixed or set by natural laws and personal history. But one common thrust to anti-dual power/externalist arguments is that externalist explanation remains indispensable for decision and action. There is an explanatory indeterminacy when only internal sources of behavior are included. There is an inability to account for decision and action in terms of internal factors alone.

Dual power/anti-dual power. Internalism/externalism. Backtracking/sub-personal. Incompatibilism/compatibilism. Folk psychology/science. Philosophers don't lack for terms and contrasts in discussing the conviction of freedom.

What of Searle's dilemma? Searle's dilemma is pressing and genuine, and it would be grand to dissolve it right here and now. But we are not in a position to do that. It would not be much of an understatement to say that philosophers are far from the last word on freedom. Here we have examined only first words.

On one occasion the philosopher Ludwig Wittgenstein observed that some philosophers are like a tightrope walker, who look as though they are walking on nothing but air. Their support is the slenderest possible. 'And yet it really is possible to walk on it.'

Wittgenstein was not thinking specifically of philosophers discussing the conviction of freedom, embracing dual power, rejecting dual power, although it seems he could have. In any case, even if we have not dissolved Searle's dilemma, we may admire how the debaters stand. We may also nervously wonder where they will land.

9.6 Happy Ending

No discussion of what it is like to be a person is complete without mention of happiness. Three hundred years before the birth of Christ, Aristotle concluded one of the most famous passages in the history of philosophy with the thesis that, more than anything else, persons want to be happy.[29] While some people may doubt whether happiness is so singly important, none can doubt that happiness *is* important. Given the opportunity for happiness or unhappiness, no person would willingly (rationally, freely?) choose unhappiness.

However, it does not take observational genius to realize that happiness is hard to achieve. The world is not designed with the happiness of people in mind. It is filled with hardship of all sorts. Millions of people lead lives of brutal misery and suffering. Some philosophers, such as the philosophical pessimist, Arthur Schopenhauer (1788–1860), have even gone so far as to say that given the evils of the world happiness is not possible. No person of sane or sound mind could be happy. Only a fool or a madman can be happy. Others such as Bertrand Russell (1872–1970) in his book *The Conquest of Happiness* (1930) admit that life is often unhappy, but contend that many people are unhappy simply because they do not know what happiness is. Sensitive, intelligent people can be happy if they set their minds to it, although before seeking happiness, people should ponder what they seek.

What is happiness? My dictionary defines 'happiness' as a feeling of pleasure or contentment, in short happiness is identified with 'happy feeling'. To be happy is to feel happy. However, philosophers and psychologists often distinguish happiness as a feeling from happiness in one's person. Georg Henrik von Wright in *The Varieties of Goodness* (1963), says that a happy person is someone who in judging or assessing the circumstances of his or her life derives pleasure or satisfaction from those circumstances. 'Happiness is not in the circumstances' but 'springs into being' because of the judgment or assessment of the circumstances.

Perhaps no psychologist has spent more time or energy in the investigation of happiness than Mihaly Csikszentmihalyi, professor and former chairperson of the Department of Psychology at the University of Chicago. In his *Flow: The Psychology of Optimal Experience* (1990), he claims that a happy person is someone who derives satisfaction from reflection on his 'life themes' – the overall character and structure of his life. He writes: 'The tide of rising expectations is stilled; unfulfilled needs no longer trouble the mind.'

What is the difference between happiness as a feeling (of pleasure or contentment) and happiness in one's person over circumstances or themes of one's life? The difference is twofold. One is that we cannot assume that just because a person feels happy that they are happy as a person. To be a happy person is to be in a certain positive relationship to one's life; and someone can be in a positive relationship to their life even though unpleasant things happen and even though they feel unhappy at the present time. Perhaps they have a severe headache or have just discovered that their car needs an expensive repair. They feel unhappy at the moment, but otherwise they are pleased with the gist or thrust of their life. If, by contrast, news of repair makes them an unhappy person, we should be pinpointing not only, or perhaps not at all, current unhappy feelings, but discouragement and regret over life itself – its themes and circumstances. Perhaps news of the bad car infects their assessment of life and turns it sour and negative.

Similar observations can be made about happy feelings and unhappy persons. As von Wright writes: 'A piece of news, say of an unexpected inheritance, can make a man jump with joy. But whether it makes him happy . . . can only be seen from effects of a longer lasting and less obvious showing on his subsequent life.' Happy feelings – pleasure, contentment, gladness – may make important contributions toward being a happy person, but they can occur in a person without making them happy as a person. To be a happy person they must pass positive judgment on their life; perhaps not each and every moment, but on the living of it and on whether they are satisfied with its course and character.

Another – the second – significant difference between happiness as a feeling and in one's person can be described as follows: Happy people are not crushed or degraded by negativity. Someone engulfed by negativity, such as a severely guilt-ridden person, may still experience (albeit occasional) happy feelings. They may be pleased to see their children, take delight in an ice-cold beer, and even appreciate that on balance their days are not filled with suffering. But they are unhappy given the judgment they pass on their 'circumstances of life'. They may believe that they do not deserve to live or that they should be punished or that they are not worthy of their children's visit. Unhappy judgments may insinuate themselves into their daily routine making them feel afflicted in their person, although not for this reason precluded from pleasurable (happy) feelings.

Manic depressives are notoriously capable of happy feelings but are unhappy as persons.[30] Robert Schumann, the composer discussed in the last chapter, seems to have been a manic depressive. Schumann felt elevated, expansive, glad, for periods of weeks or even months, all the while harboring, in some sense, attitudes of inadequacy and self-reproach, and unable to function effectively or prudently socially and occupationally. His life was at loose ends and lacked positive self-assessment despite his expansive efforts to positively reconstitute it.

In a different and indirect way, nonhuman animals help to show that happy feelings are possible without being happy as a person. There are profound differences between the attitudes and capacities of animals and human beings. For instance, we human beings are capable of passing judgment on the overall circumstances of life. We can write autobiographies, keep diaries, appreciate the course of life, and so on. At the same time, nonhuman animals cannot do these things. There are limited if difficult to precisely define horizons within which animals think. Life *as a whole* cannot be a source of happiness for them. Life on balance may be pleasant for them, but they cannot reflect upon and appreciate that balance. So, although there seem to be situations in which an animal (a dolphin, chimp, whatever) has positive or 'happy' feelings, there are no situations in which it is happy by virtue of assessing the circumstances of life. People, by contrast, can be happy both in the balance and over the balance; they can possess happy feelings as well as happiness over the circumstances of life.

To sum up, when Russell asks, What is happiness? we must distinguish happiness in one's person from happy feeling. The hypothesis I offer is that although happiness comes in many forms, and has many distinguishable elements or ingredients, some of which no doubt include happy feelings, a happy person is someone who in judging the circumstances of their life and its themes is pleased and satisfied. There is in them a conviction that their life is worth living.

The thesis that happiness in one's person does not rest on mere feeling can be complemented in a number of ways. One line of complementary development consists in identifying components of happiness other than feeling.

I propose that an essential component is self-respect or self-worth. Self-respect is necessary if one is to avoid becoming defeated and helpless in the face of life's disappointments and obstacles. At some point, especially during sustained and unrelieved blows to hopes and expectations, people may begin to give up. Disappointed medical students lose enthusiasm and become alienated from medical school; famous composers (like Schumann) whose lives are littered with marital discord, financial debt, and unachieved ambition become apathetic and depressed. Defeat, Bertrand Russell remarks, 'makes people feel that nothing is worth doing.' Kierkegaard writes that a person who is consistently disappointed may feel that life is 'like a series of consonants only' and be rendered 'dumb'.[31] Such an individual may suffer from 'despair of necessity due to lack of possibility' (unhappiness over efforts which seem ineffectual and useless).

A person who respects themselves, by contrast, and who values themselves despite faults and failures, may be able to swing free of unhappiness over disappointment and defeat. Indeed, self-respecting people often seem able to press forward with renewed efforts invigorated by otherwise negative occurrences.

Another and related essential component in happiness is autobiographical memory. Without autobiographical memory an individual may experience happy feelings but cannot be happy as a person. Even if such a subject may somehow qualify as a person they cannot count as a happy person.

Memory and recollection are necessities of the happy person, providing awareness of life themes and a perspective on the present – a broad sense of what life means to the person in the way of achievement and defeat. Only in the light of memories can a person's life assume its proper depth and meaning, for in that light a person can distinguish between the conditions of life which matter to them and those which are trivial and unimportant.

Amos Tversky was a professor of psychology at Stanford University and a recipient of the prestigious MacArthur Prize in 1984. Dale Griffen is a psychologist at the University of Waterloo in Canada. Together in a 1991 paper they contend that there are two components in happiness: one is 'endowment' (roughly, how a person feels, their current experience), and the other is 'contrast'; in particular, the contrast between a person's current condition and remembered past experience.[32] Tversky and Griffen claim that a person who cannot contrast current with past experience cannot be happy as a person. For instance, they cannot be relieved when a dreaded event does not happen or cheered when a hoped for event does occur.

Here we should agree. For victims of Korsakoff's syndrome, and others unable to reappropriate their past, the capacity for happiness as a person is stolen. They cannot make intelligent, informed assessments of their life (its circumstances and themes), because they do not recall what for them is at stake. Personal perspective is lost. Sacks's Jimmie, and others like him, lack perspective on their life.

The inability to remember and thereby evaluate life does not mean that the memory-less are unable to experience happy feelings of pleasure and contentment. Sacks reports how Jimmie liked gardening and would show rapt attention in 'following' simple music or dramas. Here, for a few short minutes or (in the case of gardening) hours Jimmie seemed to find a way of, 'transcending the incoherence of his . . . disease'. His spirits rose and he seemed elated in the moment. Conscious connections with his past were cut off; he could pass no judgment on his life themes: he could not plan, self-scrutinize, sense the connectivity of his life. But neither could he judge his life worthless or himself a miserable wretch. He would get satisfyingly lost in the moment.

Jimmie impressed Sacks as like a young child with a cheerful heart. So, perhaps Jimmie's freedom from unhappiness was merciful compensation for not having his consciousness, in Locke's terms, reach back into the past. Unhappiness is woven into the fabric of many people's lives. Jimmie's loss of memory liberates him from that net.

However, lacking a capacity for happiness as a person perhaps is the most tragic part of the destruction of autobiographical memory. Minds occluded from unhappiness are cut off from happiness as well. Their inner life as persons is mutilated or truncated. 'If the gods give any gift at all to human beings, it is reasonable for them to give happiness also; indeed, it is reasonable to give happiness more than any other human

[good], in so far as it is the best of human [goods]' (Aristotle, *Nichomachean Ethics*, Bk 1, ch. 1).

NOTES

1 Mary Anne Warren, *Gendercide: The Implications of Sex Selection* (Rowman & Allanheld, New Jersey, 1985), p. 70.

2 Owen Flanagan, *Consciousness Reconsidered* (MIT Press, Cambridge, Mass., 1992), p. 155.

3 John Locke, *An Essay Concerning Human Understanding* (Oxford University Press, Oxford, 1690/1969), Book II, chapter XXVII, section 9.

4 For related discussion of Sacks's patient, see J. Rachels, *The End of Life* (Oxford University Press, Oxford, 1986), pp. 52–3; Flanagan, *Consciousness Reconsidered*, pp. 168–9.

5 J. Searle, *Minds, Brains, and Science* (Harvard University Press, Cambridge, Mass., 1984), p. 95.

6 The notion of dual power has been explored by a number of philosophers, whose ideas influence the discussion to follow, first and foremost Robert Kane in *Free Will and Values* (SUNY, Albany, 1985) and *The Significance of Free Will* (Oxford University Press, Oxford, 1996). The terminology 'dual power' is from Kane's 1985 book. Searle himself has no special term for the power (other than calling it freedom).

7 Searle, *Minds*, p. 95.

8 Thomas Nagel, *The View From Nowhere* (Oxford University Press, Oxford, 1986), p. 113.

9 Of the conviction Nagel writes: 'I suspect it is no intelligible belief at all' (*View*, p. 114). See also G. Strawson, *Freedom and Belief* (Oxford University Press, Oxford, 1986).

10 Searle, *Minds*, p. 97.

11 Ibid., p. 98.

12 Herbert Fingarette's *Heavy Drinking* (University of California, Berkeley, 1988) is a provocative attack on the thesis that alcoholism is a disease. The supposition that alcoholism is a disease is controversial. However, if alcoholism is not a disease, the points I am about to make can be made by reference to other sorts of local incompatibilities: brainwashing, kleptomania, and numerous other disabling conditions.

13 Searle, *Minds*, p. 93.

14 For the reformulation, see Lyn Y. Abramson, Martin Seligman, and John Teasdale, 'Learned helplessness in humans: critique and reformulation', *Journal of Abnormal Psychology*, 87 (1978), pp. 50–70. Seligman's theory has been found relevant to debate over free will by Bruce Waller, *Freedom Without Responsibility* (Temple University Press, Philadelphia, 1990).

15   Peter Van Inwagen, *An Essay On Free Will* (Oxford University Press, Oxford, 1983). See also Kane, *Significance*, pp. 44–59.

16   Van Inwagen, *An Essay*, p. 16. The fullest statement of the consequence argument invokes as well the inability to control the forces or laws of nature and refers to something called 'determinism'. I shall discuss that doctrine momentarily.

17   Searle, *Minds*, p. 92.

18   Ibid., p. 95.

19   Ibid., p. 92.

20   The array of versions of explanatory internalism is varied. Versions go by different names including 'free-willism', 'libertarianism', 'the theory of self-determination', and 'agency theory'. Each version bears a distinct theoretical load. Profession of agency theory, for example, requires distinguishing between two different types of causation or causal explanation: event causation and agent causation. The theory of self-determination directs attention to considerations of selfhood and personal identity.

21   Wilfred Sellars, 'Philosophy and the scientific image of man', in *Science, Perception, and Reality* (Routledge & Kegan Paul, London, 1963).

22   'Theory' may be too sophisticated a word to describe the status of manifest image psychology. Perhaps it would be better to call it a network of concepts or principles – a story.

23   See, for example, Frederick Ferre, 'Self-determination', *American Philosophical Quarterly*, 10 (1973), pp. 165–76.

24   See, for instance, Paul Churchland, 'Eliminative materialism and propositional attitudes', *Journal of Philosophy*, 78 (1981), pp. 67–90.

25   Terence Horgan and James Woodward, 'Folk psychology is here to stay', in *Mind and Cognition*, ed. William Lycan (Blackwell Publishers, Oxford, 1990), p. 390. This paper first appeared in *The Philosophical Review*, XCIV (1985), pp. 197–225. See also Terence Horgan and George Graham, 'In defense of southern fundamentalism', *Philosophical Studies*, 62 (1991), pp. 107–34.

26   Searle, *Minds*, p. 89.

27   The marvelous expression 'sparkle, glitter, and noise' I owe to Owen Flanagan, *Consciousness Reconsidered*, p. 133.

28   Nagel, *The View*, p. 110.

29   Aristotle, *Nichomachean Ethics* 1097b.

30   See *Diagnostic and Statistical Manual of Mental Disorders*, 3rd edn, American Psychiatric Association, Washington, DC, 1987), pp. 214ff.

31   S. Kierkegaard, *Fear and Trembling and The Sickness Unto Death*, trans. with introduction by W. Lowrie. (Princeton University Press, Princeton, 1969), p. 171.

32   A. Tversky and D. Griffen, 'Endowment and contrast in judgments of

well-being', in *Strategy and Choice*, ed. R. Zechhauser (MIT Press, Cambridge, Mass., 1991), pp. 297–318.

10

Consciousness, Matter, and Morality

'I have led you through a very sandy desert', remarked William James, explaining: 'But now, if I may be allowed so vulgar an expression, we begin to taste the milk in the coconut.' From the perspective of the reader of this book, the irony in James's remark should be transparent, for I hope that the earlier chapters have been neither dry nor sandy. It is also true, though, that we have not yet 'tasted' the milk in the coconut or discussed the way red looks or pain feels. We have not yet focused exclusively on one major and challenging topic in the philosophy of mind: consciousness. True, the topic of consciousness has surfaced in earlier chapters. However, it has not yet had chapters to call its own. These next two chapters remedy that.

10.1 Consciousness Defined

What is consciousness? Let us answer this question by asking and answering another question. What do we know about consciousness, not as a professor of philosophy or student of brain science, but simply in our capacity as subjects of conscious experience?

We know the following:

It is like something to be conscious; by contrast, it is not like anything not to be conscious. Conscious states appear like something from the inside; they seem a certain way to those in them. Being nonconscious does not seem any way at all.

In saying that conscious states appear like something from the inside, we mean that these states not only are *there* in subjects, but that they possess a specific quality or *like-thisness* to them. To someone in pain pain hurts, which is different from what a pleasurable sensation feels like. Perceiving a ripe tomato may mean one visually experiences red. There is a qualitative difference between how red looks to us and green. Coconut milk may offer a sweet taste and, once again, there is a qualitative difference between the taste of coconut milk and the taste of bitter beer.

The word philosophers sometimes use to designate the qualitative like-thisnesses of conscious experience is 'qualia' (or 'phenomenal qualia'), the singular of which is 'quale'. The expression philosophers sometimes use to designate consciousness which goes with talk of 'what it is like' is 'phenomenal consciousness'.[1] 'There is a peculiar quale to my whole personal consciousness', wrote C. S. Peirce (1839–1914), 'I appeal to your introspection to bear me out.'[2]

Additional examples of qualia? Philosopher Frank Jackson offers: 'the itchiness of itches, pangs of jealousy, . . . the characteristic experience of tasting a lemon, smelling a rose, hearing a loud noise, or seeing the sky.'[3] Peter Bieri contributes the following examples: 'sensory experiences like . . . hearing sounds; . . . emotions like fear and hatred; moods like melancholy and serenity.'[4]

In saying that conscious appearances or qualia are *there* in subjects, we do not mean that if a brain surgeon took off the top of our skull and peered into our brain while we savored coconut milk, they would see sweet qualia. Evidently, all they would see, in the words of Thomas Nagel, 'is a grey mass of neurons'.[5] We mean that qualia are interior with a type of interiority that is different from the way that our neurons are inside our head. Qualia are inside in the sense that there is something it is like to experience sweet tastes, and there is no obvious reason to think that this inside something can be open to public inspection.

By contrast, there is nothing it is like not to be conscious: to be a stone, ocean wave, or pencil. Things do not appear to them in any way at all. The interior of a stone can be open for public inspection. A surfer may relish a wave's qualities, but there are no qualia in waves. Relish is in the eye of the beholder and not in the wave itself. Should you accidentally stab a school friend with a pencil and he retort 'It hurts', he does not mean that the pencil is in pain. He means of course he is.

10.2 Six Roles of Consciousness

Consciousness plays six major roles in the philosophy of mind and related areas of philosophy. Each poses problems and excites controversy. Some roles should be familiar to readers of earlier chapters. Others should be familiar by the end of the book.

First, the qualitative character – the subjective like-thisness – of consciousness is a *troubling impediment* to materialism (physicalism) about consciousness. There seem to be two very different kinds of things occurring in the world: the physical goings on that can be studied by physical science and exposed to public inspection, and those other things – qualia – that belong in consciousness and must be experienced from the inside. There are brains; and then there are looks, tastes, and pains.

Second, conceptions of consciousness serve *to orient and justify skepticism* about other minds. The person who consciously doubts whether other conscious minds exist cannot doubt whether they themselves are conscious. The one and only conscious mind of which they can and should be sure is their own.

Third, the concept of consciousness rests at the foundation of the *causal explanation* of human behavior. I withdraw my hand from the flame because it induces pain; you emulate another person's behavior because you feel envy over her popularity and success. Without feeling envy, you would not emulate. Absent feeling pain, I would not withdraw.

The fourth role played by consciousness is as the alleged bearer of *personal identity*. John Locke is probably the most notable exponent of the view that the historical identity of a person hinges on the backward or retrospective stretch of their autobiographical consciousness. If I should happen to consciously remember experiencing the things that 4-year-old Georgie Graham experienced on the streets of Brooklyn, New York, in 1949, then I am one and the same person as that boy. He grew up to be me. The chain of identity – the chord of personal history – is as strong and expansive as connections provided by the conscious reach of the person.

Fifth, relatedly, consciousness plays a *self-conscious* role. When we attend to our own convictions, report our own beliefs and desires, describe our own hopes and fears, these things appear to have a personal 'my-ness' about them. Sometimes we are self-conscious in an especially perplexed way, for example, when we are trying to figure out who we are and where we are going with our lives. The actress Marilyn Monroe has had about fifty biographies written about her. To outsiders, by now, she should be transparent. But the feel of her own attitudes and desires was a source of self-alienation and confusion to her. 'I seem to have a whole superstructure with no foundation', she once told reporters, 'but I'm working on the foundation.'⁶ How should we understand Monroe's remark? The best answer is that there is a way Monroe's life felt to her and that this way is different from the confident and self-transparent feeling and self-direction she wished to possess.

Sixth, and finally, consciousness plays a *moral* role. A number of philosophers contend that all and only conscious creatures morally count. Nonconscious things (waves, stones, pencils, etc.) do not count, morally.

William James (1842–1910), the great Harvard philosopher and psychologist of the turn of the last century, whose words began the chapter, writes: 'Neither moral relations nor the moral law can swing *in vacuo*. Their only habitat can be a mind which feels them.'⁷ The Australian philosopher Peter Singer, a powerful voice in the Animal Liberation movement, writes: 'The only acceptable limit to our moral concern is the point at which there is no awareness . . . no conscious preference, and hence no capacity to experience.'⁸ James and Singer believe that the fact that a creature is conscious means that it counts, morally. Conscious creatures possess moral standing. This is not to say that every animal has moral standing. (What about worms and paramecia? It is doubtful whether they are conscious.) But it is to say that if things seem a certain way to animals, if they feel, sense, and perceive, then such animals possess moral standing.

What does it mean to possess moral standing or to morally count? To possess moral standing is to be the sort of thing which deserves respect and ought to be given consideration by fair-minded moral agents. A person, for instance, can be treated fairly or unfairly; a stone cannot. A person can be wronged or disrespected; a wave cannot. Persons possess moral standing; stones and waves do not.

Suppose on a hot day I dig a hole. To take a rest I sit on a stone. If the stone is owned, the owner may protest, but the stone itself is indifferent to what happens. For the sake of the owner I may refrain from sitting, but I show no disrespect to the stone by sitting upon it.

At the base of the hole I set a trap to kill a rabbit for my private collection of stuffed animals. The rabbit is not indifferent to what happens; it strongly prefers not to be trapped. Do I wrong the rabbit in trapping it?

According to James and Singer, the answer is yes. Take any form of consciousness, James exclaims, 'however slight', which any creature may have, and this form of consciousness makes its own moral demands, carries its own moral imperative.[9] The rabbit 'asks' that I not trap it, and to be fair-minded – given that I wish the poor creature for no more serious purpose than my collection – I must refrain.

The six basic roles played by consciousness rotate in the center of several controversies. This chapter explores two. The next and final chapter explores one.

10.3 Is Consciousness a Brain Process?

No philosopher should be without opinions concerning controversies surrounding consciousness. One of the most conceptually vexing controversies concerns whether consciousness is material or physical, although an equally interesting question concerns the moral role of consciousness. Let's take the first first.

Is consciousness – phenomenally conscious experience – something material? Physical? A brain process? If it is, I assume this means it is something describable in terms of physical science. If it is not describable in terms of physical science, I assume this means that consciousness is not material, not a brain process. J. J. C. Smart endorses materialism about conscious experience as follows: 'experience should be identified with brain processes'.[10] If Smart is right, conscious experience should be described in terms of the physical brain sciences.[11] If conscious experience cannot be described in terms of the physical brain sciences, conscious experience is not a physical process.

As readers of the eighth chapter may recall, Franz Brentano charged, over a hundred years ago, that materialism about the mental should be resisted. Brentano argued that materialism runs foul of the Intentionality (aboutness) of the mental. To take a simple illustration, suppose that I feel envy over your popularity. My envy is *about* your popularity. If Brentano's charge is correct, nothing physical can be envious. Nothing physical can possess envy's Intentionality.

Brentano's case for the immateriality of the mental concerns the immateriality of phenomenal consciousness only indirectly, however. To

Brentano the immateriality of envy consists in its Intentionality, not in *feeling* envious. It consists in the fact that envy is about something, not in the fact that envy is 'like-this'.

Are there difficulties distinctive to materialism about conscious experience which are independent of Intentionality? As readers of the first chapter may recall, in his thought experiment about Mary the super neuroscientist, Frank Jackson attacks the sufficiency of physical science for describing the qualitative like-thisness of conscious experience. In Jackson's view, demonstrating that there is an aspect of consciousness that physical science cannot describe offers a simple and decisive argument for the immateriality of consciousness. Here is the gist of the Jacksonian argument in two sentences:

Nothing physical science can describe succeeds in capturing the red look of a ripe tomato. So, consciousness is not something physical.

I don't wish to re-review Jackson's argument (although I will re-employ Mary). It is controversial, though quite compelling.[12] However, I would like to reinforce Jackson's misgiving about whether consciousness is physical or a brain process by identifying a closely related difficulty with materialism about consciousness. (It may actually be the same difficulty as Jackson's or an aspect of the same difficulty.) There are several ways in which to describe the difficulty. One goes as follows.

Materialism about conscious experience must assign greater authority to neuroscience (physical science) in identifying the qualities of conscious experience than to subjects who undergo the experience. But there is a general principle which stands in the way of deference to physical science in identifying the qualities of consciousness. This principle may be called the 'first-person authority principle' and it goes roughly as follows:

First-person Authority Principle: The specific like-thisness of conscious experience is authoritatively known by and only by someone undergoing the experience and attending to it from the subjective, first-person point of view. The first-person view when it conflicts with any other view of the like-thisness of conscious experience is decisive.

This principle is deeply embedded within our common-sense conception of ourselves as conscious subjects. For us, it seems, we know better than anyone else what things are like to us. Marilyn knew as her biographers did not what it was like to be Marilyn. The problem with materialism is that it requires abandoning the first person principle. Materialism requires embracing a contrary principle which may be called the 'impersonal authority principle' and it goes roughly as follows:

> Impersonal Authority Principle: Physical science embodies an impersonal, objective point of view. If materialism about consciousness is true, the like-thisness of conscious experience is known or knowable from a physical scientific point of view. If this impersonal view conflicts with a first-person view of experience, the impersonal physical scientific view is decisive.

This is a bald and bold idea. But materialists – or many materialists (some complicating exceptions will be mentioned later) – embrace it. J. J. C. Smart willingly engages in the embrace. When one adopts the perspective of physical science, he writes,

> One tends to get a certain way of looking at the universe, which is to see it *sub specie aeternitatis*.... To see the world *sub specie aeternitatis* ... is to see it apart from any particular or human perspective. Theoretical language of science facilitates this vision of the world because it contains no indexical words like 'I', 'you', 'here', 'now', 'past', 'present', [and] 'future'.[13]

According to Smart, one fruit of physical science is that it enables us to grasp conscious experience as well as the rest of the world 'under the form of eternity' (*sub specie aeternitatis*, impersonally). 'The poet or traveller', he says, 'describes the brilliant colors of trees and mountains; the physicist speaks of wavelengths of light. To see the world "under the form of eternity" we must follow the physicist here.'[14]

Suppose that consciousness somehow is a brain process. Suppose materialism about conscious experience is true. This would mean that creatures exactly like us physically (molecule for molecule duplicates) must be exactly like us in their qualitative interior. Otherwise consciousness is not a brain process, for although we and they are in the same brain states, they would differ from us consciously. However, it seems to make perfectly good sense, not to be conceptually muddled or incoherent, to imagine creatures exactly like us physically who nevertheless do differ from us in their qualitative interior.[15] On 'absent qualia' versions of this thought experiment these creatures are *zombies* or *imitation* conscious subjects. They lack qualitative consciousness altogether; there isn't anything at all that it's like to be them, although they act as if they are phenomenally conscious creatures and refer to themselves using the language of consciousness. On 'inverted qualia' versions, one imagines that the qualia that occur in them are somehow inverted relative to their occurrences in us: for instance, the qualitative aspects of color-experience are systematically reversed. What it is like to us to see red is what it is like to them to see green; and so forth.

To simplify let's focus on inversion and me. Imagine that a molecule for molecule duplicate of me, Physical Twin-me, looks at a ripe tomato. Can we coherently suppose that he visually experiences green when I experience red, although he and I both perceive the same tomato in the same lighting conditions?

The possibility is bizarre, you will object. If Twin and me are exactly alike physically, we should be exactly alike consciously as well. That was my first reaction on imagining my physical twin too. Qualia, on this reaction, 'fit' the underlying neurophysiology. Same physiology spells same qualia. If, however, we set aside the first reaction, the possibility of qualia inversion seems intelligible and coherent (a point to which I return shortly).

Inversion in a thought experiment or hypothetically possible world is not something against which *Trends in Neuroscience* (a distinguished neuroscientific journal) should defend itself. However, perhaps oddly, it is something against which materialism has trouble defending itself. How can a mere conceptual or imagined possibility threaten materialism? It does, since the experiment expresses the first-person authority principle. The imaginative possibility of inverted qualia stems from conceiving of the subjective, first-person point of view as authoritative concerning the qualitative character of conscious experience. It stems from taking the first-person view to be decisive even when it conflicts with all the physical evidence. Another tale shows how and tells why. It illuminates the trouble consciousness poses for materialism.

Once upon a time there was a super neuroscientist, Mary. Mary examined my brain when I looked at a ripe tomato and insisted that it looks green to me, although I sincerely insisted that it looks red. Mary pondered how she could prove to me that the tomato appears green to me, my protestations to the contrary. Of brain regions which she claimed were associated with color experience, she took computerized axial tomographic scans and claimed that they were evidence of my being appeared to greenly. I was unmoved. She took positron emission tomographic scans; I did not budge. She took a series of magnetic resonance images; I was strident about red. Then came what she believed would be the ultimate if expensive refutation. She cloned my absolutely identical physical twin. Physical Twin-me sincerely asserted that the tomato looks green. Must I be shaken by twin? Must I announce, like him, that the tomato appears green – to me?

Notice that this is not disagreement over whether the tomato really *is* green, whatever that may mean. It is discord over the tomato's subjective visual appearance. It is discord over qualia. Can I be mistaken in how the tomato looks to me?

If I must say that the tomato looks green (to me) because my physical twin insists that it looks green (to him), then I am abdicating first-person authority over how things appear to me. I am admitting that I mistook how the tomato looks. If materialism is true, mistakes about our own conscious experience are possible (even if they do not occur). They are possible since materialism requires rejecting the notion that we each are the final or decisive authority over what conscious experience is like to us. Material authority is *sub specie aeternitatis* authority. It is not 'I' or 'you' or *subjective* authority. In the imagined conflict between Twin/Mary and me, Twin/Mary can win. My qualia can be green and not red, my protestations to the contrary.

Much can be learned about consciousness by examining the first-person authority principle and contrasting this with materialism's impersonal principle. I would claim, for example, that subjective authority though real is limited. It operates in cases of simple sensations and perceptions (pains, red looks, and so on) but not in cases of complex emotions and conscious attitudes (desires, beliefs, and so forth). The representational content of some attitudes (even when conscious) is best determined by third parties including science. This is because of a certain systematic elusiveness in attitudinal qualia, due to the manner in which their qualitative character may be interwoven with conceptual content (or Intentionality), and, finally, due to something which I would dub the 'Monroe doctrine', viz. that self-confusion exerts an ineliminable tug on all of us in reckoning our attitudes. Fascinating issues all, which I must keep subvisible here, lest I destroy my own argument with six nuances and a dozen qualifications. My concern here is not to explore the scope and limits of first-person authority. My point is to post a difficulty for materialism which stems from taking such authority seriously (no matter if narrowly confined). Materialism overthrows my entitlement to sincerely conflict with my molecule for molecule twin. More generally, materialism subverts our subjective authority over what conscious experience is like to us. If we possess a decisive role in determining what conscious experience is like to us, then materialism should be rejected.

Materialists get unnerved by this argument and its appeal to first-person authority. Some are driven to extremes. In his paper 'Quining qualia' Daniel Dennett recommends the massively counter-intuitive action of denying the existence of qualia. *Sub specie aeternitatis* there are no qualia – no phenomenal qualia.[16]

Other defenders of materialism adopt less extreme measures. Owen Flanagan denies that materialism endorses an impersonal authority principle. According to Flanagan, consciousness can be a brain process even if physical science cannot describe its phenomenal character.[17] Consciousness is a neurophysically constituted process, although its 'like-thisness' cannot be described by brain science.

Dennett's action is an impertinent if in some ways theoretically courageous move. The qualities of conscious experience are so obvious within experience that it is difficult to trust any philosophical position like his that denies them. Flanagan's tactic while certainly not impertinent still is unattractive. Is it consistent with materialism to deny that there is no link between whether conscious experience is a brain process and whether looks, tastes, and feels can be described by brain science? How, then, is the expression 'brain process' to be interpreted? It is unclear whether it is even intelligible to call something a physical brain process, if it is not to connect its description with physical science.[18] If Dennett is too intolerant about qualia, Flanagan seems too tolerant about materialism.[19]

Other defenders of materialism make a third move. They reply that *they* do not accept the first-person authority principle. Consciousness is a brain process. So the principle that they accept – the impersonal principle that physical science is decisive – means that absent and inverted qualia are inconceivable. We *think* we can imagine such things only because we operate with the wrong concepts: common-sense concepts in which first-person authority is rooted. So long as we deploy common-sense concepts of consciousness in which first-person authority is rooted, the possibility of absent or inverted qualia seems unproblematic. We imagine someone just like us *impersonally* (our exact physical twin) but unlike us *personally* (in their conscious interior). Who is to say whether this person is possible? If we *subjects* are the final authority, only us. But our powers of conceptual imagination lose their anti-physicalist impact if we restrict ourselves to proper materialist concepts. Are absent and inverted qualia imaginable? No, not if we think of consciousness as nothing but a brain process. It is inconceivable that my molecule for molecule duplicate differs from me in his visual color experience of the tomato. If the tomato looks red to me it must look red to him. Or if somehow the tomato doesn't look red to him, than Mary needs to hone her cloning skills. She hasn't produced my physical duplicate.

Can materialist views of inconceivability be defended? Those who accept them usually offer the following sort of argument.

The conceptual possibilities of absent and inverted qualia are embedded in common-sense non-neuroscientific concepts of conscious experience. These concepts enjoy currency in philosophical thought experiments. As concepts they seem safe enough if philosophers blind them to materialist futures. But common-sense concepts of the mental will be dispensed with in the final accounting – in the Golden Age of Neuroscience. The principle of first-person authority will be subverted by future scientific neuropsychology. Concepts which preclude imagining absent and inverted qualia somehow will displace common-sense concepts. The Impersonal Form of Eternity will be regnant.

So far, perhaps inspiring. Materialism may seem like a valuable distrust of self-serving indifference to the future development of science. William James wrote:

> I admit that were I addressing the Salvation Army or a miscellaneous popular crowd it would be misuse of opportunity to preach . . . as I have in these pages preached. . . . What such audiences most need is to have their faiths broken up and ventilated, that the north-west wind of science should get into them. . . . But academic audiences, fed already on science, have a different need.[20]

Materialism may feel like a needed north-west wind. But there is a rub. A different need. The rub is this: Predicting that golden age neuroscience will become orthodoxy, what should we do *now*? Claim that we cannot imagine absent or inverted qualia? Should I forget about the apparent conceptual possibility (to me now) of Physical Twin-me possessing inverted qualia?

The materialist prediction is interesting, but remains far from compelling. All talk of abandoning common-sense concepts of conscious experience is idle if the golden age either does not arrive or arrives but leaves materially contrarily answered or indeterminate questions of just which concepts for consciousness are being used by science.

Suppose the following happens. Future physical scientists inform us that common-sense concepts we are using to refer to qualia actually identify basic features of the universe such that a scientific worldview needs to be expanded *beyond* materialism. Subjectively authoritative qualia are no less fundamental to the universe than the most basic properties posited in theoretical physics (mass, charm, spin – whatever they turn out to be).[21] Positing basic properties of the universe outside physical science, and the additional fundamental natural laws which go along with them, would seriously complicate our picture of the natural world but it will mean that absent and inverted qualia will remain conceivable even when we restrict ourselves to golden age scientific concepts.

In order for it to be reasonable for us now to deny that we can conceive of absent and inverted qualia, we must have good reason to predict that golden age neuroscience will confirm materialism. On the other hand, *given* our common-sense concepts we now seem unwarranted in making such a prediction. Predicting the future of neuroscience is at best a dubious advertisement for materialism.

Dennett writes, 'contrary to what seems obvious at first blush, there simply are no qualia'.[22] But that's not how it seems to me – or to us, I trust. Qualia exist, but on second blush, there are no material qualia. Phenomenal consciousness is real, but (in the words of Stephen Kosslyn and Oliver Koenig, two scientists) it 'is not the same as neural activity; experience cannot be described in terms of ion flows, synaptic connections, and so forth'.[23]

10.4 Consciousness and Animal Liberation

No philosophical debate has stirred more attention in moral philosophy and the popular press in recent years than the debate inspired by the publication in 1975 of Peter Singer's *Animal Liberation*. In that book Singer argued that human treatment of nonhuman animals is fundamentally morally objectionable. He argued that we should be forced

> to make radical changes in our treatment of animals that would involve our diet, the farming methods we use, experimental procedures in many fields of science, our approach to wildlife and to hunting, trapping and the wearing of furs, and areas of entertainment like circuses, rodeos, and zoos. As a result, a vast amount of suffering would be avoided.[24]

As rarely happens with a philosophy book, people sat up and took notice. Some made deep changes in their lives, by dropping meat from their diets and animal products from their lifestyles. Here is how one reader described his reaction.

> I have most of my adult life paid people to axe-murder and bludgeon to death a considerable variety of creatures, some of whom were babies, so that I might eat them; they were, in fact, tasty. That this description applied to my actions or that there were moral questions about those practices is something to which I was largely oblivious until reading [Singer].[25]

I have three objectives in the rest of this chapter. First, I want to discuss the idea that nonhuman animals count or matter, morally, just because they are conscious. Second, I want to explore, and ultimately to criticize, the moral weight which Singer says attaches to different forms or types of conscious life. Third, I would also like to suggest the importance for moral philosophy of having a proper theory of consciousness.

Philosophers have long felt that there is something inescapable but also elusive about the moral status of animals or at least conscious animals. Assuming that conscious animals possess moral standing, how do we know whether animal A, who might be a member of a very different species from our own, counts more heavily, or less heavily, than creature B, another animal or perhaps a human person? To take a popular illustration, when used in medical research, nonhuman animals often suffer. Are we morally justified in imposing burdens on animals by using them in research? Suppose suffering animals count. Do they count more (or less) than the gains or benefits primarily to humans of research?

One of the chief problems facing the idea that conscious animals count is how moral consideration ought to be distributed or parcelled to all conscious creatures. It is useful to distinguish between *unscaled* and *scaled* ways of distributing moral concern. To the unscaling distributor the brilliant physicist Albert Einstein counts no more (or less) than a frog. Killing Einstein is equally evil to killing a frog. The scaling advocate, in contrast, acknowledges morally relevant differences between Einstein and frogs. The scaling distributor asserts that some forms of consciousness are inherently superior to other forms. The death of Einstein is much worse than the death of a frog.

There are two main approaches to scaling moral concern for conscious creatures. One approach scales or differentiates by species: members of the human species count more than members of nonhuman species. Einstein counts more than a frog because Einstein is human. The other approach scales by judgments about the superiority of some individual conscious lives over others. Einstein matters more than a frog because *his* life is superior to the frog's. Einstein's life matters more, not because he is human, but because his life is superior as a life. If contrary to fact Einstein really was not human, his life would still matter more just because his life is superior.

Of course, superiority according to the second approach is not absolutely unrelated to superiority according to the first approach. The life of a human being may often be judged superior to the life of a member of another species. Humanity may typically come out on top. But that is not incompatible with the second approach. The point of the second approach is to resist rote application of species preference and to consider each and every conscious creature in its own terms.

Here I will not consider unscaled distribution, but will concentrate only on distributing in the manner recommended by Singer, who favors a version of the second form of scaled distribution. Happily for science in the twentieth century, Einstein's mother did not distribute her moral sympathies without differentiating between her son and his pet frogs. (Did Einstein have pet frogs?) Singer's proposal for attaching different moral weights to different forms of conscious life goes as follows.

Some lives are inherently superior to others. Those which are inherently superior count more, morally, than those which are inferior. Meanwhile, the inherent superiority (inferiority) of a life is a function of whether the life would be chosen or preferred, in contrast to other lives, by a neutral or impartial imaginative participant in that life. Creatures whose lives would be preferred from such a standpoint are superior and carry more moral weight than creatures whose lives would not be chosen.

In short, if A's life is preferred – compared on the inside – to B's, A counts more heavily than B. Let's illustrate.

Suppose that I have suddenly been placed in a situation where I have a choice of saving one of two creatures from a fire. One is a barnyard hen; the other is a mentally handicapped human infant. According to Singer, then I must try to imagine myself as living the conscious lives of both hen and handicapped child. I must consider what conscious experience is like to the child and I must 'do my best to grasp what it is like to be a hen'.[26] I do not then discount the hen just because it is a hen. The point is that once we grasp hen and handicapped infant consciousness, we can understand which form of consciousness – whose conscious life – is preferable. If we as impartial imaginative participants prefer to be the hen, despite the difference in species, then the hen carries more moral weight than the handicapped infant. Between saving the hen or infant, morally, I ought to save the hen.

I shall call Singer's idea for scaling or ascertaining the relative moral weight of different forms of conscious life, the *principle of imaginative interior impartial comparison*. The principle is a verbal mouthful because the idea behind the principle is a conceptual mindful. It may be abbreviated as the *inner comparison principle*.

The principle of imaginative interior impartial comparison, or the inner comparison principle, plays an important part in Singer's moral scheme. Singer rejects preference for species membership as the bench mark of moral weight. Mere difference in species between child and hen is morally irrelevant. He dubs species preference 'speciesism', which means that, in his moral universe, it is a moral evil similar to sexism or racism. In order to avoid speciesism, he appeals to the principle; it says avoid pegging the moral weight of a creature on species. Peg moral weight on the character of the creature's conscious life. The principle also tells us to factor out social externalities in determining the value of a life. Singer would urge that to be fair to the infant, I cannot save the hen just because it is my pet; and to be fair to the hen, I cannot save the infant just because it is my child. A creature's relation to me (or to us) cannot be what makes its life superior or weighty, morally. The superior form of conscious life must be fixed by internal considerations: by what it is like on the inside. In comparing horses and humans, for instance, Singer says, one must decide, in effect, 'between the value of the life of a horse to the horse, and the value of the life of a human to the human.'[27]

Singer admits that the principle imposes conceptual strains, but he fails to appreciate the gross difficulties which actually undermine the principle. Some difficulties are familiar to students of moral philosophy. Singer's principle is a version of what moral philosophers call 'the choice criterion of value'. The key idea behind the choice criterion is that the value of something (in this case, a conscious life) rests on whether it would be chosen by a certain type of chooser (in this case, an impartial imaginative and comparative participant).

Certain moral difficulties are built into the choice criterion. These are neatly summed up by Vinit Haksar in his book *Equality, Liberty, and Perfectionism*: 'To be fair between different forms of life requires a choice from some sort of neutral value-free standpoint, but such an idea is not a coherent one.'[28]

For the principle to work comparison has to be made by choosers who are not biased. If we assume people can project themselves into genuinely different forms of conscious life (an implausible assumption at the animal limit as it turns out), which types of consciousness actually end up being preferred may depend partly on background moral beliefs or values which the projectors possess. Anti-speciesists like Singer may prefer being a hen; whereas speciesists may select the existence of the handicapped child. What constitutes impartiality or neutrality in choosing between different forms of consciousness? Is anti-speciesism necessarily the only impartial position? How much influence should background moral beliefs have in choosing a form? Are only certain sorts of background beliefs morally acceptable?

The principle says that the moral agent's project is to choose among various forms of conscious life. But what moral attitudes may they carry into their imaginative projections? Is it speciesist to judge that human life is always better than animal life even after one has imaginatively tasted animal existence?

In addition to moral questions, there is another set of problems for the principle. These are problems associated with imaginative projection – or 'imaginative reconstruction' as Singer calls the task. The most troublesome question is whether we really can grasp the consciousness of a member of another species and experience life, albeit vicariously, from the creature's point of view. What is it like to be a hen? Eagle? Horse? Is this even a coherent question? How would we discover the right answer?

In the words of Colin McGinn, a philosopher of mind at Rutgers University, 'apprehending animals as they are in themselves' should enable us to give them their proper due, morally.[29] Singer requires extraordinary imaginative feats in the apprehension of animals as they are in themselves. Singer's moral outlook is shaped by adherence to a comparison principle which requires grasping what it is like to be an animal – or as he also puts it, apprehending the value of the animal's existence to the animal.

10.5 An Impossible Consciousness

It is clear from Singer's description of how to distribute moral concern among different creatures that he intends to make the following *imagination requirement*: Between any two individuals of any species, to determine whose life is superior and carries the most moral weight, it is necessary to grasp their lives from the inside. One must imagine oneself as 'living the lives of . . . those affected . . . by my decision.'[30] One must turn one's consciousness temporarily and imaginatively into another's consciousness. One must imagine *being* them.

Let us suppose that one can imaginatively project oneself inside another person's consciousness. I can know what it is like to be you; you can know what it is like to be me. The supposition may be worth questioning, especially in cases of projection into severely handicapped and pathological human beings, but I shall not question it here. Here I wish to explore the case of animals. What about animals? Can I grasp what it is like to be an animal? Or more precisely: Assuming that there is something it is like to be an animal, can I grasp what it is like to the animal to be the animal? Singer says yes. The answer is no.

It is not obvious why Singer says yes. I suspect that this is because he assumes that grasping what it is like to be an animal is essentially analogous to grasping what it is like to be another human being. Just as I can imagine what it is like to be you, I can imagine what it is like to be a horse or hen. But can I?

The correct answer is no, and this for two related reasons.

1 *Range* Human beings do not have and never can acquire (as long we remain human) the sorts of conceptual equipment, the perceptual endowment, to imagine what it is like to *be* an animal. We are just *too*

different from them. Or more exactly: animals do not have and never can acquire the sorts of conceptual equipment, the perceptual endowment, to make it possible for us to imagine being them. They are just *too different* from us. Hence, we cannot grasp what it is like to be them. Moreover, this means that we are barred from using Singer's inner comparison principle.

The claim is not that we cannot grasp what certain experiences are like to animals. It may be possible, at least in a narrow band of cases, to imagine animal experience. Knowledge of animals, time spent observing their behavior, acquaintance with their nervous systems – these are the means through which imagining animal experience may occur. If a ripe tomato appears red to me, perhaps (given equine sensory vectors for color) it looks red to a horse as well; hence I may imagine how a horse visually experiences the tomato. But imagining an equine color experience is not the same as imagining being equine. It takes more than imagining a narrow range of experiences to imagine being an animal. It takes imagining a wide range of experiences from the animal's point of view. It requires being able to extensively and vicariously place oneself into the animal's form of conscious life.

Let me put the point in a different way. Imagine *being* Hitler. No one in their right mind would claim that to imagine being Hitler it suffices to imagine how ripe tomatoes visually appeared to this dreadful man. Some wide or large, however indeterminate, range of Hitlerian experiences must be imagined. If you cannot project yourself into a wide range of Hitlerian experiences, then you cannot imagine being Hitler. It is one thing to imagine having the same visual color experience as Hitler, and another to imagine being him having this experience and many others besides. What are the prospects for your imagining a wide range of Hitlerian experiences? I suspect: Slim to none – to hate as Hitler hated, to fear as he feared, to experience the scale of his paranoia. As Owen Flanagan puts it (though in a different sort of setting), 'chances for visits' may abound, but opportunities for more 'direct communion do not'.[31]

So, what I am claiming about Singer's principle is that we cannot project ourselves into a wide range of animal experiences. There is psychological blockage between us and animals prohibiting projection. To project to extensive levels or forms of animal consciousness is impossible.

The basis for my charge may be made vivid by considering a description offered by Kathleen Akins, a philosopher and neuroscientist, of trying to imagine what it is like to be an eagle as it spots its prey and dives at fantastic speeds. Here one is faced with imagining not just eagle color experiences, but what it is like to *be* an eagle embodied in its unique physiology, possessing its special visual acuities, and cued to salient features of its environment.

> How does a bird of prey 'attend to' a scene, look at the world? What does that mean and, more interestingly, what would that be like? Here, in my mind's eye, I imagined myself perched high in the top of a dead tree sporting a pair of very peculiar bifocal glasses. More precisely, I pictured myself in a pair of *quadra*focals, with different lenses corresponding to the horizontal band, foveal and peripheral regions of the eagle's eye. I wonder whether it is just like that, I thought, like peering successively through each lens, watching the world move in and out of focus depending on whether I look. First I stare through the horizontal section and scan the horizon for other predators; then I switch to my left central lens and make sure no one is approaching from behind; then I use the high-powered temporal lens to scrutinize the water below for shadows of some dinner. Is that how the eagle sees the world, I wondered? Is that what it is like to have [eagle eyes]?[32]

We will never know. Our eyes anatomically are very unlike those of an eagle. We also don't have the habits of perching, predation, and flight which eagles possess. The path into the conscious point of view of this predator is blocked by striking differences between us. The longer its wings, as it were, the more the ways of our getting its conscious life wrong.

2 *Self-comprehending reflexivity* Even animals (notably the higher mammals) which seem very like us are actually most unlike us – on the inside. Today's most fashionable type of animal theorizing, cognitive ethology, has provided several elegant studies of the conceptual equipment and perceptual capacities of animals. One of the most detailed is a study by Dorothy Cheney and Robert Seyfarth, two professors at the University of Pennsylvania, of the minds of East African vervet monkeys. Here is how they summarize the results of their study in *How Monkey's See the World*: 'There are ... many ways in which a vervet's view of her world is very different from our own.... Her mental states are not accessible to her: she does not know that she knows. Further, monkeys seem unable to attribute mental states to others or to recognize that other's behavior is also caused by motives, beliefs, and desires.'

Again, the scientists say: 'The inability to examine one's own mental states or to attribute mentality to others severely constrains the ability of monkeys to transmit information, to deceive, to feel empathy with one another.... *We* attribute motives, plans, and strategies to the animals, but they ... do not.'[33]

The conclusion to be drawn from this is that vervet monkeys fail to grasp that they themselves have lives – conscious mental lives – of their own. Their states of consciousness exist in a kind of self-comprehending vacuum. They don't have reflexive thoughts like 'This is what experiencing X is like to me'.

When Singeresque comparisons are made between different forms of consciousness, we should care whether animals grasp that they themselves are conscious. Self-consciousness matters because according to the inner comparison principle one consciousness has to be compared from within its qualitative interior to another's. *This* conscious life (a monkey's) has to be judged better or worse than *that* conscious life (a person's or a hen's) from within the creatures themselves. It is this realization, that animals are not on a self-comprehending par with humans, that is the trickiest yet deepest reason (of the two) why imaginative comparison is impossible.

Singer fails to realize this point, but how can the point be explained? Suppose you try, Singerlike, to grasp what it is like to be a vervet. You say to yourself, 'Despite the strain, I have a pretty good idea what it is like to be a vervet.' Do you? How can you? If Cheney and Seyfarth are right, *you* cannot grasp what it is like to be a vervet because vervets themselves don't know what it is like. They don't think of themselves as being conscious; they fail to recognize that there is anything it is like to be them. To conceive of themselves conceiving of experiencing themselves is to fail to be them.

Let us call a person who tries to grasp what it is like to be a vervet 'Vervette'. Vervette is a perfectly normal human being except for the fact that having read *Animal Liberation* she is deeply morally concerned for animals.

Suppose that Vervette is suddenly placed in a 'forced choice' situation where she has to choose between saving one of two creatures from a fire. Suppose one is a normal 4-year-old human child and the other is a monkey.

Vervette wants to grasp what it is like to be a monkey as well as what it is like to be a child so that she can allocate her moral concern according

to the impartially preferred or superior form of consciousness. Suppose
that she completes grasping child consciousness. Her second task, then,
is:

1 Imagine myself to be a monkey.

She then strains her imagination and projects herself into the conscious
mind of a monkey. What happens there? What is monkey consciousness
like? What does it seem, feel, or appear like? It would violate the
discoveries of Cheney and Seyfarth for Vervette to think:

2 I have achieved the desired imaginative reconstruction. I am now
simulating monkey consciousness. I am living a monkey's life, albeit
projectively. *This* is what monkey experience is like to a monkey.

For monkeys lack that conscious reflexivity. Although conscious, they
have no reflexive appreciation of their own states of consciousness; they
do not think of themselves as possessing lives. And, thus, Vervette
cannot picture herself living (or remembering having lived) monkey life.
She cannot project herself inside monkey consciousness and know it as
conscious.

To make the bar to monkey life still more vivid and impenetrable
imagine that Vervette tries to imagine herself as a monkey terrified by the
fire. Will she be able to imagine herself as such a monkey?
She can't think:

3 I am now terrified by the fire, monkey-like, imaginatively

because monkeys may feel terror but they do not know (unlike Vervette)
that *this* is something which they themselves feel.
Once again, let me put the point in a different way. Presumably you
once were a late-term fetus. Supposedly there is something it is like to be
fetal in late term. (Presumably late-term fetuses have conscious experiences.) Now compare what conscious life is like to you now with what
conscious life was like to you then. My point is: I bet you can't. It's not
that your autobiographical memory has failed. It's that, in the requisite
sense, there is nothing to remember. Fetuses presumably (like nonhuman animals) have no way of referring to their conscious experience.
They don't think 'This is what it's like to be here now'. And you can't
compare – from the inside – the life of a creature that does not refer to

itself as conscious with the life of a creature (like yourself) that does. That would be like comparing two faces in a mirror when only one face looks in the mirror. The fetus just does not attend to its face, that is to say, its conscious experience, in the mirror.

Parts of Marilyn Monroe's inner life are scattered among the fifty biographies about her. Each makes, or tries to make, a visit. Each tries to get inside her conscious experience and to formulate a view of what makes her tick. When they get in there the prospects are not blackened by her inability to self-attend to her own conscious experience. To Marilyn her life had a certain feel; it wasn't what she wanted.

The moral to be drawn from these two reasons is that to the question of what it is like to be an animal (hen, eagle, horse) we can only plead ignorance. So, it is futile to frame an imaginative comparison requirement because animals possess a subjectively alien form of conscious life. No matter how resolute and sympathetically disposed a person is, they cannot bring about the desired projection into the animal mind. There are profound differences between us and other species.

Aware that people may have difficulty projecting themselves into animal lives, Singer says, 'Nevertheless I think I can make some sense of the idea of choosing . . . and I am fairly confident that . . . some forms of life would be seen as preferable to others.'[34] Perhaps. But perhaps this is only because some forms of life could not be seen *at all*. If human/animal comparisons are impossible, humans might prefer humanity by default. If she is occluded from monkey life, Vervette inevitably will prefer any human life to which she may gain imaginative admission. Or perhaps Singer is confident only because he is confusing two questions. One is the question of whether some lives are preferable to others; the other is the question of whether preferability consists in comparisons made from within interiors. Many moral philosophers argue that some lives can and should be preferred to others, but they also argue that it is a mistake to believe that states of consciousness alone make them comparable. Better to be an Einstein unsatisfied than a happy hen, or a happy hen than a suicidal Monroe.

Of course Singer may have replies to the above two-reasons case against imaginative projection. Perhaps my arguments rest on notions which he rejects. For example, projection, he may say, is not consciously reflexive or self-comprehending. Yet I say that it is reflexive. I claim that if we must compare the conscious lives of creatures from the inside, they must somehow comprehend those lives or experiences as their own if we are to make comparisons. But, truth be told, the insistence on the possibility of self-comprehension ultimately is not mine; at least implicitly, it is Singer's. (Recall his remark about the value of a horse's life *to* the horse.) If I am to compare the value of my life *to* me with the value of a horse's life *to* the horse, I must assume that the specific *like-thisness* of his life is something *to* which he (or I when imagining being him) can attend. Comparative projection is not a procedure alternative to self-comprehension; it is a case of self-comprehension, albeit self-comprehension can occur in different ways and degrees.

Singer may object to my denial that animals lack powers of self-comprehension. I don't expect universal agreement on the denial, though I am confident that Cheney and Seyfarth are right about vervet monkeys, and that self-comprehending nonhuman animals are at best few and far between.

To substantiate the charge that self-comprehending nonhuman animals are few and far between, I must carefully distinguish self-comprehension from related phenomena with which it may be confused. Here is a short example. Readers of the fourth chapter may recall the discussion of Gordon Gallup's self-recognizing chimps. These animals recognize themselves as themselves in mirrors. The central concept in Gallup's studies is self-recognition. Deciding whether a chimp self-recognizes is determining whether it discriminates itself on the basis of its appearance in a mirror. The empirical evidence for self-recognition lies in the observed behavior of self-attentive chimps. Although Gallup speculated that mirror self-recognition implies self-comprehension (conscious reflexivity), there is no solid evidence that self-recognizing chimps also self-comprehend.[35] Self-comprehension, in contrast to self-recognition, depends critically on the ability to attend to the character of one's conscious experience; self-comprehension taps into one's own conscious mental life. Self-recognition may play a role in certain forms of self-comprehension, but self-comprehension carries a more sophisticated or at least different psychological or conceptual load than self-recognition. Part of what is critical about self-comprehending creatures is that they represent themselves to themselves as having experiences: as possessed of conscious lives and not just of images in mirrors.

Singer's motives for making the imagination requirement, of course, are morally commendable. Certainly none of the above criticism of

Singer means that we do not have moral duties to animals. However, for people like Singer who assume that animals count, morally, there needs to be a method by which to determine how *much* they count. Generally speaking, people know which side their toast is buttered on, and will prefer that side unless they can be shown that something is to be said for the other side. What counts as a benefit to humans which would be defeated by a burden to animals? We need answers to questions about experimenting on nonhuman animals, whether we should refrain from eating them, hunting and slaughtering them, and so forth. Singer's suggestion even if emotionally appealing ultimately is implausible: take their conscious standpoint, and feel what is, from their subjective point of view, their mode of existence; then make an intrinsic comparison. Is it worse to be a factory farmed chicken or a person without cheap eggs? Is it worse to be a rabbit caught in a trap or a collector with a gap in his collection? Is it better to be an eagle spotting its prey or a human hunter spotting an eagle as its prey?

In this comparative interior our role as Singeresque moral agents is to compare and contrast how life is to creatures affected by our actions. Animals are looked at not in terms of their real or potential usefulness to us, but as apprehensible in themselves. We discover them in themselves by vicariously living their lives.

Singer's principle would be exciting if it worked. But alas, theoretically, it fails. There is no inter-species comparative interior. Nothing can enable us to know what it is like to be an animal.

Though as a moral bench mark Singer's position is unhelpful, the long and sorry history of human treatment of animals may serve as stimulus to develop a superior position. What then of the consciousness of animals? Might it count for something, morally? Surely yes. Take the most modest animal ethic imaginable: In order to treat animals in a morally proper manner, the less animal suffering in the treatment, the more defensible the treatment, other things being equal. The moral truth about animals may be radically more demanding than such a strategy, but for a leap in the moral dark the least strenuous ethic is decent moral behavior, too, since in every action it admonishes respect for animal suffering. There is modesty, too, though of a decidedly more theoretical sort, in our earlier examination of whether consciousness is nothing but a brain process. One might succeed in knowing everything that there is to know about the brains and nervous systems of animals, but it is still uncertain just what, if anything, looking at a ripe tomato is like to them.

Monkey an imitation? Horse a zombie? Qualia-less animals? Such things are conceptually possible, to quine a phrase. However, one does not have to be fond of Singer to recognize the moral danger which lurks within *that* conceptual move.

NOTES

1 There are other non-phenomenal senses of the word 'consciousness' and its conceptual kin (like 'conscious'). To be conscious may mean, simply, being awake. To be conscious of something may mean, less simply, attending to it or perceiving it. It is sometimes argued that every state of consciousness is also a state of self-consciousness. In this chapter I am not interested in consciousness in the senses of being awake or attentive. I focus on phenomenal consciousness, although I take some interest in self-consciousness at the end of the chapter. I would deny that it is characteristic of phenomenally conscious states that they are self-conscious (in any ordinary sense of self-conscious). Suppose I am sitting in a bar having an ice-cold beer. I may be conscious that the beer tastes bitter, but not necessarily attentive to the fact that I am someone to whom the beer tastes bitter. I can shift my attention to myself as tasting bitter beer. However, it is the beer's taste of which I am initially (phenomenally) conscious, not me. The point is elusive. So here is another way in which to make it: When someone asks about the taste I say, 'The beer tastes bitter'. I do not say, 'I taste bitter beer'. It is one thing to focus on the taste, another on the taste as something that I experience.

2 C. S. Peirce, *Collected Papers*, Vol. 6, eds C. Hartshorne and P. Weiss (Harvard University Press, Cambridge, Mass., 1935), par. 223.

3 F. Jackson, 'Epiphenomenal qualia', *Philosophical Quarterly*, 32 (1982), p. 127.

4 P. Bieri, 'Why is consciousness puzzling?', in *Conscious Experience*, ed. T. Metzinger (Shoningh, Paderhorn, 1995), p. 47.

5 Thomas Nagel, *What Does It All Mean?* (Oxford University Press, Oxford, 1987), p. 29.

6 The quotation is reported in A. M. Ludwig, *How Do We Know Who We Are? A Biography of the Self* (Oxford University Press, Oxford, 1997), p. 13.

7 William James, *Essays in Pragmatism*, ed. A. Castell (Hafner, New York, 1948), p. 69.

8 Singer, 'The significance of animal suffering', *Behavioral and Brain Sciences*, 13 (1990), p. 12.

9 James, *Essays in Pragmatism*, p. 73.
10 J. J. C. Smart, 'The revival of materialism', in *Essays Metaphysical & Moral* (Blackwell Publishers, Oxford, 1987), p. 243.
11 Smart, 'Revival', p. 241.
12 For its best formulation, see J. McConnell, 'In defense of the knowledge argument', *Philosophical Topics*, 22 (1994), pp. 157–87.
13 See J. J. C. Smart, 'My semantic ascents and descents', in *Essays Metaphysical and Moral*, p. 33. See also his 'Under the form of eternity', pp. 120–31.
14 Smart, 'Under', p. 125.
15 For related discussion, see K. Campbell, *Body and Mind* (University of Notre Dame Press, Notre Dame, 1980).
16 D. Dennett, 'Quining qualia', in *A Historical Introduction to the Philosophy of Mind*, ed. Peter Morton (Broadview Press, Ontario, 1977), pp. 409–34. Reprinted from *Consciousness in Contemporary Science*, eds A. Marcel and E. Bisiach (Oxford University Press, Oxford, 1988). Reference to 'quining' is reference to W. V. O. Quine, one of the most distinguished philosophers of the later part of the twentieth century. Quine sometimes speaks of dismissing qualia, though, on my reading of his relevant texts, Quine's attitudes towards qualia are fairly (perhaps even intentionally) vague. Quine is no crude 'quiner' (and, if the full truth be told, neither is Dennett). See W. V. O. Quine, 'Mental entities', in *The Ways of Paradox*, revised and enlarged edition (Harvard University Press, Cambridge, Mass., 1976), pp. 221–7. See also D. Dennett, *Consciousness Explained* (Little, Brown, Boston, 1991).
17 See O. Flanagan, *Consciousness Reconsidered* (MIT Press, Cambridge, Mass., 1992), p. 101.
18 One of Flanagan's suggestions is that 'qualitative experience might ... yield to neural decomposition'. See *Consciousness*, p. 64. His idea seems to be this: Physical science does not capture the like-thisness of conscious experience, but the like-thisness of conscious experience has neural constituents or components. For this and perhaps other reasons, conscious experience is a brain process. However, how can something whose description does not fall within the domain of neuroscience yield to neural decomposition? Consider the following analogy: If an automobile engine yields to mechanical decomposition, doesn't this mean that the engine can be described in mechanical terms? Materialism without comprehensive reliance on physical science isn't materialism. Or else the whole physicality of conscious experience is mysterious. On materialism with mystery, see C. McGinn, *The Problem of Consciousness* (Blackwell Publishers, Oxford, 1991).
19 For a less dismissive, more conciliatory but still cautious attitude towards Dennett's quining qualia than I exhibit here, see W. Bechtel, 'Conscious-

ness: perspectives from symbolic and connectionist AI', *Neuropsychologia*, 33 (1995), pp. 1075–86.

20 W. James, *The Will to Believe and Other Essays in Popular Philosophy* (Dover Publications, New York, 1956; orig. edn 1987), p. x.

21 This picture of the future development of science is articulated in David Chalmers, *The Conscious Mind: In Search of a Fundamental Theory* (Oxford University Press, Oxford, 1996).

22 Dennett, 'Quining', p. 431.

23 See S. Kosslyn and O. Koenig, *Wet Mind: The New Cognitive Neuroscience* (Macmillan, New York, 1992), p. 432.

24 Peter Singer, *Animal Liberation* (Avon Books, New York, 1975), p. 17.

25 Donald Van DeVeer, 'Interspecific justice', *Inquiry*, 22 (1979), p. 55.

26 Peter Singer, 'The significance', p. 12. The quote is adapted from another example of Singer's, but it helps to capture the essence of his position.

27 Singer, *Practical Ethics* (Cambridge University Press, Cambridge, 1979), p. 89.

28 Vinit Haksar, *Equality, Liberty, and Perfectionism* (Clarendon Press, Oxford, 1979), p. 211.

29 Colin McGinn, 'Evolution, animals, and the basis of equality', *Inquiry*, 22 (1979), p. 95.

30 Singer, 'The significance', p. 11.

31 O. Flanagan, *Consciousness Reconsidered*, p. 107.

32 Kathleen Akins, 'Science and our inner lives', in Marc Bekoff and Dale Jamieson, eds, *Interpretation and Explanation in the Study of Animal Behavior* (Westview Press, Boulder, 1990), p. 415.

33 Dorothy L. Cheney and Robert M. Seyfarth, *How Monkeys See The World* (University of Chicago Press, 1990), p. 312.

34 Singer, *Practical Ethics*, p. 90.

35 See G. Gallup, 'Self-awareness and the emergence of mind in primates', *American Journal of Primatology*, 2 (1982), pp. 237–48; M. Tomasello and J. Call, *Primate Cognition* (Oxford University Press, New York, 1997), pp. 331–41.

11

Fear and Trembling

It came over me on high. I was flying from Atlanta to New York on a night flight. It was an 11 p.m. of November, a time of pitch black and moonless motion. From my window seat I looked into the astrophysical abyss. I felt fear. I trembled. The intimate communion of cause and effect.

Not so, says the consciousness epiphenomenalist. No event can cause anything by virtue of being conscious. Conscious events *do* nothing, they *explain* nothing. Feeling fear does not cause trembling.

Feeling fear does not cause trembling? The philosopher Peter Bieri notes: 'I am not particularly fond of this doctrine. But I find the arguments leading to it very strong.'[1]

In this final chapter we examine consciousness epiphenomenalism and the argument – the main or master argument – leading to it. As befits a final chapter, echoes from earlier chapters can be heard here. Theory and data from psychopathology are used to help to argue that consciousness epiphenomenalism, though argumentatively potent, is mistaken.

11.1 Consciousness Epiphenomenalism

Our being conscious in the sense of having subjective experiences means that there are things it is like to be us and to have things happen to us and to act in various ways. The specific *like-thisness* of subjective experience constitutes its phenomenal character or quality (or 'quale' [plural 'qualia']). The hurtfulness of pains, the itchiness of itches, the emotional quality of fear: these and other phenomenal qualities not only occur in us but it is like something to experience or undergo them.

What, if anything, does being conscious do for us as persons? How, if at all, do the qualities of conscious experience matter for us? The following answer seems appropriate. It seems nothing less than common sense:

> Consciousness matters for the behavior that we produce. Because I feel a sharp, stabbing sensation at the base of my foot, I scream; since you feel deeply depressed, you act fatigued and socially withdraw; because I feel itchy on the back of my neck, I scratch; feeling happy I smile; feeling fear I tremble.

However, perhaps consciousness fails to matter. Perhaps conscious experience is inessential for our behavior. Perhaps we are victims, in the words of Peter Bieri, of a 'permanent, massive, and irresistible error' that consciousness makes a behavioral difference.[2]

Consider the following analogy between consciousness and a computer printer, offered by Owen Flanagan to make intelligible the possibility that consciousness doesn't matter.

> My computer printer reveals my thoughts in tangible form. But my printer is not in any important sense involved in the process of composing what I write. Despite the perspicacity, noisiness, and fulfilling role it plays in the display of my written words, my printer is really, truth-be-told – just a public relations device. It gives voice to, or makes public, what has already been produced. Just as one might overrate the role of one's printer in the process of writing, one might overrate the causal efficacy of the conscious mind in the generation of action. It is possible, after all, that conscious mental states lie at the end of causal chains. Perhaps they are broadcasts of what has happened or is happening in some ... unconsciously driven system, and not, as they seem, critical initiators of action.[3]

Is consciousness just a private relations device, somehow announcing itself *in* us, individually, but not doing anything *for* us behaviorally? Biologist Thomas Huxley (1825–95) famously remarked: 'There is no proof that any state of consciousness is the cause of change in the motion of the matter of the organism.' He announced: 'We are conscious automata.'

That consciousness, the phenomenal quality or like-thisness of experience, fails to matter behaviorally is the doctrine of consciousness epiphenomenalism. No conscious event in virtue of being conscious, in virtue of how it feels, causes or causally explains behavior. To explain my trembling we should not invoke my feeling of fear. We should refer to non-conscious sub-personal brain processes. 'Our trajectory through the world would be exactly the same, down to the smallest movement' if our otherwise normally functioning brains somehow failed to produce conscious experience.[4]

Why endorse consciousness epiphenomenalism? Why embrace so counter-intuitive a doctrine? Where lies the argument?

11.2 The Master Argument for Consciousness Epiphenomenalism

The most widely used arguments designed to defend consciousness epiphenomenalism share a common structure, which may be called the Master Argument for Consciousness Epiphenomenalism. The argument has three steps and goes like this:

MA1 Every physical event, including human behavior, has, in principle, a causal explanation in physical terms – in terms of physical science.

MA2 No event can be given more than one causal explanation.

MA3 Physical causal explanation never invokes consciousness as a cause of anything. No event in virtue of being conscious – in virtue of its phenomenal quality – is cited as a cause by physical science (including the neurosciences).

MA4 So consciousness makes no difference to the behavior that we produce. Behaviorally consciousness is causally impotent, explanatorily inert.

What about the first premise? According to the first premise, the physical world has the possibility of comprehensive physical scientific explanation somehow built into its structure. If an event is physical, it can be physically explained.

Physical science casts the widest disciplinary net of any science. It includes sciences such as physics, chemistry, and biology as well as neurosciences such as neurochemistry and neurobiology. The movement of my arm and fingers when I scratch, in theory at least, says the first premise, can be accounted for in terms of chemical changes in muscle fibers and signals from the brain which produce those changes as well as by the neurochemistry of receptors on the skin and body wall which activate the brain signals.

The philosopher Jaegwon Kim calls the second premise 'the principle of causal/explanatory exclusion'.[5] The premise implies that if behavior can be causally explained without invoking consciousness, then the search for an explanation of behavior which invokes consciousness is empty. There is none.

Many contemporary philosophers are attracted to the principle of causal/explanatory exclusion in connection with understanding the history and methods of physical science. Here is a typical expression of attraction:

> When science came up with the explanation of the operation of pumps in terms of air pressure, this was taken to exclude the older explanation of their operation in terms of nature's abhorrence of a vacuum. Likewise, the explanation of lightning in terms of electrical discharges displaced the explanation in terms of Thor's thunderbolts, and the explanation of plant growth in terms of the chemistry of cell division displaced the explanation in terms of vital spirit. In none of these cases did scientists say, 'How nice. We now have two explanations, where before we had only one.'[6]

The third premise says that neuroscientific explanation does not attribute causal relevance to consciousness. Neuroscientific explanation of my scratching, for instance, does not describe the behavior as a response to the subjective quality of the itch. It refers to my neurochemistry, neurobiology, and so on. The following passage from a popular textbook in neuroscience is representative. The passage begins to sketch a story of the impact of a somatic sensation such as an itch on behavior. Absent is any reference whatsoever to what somatic sensations feel like to their subjects.

> Somatic sensation deals with many types of information from almost all parts of the body. It begins with sensory receptors in the skin and the body wall; in the muscles, tendons, ligaments, and connective tissue of the joints; and in the internal organs. Because ... stimuli vary from the mechanical ... to the chemical ... it takes many different kinds of specialized receptors to detect them. A receptor might be a simple, bare

nerve ending or a complex combination of nerves with supporting cells, connective tissue, muscle cells, or even hair.[7]

The master argument concludes that consciousness makes no difference to behavior. Ultimately it is, to borrow psychologist Howard Gardner's predatorial metaphor, 'devoured by neuroscience'.[8]

11.3 Attacking the Master Argument

Despite the unpopularity and counter-intuitiveness of consciousness epiphenomenalism, it is not easy to demonstrate that the master argument is unsound and that consciousness epiphenomenalism is mistaken. Lines of attack are distinguished by reference to which premise is chosen for rebuff.

(1) *First line of attack*   There are various ways in which the first premise has been challenged. Some charge that the physical world is at bottom something non-physical. Matter is a theoretical construction from conscious non-matter. This is the doctrine of metaphysical idealism or phenomenalism, which implies that there are no physical events and no genuine physical science. Others charge that physical science cannot account for all types of behavior, even as a matter of theoretical principle. Some behavior must be explained by invoking causes which cannot be described in physical scientific terms.

(2) *Second line of attack*   Another line focuses on the second premise. It rejects the principle of causal/explanatory exclusion. It charges that there can be more than one causal explanation of the same physical event. Some behavior may be causally *overdetermined*.[9] Scratching can be produced (independently) by itchy feeling and by brain activity. Trembling can be caused by fearful feeling as well as by neurochemistry.

(3) *Third line of attack*   The most popular and widely debated means to attack the master argument is to argue that conscious experience somehow is physical and can be described in terms of physical science. In J. J. C. Smart's materialist idiom, consciousness somehow is nothing but a brain process.[10] Then, given that consciousness is Smart and brainy, physical brain science can invoke conscious states or processes (contrary to the third premise) in the explanation of behavior. One version of this type of maneuver takes the form of appeal to the notion of 'knowledge under a description' (familiar to readers of the eighth chapter), and to the

theoretical possibility that, contrary to appearance, neuroscience *already* invokes conscious processes in the explanation of behavior. Neuroscience does this not by using phenomenal descriptions (not by talking of 'feelings') but by describing subjective qualities in neurophysical terms.

Which line of attack should be pursued? Let's briefly look at the overall argumentative situation.

The second line requires defeating the principle of causal/explanatory exclusion. That is a difficult order. Explanation is a knotty notion. Explainers, especially scientific explainers, put a lot of stock in their ability to find explanations which defeat other explanations. Electricity takes the energy out of Thor's thunderbolts. The principle of causal/ explanatory exclusion invests in that stock. A scientist's insistence on explanations which exclude other explanations also serves a pragmatic function, that of promoting telling experiments and revealing observations while discouraging the embrace of poorly tested hypotheses which may tempt the non-exclusivist mind.

What about the third line? The third line requires defending materialism about conscious experience. That, too, is a difficult order. Trouble brews for materialism in the form of forceful arguments that consciousness is not a brain process. The qualitative like-thisness of conscious experience is the most troubling impediment to materialism (as observed in the last chapter).[11] The remarkable thing is that possessing phenomenal quality just is what it means for an event to *be* conscious. For any conscious experience, what it is like to undergo it is essential to it. Critics of materialism also complain that materialism too often legislates against sciences other than materialism's favorite theoretical brands. Materialists picket anti-materialist complaints, but their counter-strikes have yet to shut down anti-materialist labor.

Alternatively, what about the first line? What about attacking the first premise that all human behavior admits of physical scientific explanation? Leaving idealism and phenomenalism aside, there are two types of approaches that critics of consciousness epiphenomenalism take in attempting to attack the idea that all behavior admits of physical explanation.[12] Some critics argue that conscious experience is not a brain process or something physical, and thus it is not invoked in physical scientific explanation. However, they argue, conscious experience figures in the causation of behavior. So, something non-physical helps to cause behavior. This may be called the 'bold attack': 'bold' because it rejects materialism about conscious experience. Other critics argue that on the question of whether conscious experience is something physical, there are many problems and unresolved issues. These critics claim to be unwilling to defend anti-materialism. Instead they begin with the observation that consciousness certainly appears to cause behavior, and then argue that it seems impossible to always account for behavior on the basis of brain or physical science. They find that this gives reason to deny that human behavior always admits of physical scientific explanation, but remain reluctant about concluding that materialism is false. This may be called the 'cautious attack': 'cautious' because it does not consist in rejecting materialism.

The cautious attack erects itself around the case for consciousness as a cause of behavior in spite of the fact that it is not cited as a cause by physical science. The cautious attack plots an argument against the comprehensiveness of physical science, but leaves undecided whether this squeezes plausibility out of materialism about conscious experience.

At least for the time being, we will be cautious. We will not assume that consciousness is something non-physical and that materialism is false. We will try to defeat the master argument by attacking the first premise and leaving the second and third premises unquestioned. However, we reserve the opportunity to worry, later, about what reasons materialists can hope to muster in support of their faith that consciousness somehow is nothing but a brain process, given the failure of the first premise.

So what's wrong with the first premise? Is there evidence to suggest that physical science, assuming (with the third premise) that it does not invoke consciousness as a cause, is not comprehensive? When behavior is caused, can consciousness be a cause?

11.4 Defeating the Master Argument

Science both physical and otherwise is widely esteemed. The strongest evidence that consciousness packs clout comes from science. If we were to express in a single expression the main liability of the first premise – if we were to label the best case for consciousness mattering for behavior – it would be that the first premise is *scientifically disrespectful*. The notion that consciousness matters is central to scientific inquiry into human behavior (albeit not physical scientific inquiry). In upshot, we have good reason to believe that (contrary to MA1) some behavior cannot be explained in physical scientific terms.

There is, of course, a qualification. The scientific study of human behavior isn't finished yet. At its present state of maturation it is not all of one piece. So how do I propose to argue that explanation by reference to consciousness is scientifically central? I plan to concentrate on theory and data primarily in psychopathology. Psychopathology (also known as clinical or abnormal psychology) is a vivid and in many ways representative domain of scientific inquiry into human behavior in which there is a presumption that consciousness makes a behavioral difference. The current best explanations of various psychopathological behavior invoke consciousness. Indeed, it is hard to imagine how various behavior could be explained without invoking consciousness. After a brief discussion of some deficits in visual perception, I turn to focus primarily on two sorts of psychopathological disorder: depression and schizophrenia.

Before setting out the argument, we need briefly to clarify two concepts or ideas which will be used in the rest of the chapter.

(1) *Psychopathological disorder*   I use the expression 'psychopathological disorder' in a broad sense to include not only mental disorders or deficits with no known organic etiology or neurological basis, but deficits which stem directly from brain lesions and other neuropathologies.

A major function of focusing on psychopathological disorders to gain insight into the role of consciousness in behavior is that disorders often provide better insight into the behavioral role of consciousness than does non-disordered, smoothly operating conscious activity. Disorders and deficits allow us to determine the contributions of conscious experience to behavior by exhibiting alterations within behavioral activity due to breakdowns in the operation of consciousness.[13]

(2) *Psychopathology*   I use the term 'psychopathology' for psychopathological disorders as well as for the loose network of principles, ideas, hypotheses, and treatments which constitutes their medical-scientific study.[14] It should be clear from the context in which sense, whether for the disorders or the network, the term is employed. It should also be mentioned, in advance, that the network is loose and various. Psychopathology sometimes deploys physical scientific explanations, such as neuroscientific explanations, for disorders or features of disorders; sometimes not. Sometimes explanations of non-neuroscientific but still scientific sorts are deployed.

An attractive feature of focusing on psychopathology, from an anti-epiphenomenalist perspective, is that it permits the hypothesis that consciousness is behaviorally potent to be scientifically trustworthy without having to be *physically* scientifically respectable. Psychopathology encourages conceiving of conscious experience as mattering for us without, as it were, mandating that it be subject to neuroscientific description.

In the remainder of the chapter I examine a currently popular hypothesis among philosophers and others for the causal role of consciousness in behavior, the intelligent behavior hypothesis, which depicts conscious experience as contributing to the overall intelligence or adaptivity of behavior. In my judgment, this depiction, though likely correct in some qualified form, under-represents the complexity and investigatory elusiveness of the power of consciousness. I offer a complementary alternative conception of the lessons of psychopathology for the causal role of consciousness, the divided labor hypothesis, which is incompatible with consciousness epiphenomenalism but admits that there is much we just do not know about the power of consciousness. I then briefly examine the implications of this conception for our understanding of the relations between consciousness inquiries and those aimed at neurophysical activity.

11.5 The Intelligent Behavior Hypothesis

- While shaving Sam reached for an aspirin bottle because he felt headachy and recognized the bottle on the shelf.
- Samantha surreptitiously nudged the bottle away from Sam, for she felt envy over the good night's sleep which he had had the night before.
- Little Sammy cried uncontrollably and ran from the bathroom. He feared that his parents were about to fight.

One striking feature of the above commonsensical claims is that they causally explain behavior by reference to states of consciousness. Sam reached for aspirin because of the subjective quality of his headache. Samantha moved the bottle because she felt envy towards Sam. Little Sammy ran away in tears because he feared that his parents would fight.

To common sense it seems obvious that consciousness makes a difference to behavior. If the headache had been missing or less intense Sam would not have sought aspirin. If he had not visually recognized the bottle, he would not have reached. However, which feature or features of Sam's activity are produced by consciousness? Did Sam's headachy feeling govern smooth muscle motility, mucous and digestive secretions, the diameter of blood vessels as he reached? Or did it affect his behavior only in some broad macrobehavioral sense? Did the headache produce the detailed character of his motor response or only its overall goal and general occurrence?

Features of behavior produced by consciousness, call these 'produced-by-consciousness features', are not completely transparent to common sense. The proposal to which some philosophers and other theorists turn is: Focus on deficits or disorders of conscious perception and visual awareness. Various pathologies of visual awareness reveal produced-by-consciousness features of behavior. These pathologies offer rather detailed evidence of the causal role of consciousness in behavior. Visual deficit data may not speak to the level of microstimulation of muscle fibers, but it does tell which broad behavioral features are due to consciousness. A person or patient pathologically truncated in visual awareness may display this deficit in behavior and therein help to demonstrate the causal role of conscious experience in behavior. Consider, for often cited examples, blindsight and prosopagnosia.[15]

Blindsight is a visual field deficit, in otherwise sighted subjects, stemming from damage to the primary visual cortex. The path for processing visual information about an external stimulus in 'blind' portions of the field is impaired, though, interestingly, some information is processed in an abbreviated or truncated way. Victims of blindsight gain information about some but not all visual properties of a stimulus, including stimulus motion and orientation, for which they take themselves to be blind. To them, for example, there is nothing it is like to see stimulus motion. Subjectively or phenomenally they don't 'see' the motion. However ingenious behavioral tests (including so-called forced-choice questionnaires) reveal that victims of blindsight extract motion information from presented stimuli. They discriminate stimulus motion although they are phenomenally unaware of the motion.

Prosopagnosia is a deficit in recognizing faces of relatives or friends as familiar. Victims see a familiar relative in full view but take themselves to miss the corresponding fact of familiarity. 'That's mother's face?' Once again, however, there are intriguing tests which show that victims extract information about familiarity from presented faces. Their electrodermal responses, for example, discriminate familiar from unfamiliar faces even though they themselves disavow that they can do this. One patient reporting his difficulties exclaimed: 'I can tell the difference between a man and a woman from across the street, but I failed to recognize the face of an old friend and I mistook my mother for my wife'.[16]

Nonconscious informational sensitivity to stimuli or stimulus properties occurs in blindsight and prosopagnosia. However, conscious awareness of those stimuli or properties does not occur. Impressed by these and related visual deficits a number of philosophers and others advance an hypothesis about the produced-by-consciousness features of behavior.[17] For reasons which will be obvious shortly, I call this the 'intelligent behavior hypothesis'. Ran Lahav summarizes the hypothesis:

> Nonconscious information evokes nonselective, nonflexible responses that are relatively insensitive to circumstances.... [Whereas] conscious experience expresses information available for an entire spectrum of global, integrated, and flexible (non-automatic) behaviors.[18]

According to Lahav and others, when stimulus information enters consciousness, all else being equal, the intelligence of behavior is enhanced. When information is conscious it is deployed in flexible and adaptive behavior. I recognize the familiar face of my mother and hug her accordingly. However, when there are lacunae or gaps in perceptual consciousness, as in prosopagnosia and blindsight, information possessed by the subject may influence behavior in various ways but is not brought into flexible play in action. A prosopagnosic Little Sammy will exhibit galvanic skin responses, but he won't run when he spots his father's frown. A blindsighted Sam wouldn't reach for the bottle if this is in the 'blind' portion of his visual field, although in a forced-choice questionnaire in which he is asked to choose between a small number of alternative responses to questions, he will report, in effect, whether the bottle is marked with vertical or horizontal lines.

The intelligent behavior hypothesis claims that consciousness makes, or tends to make, a positive difference in the intelligence or performance of behavior. Provided of course that the subject is awake, some sort of stimulus-specific behavior (such as electrodermal response) occurs without visual consciousness of the relevant stimulus. This behavior, however, typically is not nearly as flexible, adaptive, or integrated as when phenomenal awareness of the stimulus occurs. Why? The answer according to Lahav and others is, briefly, that in conscious states stimulus information is broadcast or made available throughout a subject's psychological economy. Internal distribution of information enables the person to adjust behavior to circumstance and to perform actions that they would not be able to perform without that distribution – to hug mother, to reach for aspirin, or to flee.[19]

The hypothesis that conscious experience is an intelligent behavioral enhancer takes many forms. In some versions of the hypothesis it is connected with claims about the evolutionary function of consciousness: in some models, consciousness in organisms is said to have been selected for by Mother Nature because of its role in integrated, flexible behavior. However, there are always caveats ('all else being equal' clauses) in any version of the hypothesis. Dissecting – differentially isolating – the role of consciousness in intelligence is no easy business. At least two factors cloud the clarity or precision of the hypothesis that consciousness improves or tends to improve performance. The first is that the hypothesis may not readily generalize or extend from visual or perceptual consciousness of an external stimulus to somatic sensory consciousness since, on the face of it, a somatic sensation such as an itchy feeling is not like visual experience of a bottle. One could be blind to and yet responsive towards the bottle, but not, it seems, to an itch. Take away the itchy feeling and there doesn't seem to be anything of the itch left to which a person could respond (intelligently or otherwise). Take away visual consciousness of the bottle, and it still perches on the shelf to be discriminated nonconsciously. The contribution of consciousness to intelligence may be different in the two sorts of cases (sensory and perceptual conscious experience). This is not to say that the contribution is different. But why think that sensory consciousness contributes in the same manner as perceptual consciousness, if gaps or deficits in the former are quite unlike those in the latter?

The second factor is recognition that keeping or getting information *out* of consciousness often is as important for performance quality as channeling information in.[20] To take an example from non-perceptual psychopathology, to which we will return again, consider schizophrenia.

Victims of schizophrenia are bombarded with conscious information. They can't filter it out or, on an alternative interpretation of relevant abnormalities of schizophrenia, they can't properly monitor and control its broadcast through their consciousness or conscious psychology.[21] Information which normally does or should remain unconscious and screened off from consciousness by perceptual and response biases enters and preoccupies attention. Then schizophrenics, unable to cope with their own activity, degrade behaviorally into stereopy, inflexibility, and abortive bodily movement. Intelligence is degraded, not enhanced. A former patient puts it effectively: 'What happened to me was ... a hodgepodge of unrelated stimuli were distracting me from things which should have had my undivided attention.'[22] While another reports: 'I feel my mind cannot cope with everything. It is difficult to concentrate on any one sound. It's like trying to do two or three different things at one time.'[23]

The lesson of schizophrenia (and various other psychopathological disorders)[24] is that truly to isolate the distinctive contribution of consciousness to intelligent behavior it is necessary to specify which types, configurations, and frequencies of conscious information contribute to intelligence and which, to put it simply, confound a person with irrelevancies. Conscious awareness may be seized by extraneous information. Consciousness puts intelligence in jeopardy if what is broadcast is a lot of noise and channel switching.

Scientists and philosophers are far from knowing the detailed truth about the contribution which consciousness makes to intelligent behavior. So even though it seems that types of behavior gain in performance quality when initiated or controlled by consciousness, it is not clear how assigning a causal role to consciousness in intelligence is compatible with appreciating the contribution which disengaging consciousness from behavior also makes to intelligence.

So much the worse for psychopathology's relevance to identifying evidence in favor of the behavioral role of consciousness, an epiphenomenalist skeptic may say. If, however, one wants to make a case for a behavioral role for consciousness, as I wish to do in this chapter, the recognition must be explicit that consciousness has – to use Owen Flanagan's apt metaphor – a hidden depth and structure.[25] Part of that depth and structure involves its causal role in behavior. Little about that role is obvious to common sense, except perhaps that consciousness makes a difference. If the pathologies of blindsight and prosopagnosia tempt us into overgeneralizing that consciousness makes behavior more intelligent, then we need to consider *more* disorders, not less. Perhaps we also need to admit that consciousness has a variety of behavioral effects. Contribution to *some* forms of behavioral intelligence is but one. Understanding the difference that consciousness makes to behavior requires framing the discussion in broader clinical and psychopathological terms.

11.6 The Divided Labor Hypothesis

Let's begin with two basic and closely related assumptions of contemporary psychopathology theory and research.

> Assumption One: Often there are various ways – vocabularies at various levels of description and analysis – in which one and the same behavior can be analyzed and explained. We cannot say that one mode of explanation (the neuroscientific) is favored over all the others prior to clinical and empirical investigation.

Assumption One (which I will explain shortly) underlies discussion of psychopathology's most explanatorily troubling disorders, of which there notoriously are plenty. Consider schizophrenia and depression.

The psychopathologist David Hemsley writes of schizophrenia as follows: 'Clearly the abnormal behaviors and experiences that we characterize as schizophrenic require analysis at a number of levels – social, behavioral, cognitive, psychophysiological, and biochemical. A major task is to demonstrate how these are interrelated.'[26] Anthony Marsella and his colleagues offer a similar comment about depression: 'Depression involves the totality of human functioning – biological, psychological, and sociocultural. We need to understand the relationships across all these levels.'[27] Dale Johnson writes of depression almost in chorus: 'A more comprehensive model is necessary ... [involving] a hierarchical organization from molecular at one extreme level to sociocultural at the other extreme.'[28]

What does the assumption mean? It means that psychopathology research conducts investigation into the possible causes of psychopathological behavior on many levels, from various points of view, sometimes using elements from several perspectives at once. It means that psychopathology research assumes that in the domain of explanatorily vexing

conditions paying exclusive attention to descriptions at lower neurophysical levels is not a promising research program. Some questions
demand non-neuroscientific, non-physical scientific answers.

Consider reports of auditory hallucinations in schizophrenia. (These
hallucinations are false auditory experiences which subjectively to schizophrenics seem compellingly and often terrifyingly real.) Why do some
victims report hearing the voice of Jesus, others their chiefs bound for
the open waters in an outrigger? Questions of hallucinatory report appear
to turn not on brain processes per se but on various facts about the
society or culture within which victims are embedded and the conscious
representation of those facts. Victims who claim to hear Jesus may be
natives of the southeastern United States; those who report hearing their
chiefs may be native to Hawaii or Malaysia.

Consider patterns of behavioral symptom formation in depression.
Why do depressive behavioral symptoms – fatigue, social withdrawal,
and so on – in individuals from non-western cultures tend to include a
dominance of bodily complaints, whereas in Americans or Europeans
complaints of guilt and despair? The answer seems to lie not in neurochemistry or neurobiology but in varying cross-cultural roles of body
image and feelings of individual responsibility as culturally alternative
sources of self-esteem. High rates of bodily complaint have been
observed in countries such as Saudi Arabia, the Philippines, and the
People's Republic of China. Withdrawal, despondency, and loss of
interest in the social environment are often connected in those cultures
with feelings of deficiency in one's body. In America and Europe
behaviors of withdrawal and despondency tend to be associated with
feelings of personal and moral failure.[29]

Assumption Two: In the causation of behavior sometimes conscious
processes are active in behavior; sometimes not.

To clarify the second assumption, again consider schizophrenia.
Psychiatrist Michael Schwartz and philosopher Osborne Wiggins have
written approvingly of the role of verbal psychotherapy ('talk therapy')
in reducing schizophrenic delusions and the behavior which follows
upon them. Delusions are among the most dramatic symptoms of
schizophrenia. They consist of conscious, severely contrary-to-fact convictions, deeply if disruptively held, and out of harmony with a victim's
general level of understanding or cultural group. The belief that one,

though male, is Mother Teresa or that the King of Sweden is 'out to marry me' would be examples of delusions.

Schizophrenics, Schwartz and Wiggins point out, often experience feelings of doubt or misgiving about their delusions. They may worry that their convictions are false or in error. Schwartz and Wiggins write: 'Treatment can aim at increasing and extending this doubt until the delusions play only a marginal and minimal role in the patient's experience.'[30] For example, if a male schizophrenic believes that he is Mother Teresa and he encounters a picture of himself in which he obviously is male and asks 'Can this be me?', the therapist may try to offer a cohesive and more satisfying account of the evidence than the schizophrenic can himself. One possibility, according to Schwartz and Wiggins, is that in time and under therapeutic guidance the subject may infer that he has been mistaken. His Mother Teresa delusional activity may disappear.

Suppose Schwartz and Wiggins are right. Suppose that psychotherapy can reduce troublesome elements in schizophrenic consciousness. When Schwartz and Wiggins say that psychotherapy reduces delusions and delusional activity, they refer to conscious processes which appear utterly opaque to neuroscience. Schizophrenic delusions straddle brain processes which are so massively heterogenous in pattern and configuration that little if any relevant information about either psychotherapeutic efficacy in schizophrenia or the causal role of doubts concerning delusions can be gleaned from neuroscientific investigation. What seems obvious from therapeutic data is that conscious experience positively contributes to reduction in delusional behavior.

I like to call the combined two assumptions that causal relevance can be distributed or divided over different levels of analysis or explanation (the first assumption), including conscious experience (the second assumption), the *divided causal explanatory labor* hypothesis (*divided labor* hypothesis, for short). If the divided labor hypothesis is correct, then neuroscience is explanatorily gappy or insufficient, although exactly where and why needs to be uncovered clinically and empirically.

Consider depression. Various researchers, including the English sociologists George Brown and Tirril Harris, have shown that reference to stressful events and losses such as the death of a parent, financial setback, and abandonment by one's spouse help to explain the onset of depression.[31] However, losses do not always bring about depression, quite obviously. Why do losses in some people trigger depression, whereas similar losses in others do not?

No exclusively neuroscientific characterization explains how stressful loss is linked to depression, that is, no explanation which fails to impute conscious experience to the subject of the loss. Indeed, merely invoking brain processes seems not to offer the slightest hint or clue as to how or why personal loss contributes to depression. Connections between loss and depression require conscious interpretation of those events.[32] The causal impact of loss, to put things crudely, turns on how it *feels* to its subject. If a person experiences parental death, spousal abandonment, and so on, with feelings of general personal helplessness or agentic impotence, there is a tale to be told about how certain losses affect depressed behavior. Focusing on facts such as that the loss had the conscious quality of helplessness is causally relevant in the situation. Indeed (as readers of the ninth chapter may recall), an influential behavioral/cognitive theory of depression known as the learned help-lessness model claims that the basic cause of some depression is a subjective sense of personal helplessness, which among other things undermines a person's motivation to act and produces social with-drawal.[33] Feeling helpless gives subjects a *reason* to withdraw. Nothing they do seems effective.

What about neurochemistry? What about a thesis like the following: Depression is caused by deficiencies of the biogenic amines.[34] Biogenic amine changes may explain why depression occurs when no stress or loss is experienced. No doubt neurochemistry also partially contributes to loss or stress-induced depression. However, neurochemistry by itself is insufficient to account for all depression. Explanation of depression invokes a variety of contributing factors of different types, sometimes including the conscious experience of helplessness, all of which cooper-ate or conspire to produce the condition and its behavioral components.[35]

The point I am making is that theory and data from psychopathology reveal that some conscious events cause behavior (at least in part) by virtue of being conscious. When developing an account of behavior – contrary to the first premise of the master argument for conscious epiphenomenalism – one can and should assume that conscious experi-ence plays a causal role. The divided labor hypothesis assumes that the relevant role may be complex. It also acknowledges the variety of effects that consciousness can have on behavior. It is perfectly compatible with the hypothesis, for instance, that some cases of intelligent behavior are best explained by reference to conscious experience of stimuli and their properties. Perhaps some version of the divided labor hypothesis can explain just when conscious experience contributes to behavioral intelligence or just how the intelligent behavior hypothesis should be restricted or qualified.

11.7 Criticism and Commitments

I can imagine someone following everything we have said thus far in this chapter but feeling unsatisfied with the case, indeed with *any* case for the power of consciousness. I can imagine in particular one major epiphenomenalist complaint.

It may be objected that, when all is said and done, what is needed to defend the causal power of consciousness is nothing less than a robust form of *dualism*: consciousness with causal powers dissociated from the brain. In the words of Daniel Dennett, 'dualism wallows in mystery, accepting dualism is giving up.'[36] 'It seems very implausible', Michael Tye writes, 'to suppose that there is no wholly physical story.'[37]

I am not sure that I can satisfy this complaint quickly. But I will be brief.

Some philosophers believe that one can admit to the causal power of consciousness, while, at the same time, maintaining physicalism or materialism about conscious experience. In certain variations this is one version of the cautious attack on the first premise of the master argument to which I referred earlier, although there are other less materialistically committed brands.

Among physicalistically oriented philosophers who have examined psychopathology for insights into the power of consciousness, Owen Flanagan has advanced a position designed to secure a modest if principled autonomy of conscious experience from neurophysical investigation. On Flanagan's model, it is true both that the subjective qualities of conscious experience fail to admit directly of physical scientific description and that physical brain science never (at least explicitly) invokes phenomenal consciousness in the causal explanation of behavior, but true also that consciousness is a brain process.[38] Flanagan's model presupposes that there is some philosophically adequate account of consciousness causation, and of neuroscientific explanation, that legitimatizes them both while also admitting that materialism is true and that the conscious mind is composed of nothing but neural processes and activities.

This produces a worry associated with his position. Reluctance to challenge materialism may strain credulity. It is not clear how Flanagan means to understand the physicality of consciousness if not by means of physical scientific description. Offhand it seems that if something (the quality of conscious experience) cannot be physically described, it is not physical. However, if Flanagan's model is sound, it offers a means of avoiding dualism and embracing materialism, while permitting conscious events to make a behavioral difference by virtue of being conscious. Foes of consciousness epiphenomenalism may endorse it.

What if Flanagan's model isn't sound? This is the field of the bold attack into which, despite its temptation, I have refrained from marching the reader. However, suppose that the temptation cannot be resisted. Then the bold response is to take the fear of dualism and anti-materialism as unfounded. It is to argue that such fear makes clear and trembling sense only if we don't look at the behavioral and clinical evidence and ask certain questions of the data. If we look at the data, the evidence – if we examine, for example, depressive and schizophrenic behavior – ask certain questions of the data, and examine our current best answers to those questions, the divided labor hypothesis presents itself as a strikingly plausible hypothesis even if it means that something conscious and (herein boldness) non-physical affects goings on in the physical world. Whatever sort of dualism or anti-materialist/non-materialist 'ism' psychopathology supports appears too shallow a mystery in which to wallow even if depressed.

Let me spell this out a bit more. Skepticism about what, if anything, consciousness does for us as persons stems in some philosophers from allegiance to stringent standards of causal potence or behavioral relevance.[39] Some philosophers assume that potence or relevance is lawful determination of behavior. If and only if being conscious, or conscious of something, lawfully determines behavior does consciousness make a difference to behavior. Additionally, various philosophers endorse rigid criteria for lawfulness, insisting, for example, that to be a law a law must hold absolutely (strictly or exceptionlessly) or universally (throughout all space-time) and not just on planet earth. This last criterion is a supposition which presupposes the supremacy of physical science and, indeed, of physics. It is not to be wondered that physics alone covers all space-time. Consciousness occupies non-numerous, earthy locations.

The anti-epiphenomenalist should not fall in uncritically with stringent standards of causal potence or behavioral relevance. As for the notion of behavioral relevance which fits with the anti-epiphenomenalist argument of this chapter, we may adopt the following less stringent and independently defensible view. Take away my consciousness, or consciousness of something, and my body would tend not to behave as it does – in this and similar circumstances; given my consciousness, or consciousness of something, and my body tends to behave as it does – again, in this and similar circumstances. Circumstantially rooted behavioral tendencies may best be understood in terms of lawfulness, but the nature of lawfulness is far from straightforward. Perhaps some laws, such as those which figure in the impact of consciousness on behavior, are at bottom tendencies or regularities which are characterized by generalizations which hold neither absolutely nor throughout all space-time. They hold more or less tightly in certain pockets of the universe (like planet earth). These laws or generalizations may be called (following Harold Kincaid)[40] *ceteris paribus laws* or (following Terence Horgan and John Tienson)[41] *soft laws*. Soft laws could be viewed as independently confirmable scientific truths, innocent by themselves of commitment to materialism.

One may be fond of the soft laws approach to laws. However, nothing more is required for making a case against consciousness epiphenomenalism, and nothing less will suffice, than the demonstration that being conscious matters for behavior. The loss I suffered made me feel helpless, it made me feel that nothing I did made any difference, and so socially I withdrew. If helpless feeling matters for my depressed behavior, then if I had *not* felt helpless, behavioral withdrawal would not, or would tend not, to occur.

A few more closing observations in a bold mood may be made. One way to think of the falsity of the first premise of the master argument is to think of it as evidence of the falsity of materialism. Put this together with other consciousness-based anti-materialist arguments (like those of the first or tenth chapters) and materialism can seem refuted. One may then go on to ask questions about the possible dualist implications of rejecting materialism. It is worth pointing out, for example, that dualism is not part of the very idea of anti-materialism. One can be opposed to materialism without being a dualist. The shape of the philosophical landscape is highly convoluted, spreading a plurality of different 'isms' (dualism and otherwise) down a variety of anti-materialist and non-materialist slopes.

Caution again. One should also be aware that materialism is a dexterous doctrine. Its ability to self-defend in the fullness of time and evolution of science should not be underestimated. If one wishes to be bold in materialism's rejection, one should be humble in its admiration.

11.8 Final Feeling

William James urged Gertrude Stein (1874–1946), when a special Radcliffe student of his at Harvard, to make a career of philosophy.[42] Stein, who later distinguished herself as a writer and spokesperson for modernistic arts, declined. She declined not for dislike of James. Stein admired James as a teacher and person, calling him 'truly a man among men', but she disliked certain areas of philosophy, foremost logic.

One day, at the start of Stein's final exam with James, it came over her on low. After reading the questions, she wrote in her examination book: 'Dear Professor James, I am so sorry but really I do not feel like an examination paper in philosophy today.' She submitted her book and left the classroom.

The next day Stein received, together with the highest course grade in the class, the following comment from James: 'Dear Miss Stein, I understand perfectly how you feel. I often feel like that myself.'

We feel like that ourselves. It is time to end the book. The philosophical jury is still taking their exams, however, on many of the issues we have considered herein. There is a lot of writing to be done, the exam is complicated, and the issues complex. Stein has left, James no longer is teaching, and the book's purpose, I hope, has been fulfilled. If all this looks like an opportunity for you to contribute, then you are urged to begin.

NOTES

1 P. Bieri, 'Trying out epiphenomenalism', *Erkenntnis*, 36 (1992), p. 283.
2 Bieri, ibid.; see also Bieri, 'Why consciousness is puzzling', in *Conscious Experience*, ed. T. Metzinger (Shoningh, Imprint, 1995), p. 54.
3 Owen Flanagan, 'Consciousness', in *A Companion to Cognitive Science*, eds William Bechtel and George Graham (Blackwell Publishers, Oxford, 1998), p. 177.

4   The quoted phrase is from Bieri, 'Why consciousness is puzzling', p. 54. For additional relevant discussion, see P. Bieri, 'Trying out epiphenomenalism', pp. 283–309; J. Kim, *Philosophy of Mind* (Westview Press, Boulder, 1996), pp. 125–54; B. McLaughlin, 'Epiphenomenalism', in *A Companion to the Philosophy of Mind*, ed. S. Guttenplan (Blackwell Publishers, Oxford, 1994), pp. 277–88.

5   See Kim, *Philosophy of Mind*, p. 148; 'Mechanism, purpose, and explanatory exclusion', in J. Kim, *Supervenience and Mind: Selected Philosophical Essays* (Cambridge University Press, Cambridge, 1993), pp. 237–64. Another (somewhat more exact) version of the second premise or exclusion principle states that no physical event can be given more than one complete and independent causal explanation. A version of the master argument can be couched in terms of distinctions between complete/incomplete and independent/dependent explanation, but these conceptual nuances I avoid here. For discussion, see Bieri, 'Trying out epiphenomenalism', pp. 291–2.

6   David Braddon-Mitchell and Frank Jackson, *Philosophy of Mind and Cognition* (Blackwell Publishers, Oxford, 1996), pp. 10–11.

7   Mark Bear, Barry Connors, and Michael Paradiso, *Neuroscience: Exploring the Mind* (Williams & Walkins, Baltimore, 1996), p. 310.

8   Howard Gardner, *The Mind's New Science* (Basic Books, New York, 1987) p. 285.

9   For detailed defense of the possibility of overdeterminaton, see Paul Pietroski, 'Mental causation for dualists', *Mind and Language*, 9 (1994), pp. 336–66.

10 See J. J. C. Smart, *Our Place in the Universe* (Blackwell Publishers, Oxford, 1989); J. J. C. Smart, 'Sensations and brain processes', in V. C. Chapell, ed., *The Philosophy of Mind* (Prentice-Hall, Englewood Cliffs, NJ, 1962).

11 See J. McConnell, 'In defense of the knowledge argument', *Philosophical Topics*, 22 (1994), pp. 157–87. See also chapter 10, section 3.

12 On objections to idealism and phenomenalism, see Frederick Schmitt, *Truth: A Primer* (Westview Press, Boulder, 1995), pp. 5–51; John Searle, *The Social Construction of Reality* (Free Press, New York, 1995), pp. 149–226.

13 For discussion of what can be learned about the operation of a system (conscious or otherwise) when it breaks down, see W. Bechtel and R. Richardson, *Discovering Complexity: Decomposition and Localization as Strategies in Scientific Research* (Princeton University Press, Princeton, 1993).

14 For a standard taxonomy of disorders, see American Psychiatric Association, *Diagnostic and Statistical Manual of Mental Disorders*, 4th edn (American Psychiatric Association, Washington, DC, 1994).

15 For clinical exposition and commentary, see L. Weiskrantz, *Consciousness Lost and Found* (Oxford University Press, Oxford, 1997).

16 R. McCarthy and E. Warrington, *Cognitive Neuropsychology: A Clinical Introduction* (Academic Press, San Diego, 1990), p. 57.

17 For versions and variations of the hypothesis, see R. Lahav, 'What neuropsychology tells us about consciousness,' *Philosophy of Science*, 60 (1993), pp. 67–85; M. Tye, 'The function of consciousness', *Nous*, 30 (1996), pp. 287–305; R. Van Gulick, 'Deficit studies and the function of phenomenal consciousness', in *Philosophical Psychopathology*, eds G. Graham and G. L. Stephens (MIT Press, Cambridge, Mass., 1994), pp. 25–49. See also B. Baars, *A Cognitive Theory of Consciousness* (Cambridge University Press, Cambridge, 1988).

18 Lahav, 'What neuropsychology tells us', p. 79.

19 See Tye, 'The function of consciousness', pp. 301–2.

20 One philosopher who has given some attention to the importance of getting or keeping information out of consciousness is Kent Bach, 'Emotional disorder and attention', in Graham and Stephens, *Philosophical Psychopathology*, pp. 51–72.

21 See P. H. Venables, 'Input dysfunction in schizophrenia,' in *Contribution to the Psychopathology of Schizophrenia*, ed. B. Maher (Academic Press, New York, 1964); D. R. Hemsley, 'Perception and cognition,' in *Schizophrenia: Origins, Processes, Treatment, and Outcome*, eds R. Cromwell and C. Snyder (Oxford University Press, New York, 1993); C. D. Frith, 'Consciousness, information processing, and schizophrenia,' *British Journal of Psychiatry*, 134 (1979), pp. 225–35; C. D. Frith, 'The positive and negative symptoms of schizophrenia reflects impairments in the perception and initiation of action', *Psychological Medicine*, 17 (1987), pp. 631–48.

22 N. MacDonald, 'Living with schizophrenia', *Canadian Medical Association Journal*, 82 (1960), p. 218.

23 A. McGhie and J. S. Chapman, 'Disorders of attention and perception in early schizophrenia', *British Journal of Medical Psychology*, 34 (1961), p. 104.

24 Such as Obsessive Compulsive (Thought) Disorder; see J. Rapaport, *The Boy Who Couldn't Stop Washing* (Penguin, New York, 1989).

25 See O. Flanagan, 'Is a science of consciousness possible?' in *Self Expressions* (Oxford University Press, Oxford, 1996).

26 D. R. Hemsley, 'Perception and cognition', p. 9.

27 A. Marsella, N. Sartorius, A. Jablensky, and F. Fenton, 'Cross-cultural studies of depressive disorders: an overview', in *Culture and Depression: Studies in Anthropology and Cross-cultural Psychiatry of Affect and Disorder*, eds A. Kleinman and B. Good (University of California Press, Berkeley, 1985), p. 314.

28   D. L. Johnson, 'Schizophrenia as a brain process', *American Psychologist*, 44 (1989), p. 554.

29   See A. Kleinman and J. Kleinman, 'Somatization: the interconnections in Chinese society among culture, depressive experiences, and the meanings of pain', in Kleinman and Good, *Culture and Depression*.

30   M. Schwartz and O. Wiggins, 'The phenomenology of schizophrenic delusions', in *Phenomenology, Language, and Schizophrenia*, eds M. Spitzer, F. Uehlin, M. Schwartz, and C. Mundt (Springer, New York, 1992), p. 13.

31   G. Brown and T. Harris, *The Social Origins of Depression* (Free Press, New York, 1978).

32   One neuropsychiatrist who has given serious attention to the role of conscious experience in the onset and course of depressive illness is Peter Whybrow, *A Mood Apart: Depression, Manic Depression, and Other Afflictions of the Self* (Basic Books, New York, 1996). See also H. Akiskal, W. McKinney, and P. Whybrow, *Mood Disorders: Toward a New Psychobiology* (Plenum, New York, 1984).

33   L. Abramson, M. Seligman, and J. Teasdale, 'Learned helplessness in humans: critique and reformulation', *Journal of Abnormal Psychology*, 87 (1978), pp. 50–70.

34   Biogenic amines (neurochemicals that facilitate neural transmission) have sometimes been proposed as the neurochemical basis of depression. See J. J. Schildkraut, 'The catecholamine hypothesis of affective disorders: A review of supporting evidence', *American Journal of Psychiatry*, 122 (1965), pp. 509–22.

35   Cooperative or conspiratorial causality is not a violation of the second premise of the master argument: the principle of causal/explanatory exclusion. 'Conspiratorial' simply means that multiple factors are causally explanatorily relevant; it does not mean (as would violate the second premise) that one and the same event has more than one independent cause or causal explanation.

36   D. Dennett, *Consciousness Explained* (Little, Brown, Boston, 1991), p. 37.

37   M. Tye, *Ten Problems of Consciousness* (MIT Press, Cambridge, Mass., 1995), p. 57.

38   Flanagan writes, 'Physicalism can be true ... without being able to explain everything, let alone capture everything in the languages of the basic physical sciences.' See his *Consciousness Reconsidered* (MIT Press, Cambridge, Mass., 1992) p. 101. Flanagan's model is designed to parry the Knowledge Argument that physicalism is false because nothing we can tell of a purely physical scientific sort captures the conscious quality of experience. See J. McConnell, 'In defense of the knowledge argument'.

39   See P. S. Churchland, 'Consciousness: the transmutation of a concept',

Pacific Philosophical Quarterly, 64 (1981), pp. 80–95; K. V. Wilkes, 'Is consciousness important?', *British Journal of the Philosophy of Science*, 35 (1984), pp. 223–43.

40 See H. Kincaid, *Philosophical Foundations of Social Science: Analyzing Controversies in Social Research* (Cambridge University Press, Cambridge, 1995).

41 See T. Horgan and J. Tienson, *Connectionism and the Philosophy of Psychology* (MIT Press, Cambridge, Mass., 1996).

42 The story to follow is from Gay Wilson Allen, *William James: A Biography* (Viking, New York, 1967), p. 305.

Glossary

Action   Actions are things done or behaviors performed on purpose, like walking to a refrigerator or writing a book. Actions contrast with mere bodily movements which have causes but not purposes.

Behaviorism   Doctrine that minds are nothing more than actual and potential behavior. Minds do not initiate and control behavior. They are behavior.

Belief   To believe something – some proposition – is to take it to be true. A widely discussed philosophical problem concerns the beliefs (if any) of nonhumans: God, animals, and computers. Which of these subjects possess beliefs and what (if anything) do they believe?

Choice   Also decision. Selection among alternative possibilities or courses of action. Choices stem from wants, desires, or preferences. The term 'choice' appears in debates about free will where it is used to refer to freedom of choice, decision, or will.

Cognitive science   The multi-disciplinary scientific study of intelligent thought and action. Psychology, computer science, neuroscience, linguistics, and philosophy are its core disciplines. Cognition and information processing are its primary subject matters.

Compatibilism   Doctrine that freedom of decision and action is compatible with the comprehensive causal explanation of decision and action in impersonal terms or with the absence of ultimate personal control of decision and action.

Computer   Machine that performs computations and processes information, typically directed by a program or formalized set of instructions or rules.

Concepts   Concepts serve classifying functions. They are represented by general terms (like 'dog', 'tree', and 'pianist') and expressed in discriminatory or classifying behavior. Concepts structure what an agent can think, believe, or say. I can think of Descartes as a great philosopher only if I possess the concepts 'great' and 'philosopher'.

Consciousness   Consciousness in the sense usually discussed by philosophers is subjective experience. Sometimes referred to as phenomenal consciousness. Phenomenal consciousness strikes many philosophers as puzzling or mysterious from a physical scientific point of view. 'Conscious' may also refer to being awake, attentive, or self-conscious.

Dualism   Doctrine that minds are not identical to or composed of something physical and that together the mental and the physical make up persons. Some dualists maintain that the mind can exist even if the body and brain do not exist, as a disembodied soul.

Eliminativism   Doctrine that mental phenomena do not exist. Eliminativists about phenomenal consciousness deny that phenomenal consciousness exists; they dismiss qualia. Eliminativists about Intentionality deny that any phenomenon possesses intrinsic aboutness or Intentionality.

Epiphenomenalism   Epiphenomenalism about some aspect or other of mind asserts that this aspect, although perfectly real, has no causal impact on anything else. Epiphenomenalism about consciousness asserts that conscious experience is behaviorally impotent.

Folk psychology   Common-sense psychology. A loosely ordered network of notions or concepts used in daily life to describe, predict, and explain behavior. Folk psychological concepts include, among many others, the concepts of belief, desire, and intention.

Free will   Freedom from outside, impersonal control of one's decisions and actions; allegedly exhibited in rational choice among alternative courses of action. Dual power; the ability to chose one way or another.

Functionalism   The view that mental states are defined by their functional or causal roles and are multiply realizable. As functionalists characterize both mental and physical states, it is perfectly possible for organisms with significant physical differences to be in the same sorts of mental states.

Intentionality   Property of mind in virtue of which it is about, directed at, or of objects real or imagined. The belief that Plato was a philosopher is about Plato. Some Intentional states are conscious; some are not. The concept of Intentionality is used to argue that nothing physical can possess Intentionality.

Intentional realism   Doctrine that mental phenomena with Intentionality (aboutness) exist; they are real and not just in the eye of the interpreter. Intentional anti-realists deny the existence of Intentional phenomena.

Materialism   Also physicalism. In philosophy of mind the doctrine that the mind consists of nothing over and above physical processes; most materialists hold that the relevant physical processes are described by physical science, including neuroscience. The mind is not an incorporeal soul or spirit.

Mind   That which thinks or has attitudes and undergoes conscious experiences; that which initiates and controls intelligent behavior.

Multiple realizability   Thesis, promoted by functionalism, that one and the same mental phenomenon can be exhibited in subjects with different chemistries or biologies, perhaps with no biology at all. If computers functionally behave like human beings, then regardless of physical differences between computers and human beings, just as humans think or believe, computers think or believe.

Problem of other minds   One's own consciousness is self-evident; but the conscious minds of others are not similarly evident to oneself. So how is one justified in believing in other conscious minds?

Propositional attitudes   Mental phenomena with propositional content and described using folk psychological concepts such as belief and desire. The belief that Descartes is a great philosopher is identified, in part, by the propositional content of the 'that' clause.

Qualia   Singular 'quale'. The 'like-thisnesses' or intrinsic qualities of our conscious mental life. Qualia are the ways subjective experiences seem or feel to us; the look of red, the taste of coconut milk, the hurtfulness of pain.

Rationality   Concept used to describe and evaluate actions and attitudes. To act rationally is to act for a reason; to act reasonably is to act for a good reason. Rational belief or choice is warranted by reason.

Supervenience   A form of systematic connection between entities of two different types. Entities of one type supervene on entities of another type just in case entities of the first type cannot differ or change without entities of the second type differing or changing. The mind-brain supervenience thesis is the thesis that mind supervenes on brain: mental processes supervene on brain processes.

Weakness of will   Exhibited in acting contrary to one's better judgment; failure to live up to deliberate decisions. Examples include the overeater who abandons the sincerely formulated intention to diet.

A Philosophy of Mind
Bookshelf

The notes and citations in each chapter offer suggested readings for term papers and other projects on a topic by topic basis. The following section gives the titles of books, some mentioned in the the body of the book, some not, which may serve as the basis for a personal library or reading list in philosophy of mind. The first set of suggestions constitutes what I call 'the basic shelf'. These books in one way or another represent the whole field. The remaining sets offer recommendations on a topical basis. Recommendations end with 'virtual entries', by which I mean selected philosophy and philosophy of mind resources on the Internet.

The Basic Shelf

A good philosophy dictionary belongs on every philosophy learner's shelf. *The Cambridge Dictionary of Philosophy*, edited by Robert Audi (Cambridge University Press, Cambridge, 1995), contains a wealth of definitions as well as short sketches of the big ideas of major philosophers.

The literature on philosophy of mind is more than vast. Readers should find the following encyclopedic reference book helpful in a variety of ways: *A Companion to the Philosophy of Mind*, edited by Samuel Guttenplan (Blackwell Publishers, Oxford, 1994). In addition to excellent essays on topics in philosophy of mind and detailed topical bibliographies, each of the following philosophers of mind (among others) offers a self-descriptive essay: Donald Davidson, Daniel Dennett, Fred Dretske, Jerry Fodor, Hilary Putnam, and John Searle.

Much of the best work in philosophy of mind appears in articles in professional academic journals or chapters in classic treatises or books. *A Historical Introduction to the Philosophy of Mind*, edited with helpful student-oriented commentary by Peter Morton (Broadview Press, Ontario, 1997), contains some of the most famous chapters and articles, including Frank Jackson's 'Epiphenomenal qualia', Hilary Putnam's 'The nature of mental states', John Searle's 'Minds, brains, and programs', and Alan Turing's 'Computing machinery and intelligence'. William Lycan's *Mind and Cognition* (Blackwell Publishers, Oxford, 1990) and David Rosenthal's *The Nature of Mind* (Oxford University Press, Oxford, 1991) contain valuable papers by Paul Churchland, Donald Davidson, Daniel Dennett, Fred Dretske, Frank Jackson, and other important philosophers of mind.

You have just read a book which introduces the philosophy of mind by covering virtually the whole broad subject. There are other types of introductions to the field. *Matter and Consciousness*, by Paul Churchland (MIT Press, Cambridge, Mass., 1988), is a popular introduction that approaches the subject through the problems of mind/body (mind/brain) and other minds, together with some elementary neuroscience. Churchland also offers a brief introduction to the brand of materialism – eliminative materialism – which he favors. William Bechtel's *Philosophy of Mind: An Overview for Cognitive Science* (Erlbaum, Hillsdale, NJ, 1988) is recommended as an introduction oriented around mind/body as well as Intentionality. Jaegwon Kim's *Philosophy of Mind* (Westview Press, Boulder, 1996) is informatively focused on mind/body, epiphenomenalism, and supervenience. Colin McGinn's *The Character of Mind* (Oxford University Press, Oxford, 1997) is directed at philosophical difficulties associated with consciousness as well as mind/body.

Most introductions to the philosophy of mind (Churchland, Bechtel, Kim, and McGinn are representative) more or less center around the mind/body (mind/brain) problem. Of broader scope is the century's classic survey of issues in the philosophy of mind: Gilbert Ryle's *The Concept of Mind* (University of Chicago Press, 1949/1984). Ryle's book is wonderfully written although hobbled by reliance on a form of behaviorism.

Owen Flanagan's *The Science of Mind* (MIT Press, Cambridge, Mass., 1991) engagingly examines interdependencies among philosophy of mind, psychology, and cognitive science. Disciplinary interdependencies are amply represented in *A Companion to Cognitive Science*, edited by

William Bechtel and George Graham (Blackwell Publishers, Oxford, 1998).

The Topical Shelf

Death, identity, and survival   Miguel de Unamuno's *The Tragic Sense of Life*, translated by J. Flitch (Dover, New York, 1954) is a model of passionate yet articulate anxiety over the fact that flesh-and-blood people die. The literature on death, identity, and survival is, of course, immense. The following surveys the conceptual terrain: Fred Feldman's *Confrontations with the Reaper: A Philosophical Study of the Nature and Value of Death* (Oxford University Press, Oxford, 1992). Themes of death, identity, and survival are sensitively explored in a combination text and reader by Herbert Fingarette entitled *Death: Philosophical Soundings* (Open Court, Chicago, 1996). The reader portion includes short but revealing selections from Tolstoy, Unamuno, Bertrand Russell, and others. Fingarette's text focuses on how best emotionally to face death. Derek Parfit's 'Personal identity', which appeared in the journal *Philosophical Review* in 1971, is the clearest and most readable presentation of the deflationist approach to personal identity for which Parfit has become known among philosophers. The paper is reprinted in the following somewhat dated but still worthwhile collection of essays: Jonathan Glover, *The Philosophy of Mind* (Oxford University Press, Oxford, 1976).

Varieties of minds   Daniel Dennett's *Kinds of Minds: Toward an Understanding of Consciousness* (Basic Books, New York, 1996) is an introduction to various main ideas of this fascinating philosopher of mind as well as a survey of issues associated with the conscious minds of others (especially animals). Computer mentality is discussed in a number of fine books. Both John Haugeland's *Artificial Intelligence: The Very Idea* (MIT Press, Cambridge, Mass., 1985) and William Bechtel and Adele Abrahamsen's *Connectionism and the Mind: An Introduction to Parallel Processing in Networks* (Blackwell Publishers, Oxford, 1990) offer lucid and informed discussions of various topics associated with computer minds. Each has the virtue of explaining philosophically relevant elements of computer science without esoteric jargon. Also worth reading are Jack Copeland's *Artificial Intelligence: A Philosophical*

Introduction (Blackwell Publishers, Oxford, 1993) and Todd Moody's *Philosophy and Artificial Intelligence* (Prentice Hall, Englewood Cliffs, NJ, 1993). (Both Bechtel/Abrahamsen and Copeland are being prepared for second editions as I write.) Thomas Morris's *The Concept of God* (Oxford University Press, Oxford, 1987) collects recent writings on divine perfection, including papers on the mind of God. Personally poignant perspectives on whether God suffers may be found in the essays by Alvin Plantinga and Nicholas Wolterstorff in *Philosophers Who Believe: The Spiritual Journeys of 11 Leading Thinkers*, edited by Kelly James Clark (InterVarsity Press, Illinois, 1993).

Intentionality, action, and freedom of will   John Searle's *Intentionality: An Essay in the Philosophy of Mind* (Cambridge University Press, Cambridge, 1983) examines how best to understand the nature and scope of Intentionality. The rationality of action and much else besides is illuminatingly discussed in Stephen Nathanson's *The Ideal of Rationality: A Defense, within Reason* (Open Court, Chicago, 1994). For a clear presentation of issues surrounding compatibilism, which also considers connections between freedom and moral responsibility, Bruce Waller's *Freedom Without Responsibility* (Temple University Press, Philadelphia, 1990) is worth a careful read. A sensitive, wide-ranging discussion of the nature of action is Lawrence Davis's *Theory of Action* (Prentice-Hall, Englewood Cliffs, NJ, 1979). Robert Kane's *The Significance of Free Will* (Oxford University Press, Oxford, 1996) is a powerful presentation of the case for dual power (free will). Daniel Dennett's *Elbow Room* (MIT Press, Cambridge, Mass., 1984) is an appealing statement of a compatibilist approach to free will. Dennett's statement, unlike other defenses of compatibilism, is less interested in the issue of determinism than in which forms of freedom are desirable.

Consciousness and mind/body   No topic in the philosophy of mind has generated more books in recent years than the topic of consciousness. Michael Tye's *Ten Problems of Consciousness* (MIT Press, Cambridge, Mass., 1995) is a probing and engaging presentation of difficulties posed for materialism by consciousness, which Tye believes that materialism, broadly understood, can resolve. Owen Flanagan's *Consciousness Reconsidered* (MIT Press, Cambridge, Mass., 1992) is a captivatingly written treatment in the naturalist/materialist tradition of the nature and scope of consciousness. Flanagan is partly responsible for assembling a valuable collection of classic and new essays on consciousness: *The Nature of Consciousness: Philosophical Debates*, edited by Ned Block, Owen Flanagan, and Güven Güzeldere (MIT Press, Cambridge, Mass., 1997).

Functionalism figures as central in several post-elementary introductions to the philosophy of mind. These include: David-Braddon Mitchell and Frank Jackson's *Philosophy of Mind and Cognition* (Blackwell Publishers, Oxford, 1996) and Georges Rey's *Contemporary Philosophy of Mind* (Blackwell Publishers, Oxford, 1997). D. M. Armstrong's *A Materialist Theory of Mind* (Routledge, London, 1968; revised 1993) is a synoptic treatment in the materialist tradition of mind and the philosophy of mind.

New topics, fresh ideas, and virtual entries   There recently has appeared a large number of philosophical and non-philosophical articles and books extolling the merits of anti-individualistic, embodied-in-the-real-world approaches to the study of mind. One hears talk of minds 'distributing' or 'stretching' into the world, of brains and bodies being inseparable, of the unity of brain, body, and world. Some threads in these discussions interweave with issues discussed in chapter 8 on the nature of Intentionality. Andy Clark's *Being There: Putting Brain, Body, and World Together* (MIT Press, Cambridge, Mass., 1997) is a helpful and crisply written guide to conceptual issues which lie within the embodied, situated, and distributed cognition literature.

A second fresh topic is mental modularity (an issue related to the discussion in chapter 8 of neural modules). Broadly speaking, a mental module is a relatively autonomous component of the mind which performs its operations uninfluenced by other mental activities. Some perceptual activity, for example, is modular. When experiencing certain perceptual illusions our visual perceptual system has access only to certain properties of a stimulus and does not draw upon our background knowledge of how the stimulus is composed. There are helpful introductions to mental modularity by Jay Garfield and Irene Appelbaum in the Guttenplan and Bechtel/Graham *Companions*, respectively. Nothing matches the thrust of Jerry Fodor's *The Modularity of Mind* (MIT Press, Cambridge, Mass., 1983) as a book on the subject. Fodor is a major figure in current philosophy of mind. His distinctive views animate various systematic perspectives on philosophy of mind, such as Georges Rey's book (above mentioned), as well as many of the more heated debates in contemporary philosophy of mind, cognition, and language. Though a lively writer, Fodor is often technical and not easy to read. However, after reading the Garfield and Appelbaum chapters, *Modularity* may open a door to Fodor's conceptual world.

Finally, no shelf would be complete without noting that the Internet now is an important information source for students and professionals. Navigating cyberspace is not without serious risks or liabilities. Two are uppermost: (1) websites often lack peer review or editorial control of their contents; (2) sites are subject to discontinuation or to change in service or address often without notice.

A useful way in which to navigate philosophy of mind cyberspace is to find general philosophy sites which professional philosophers and graduate students who work in philosophy of mind and related areas seem to use. Abundant information specific to philosophy of mind can be readily accessed from these sites. Such sites include, among other items of potential interest, links to sites of philosophers of mind active in cyberspace, to sites containing bibliographies, dictionaries, and other research tools, and to sites of mind-related professional societies and organizations.

I recommend the following general philosophy sites on the worldwide web. If their own addresses change, they may be reached one from the other or by using a general search engine.

Episteme Links
http://www.epistemelinks.com

Guide to Philosophy on the Internet
http://www.earlham.edu/ ~ peters/philinks.htm

Philosophy in Cyberspace
http://www-personal.monash.edu.au/ ~ dey/phl

Index

CPSIA information can be obtained at www.ICGtesting.com
Printed in the USA
LVOW130414251112

308511LV00001BA/64/P